THE FIRST ENGLISH FEMINIST

The First English Feminist

Reflections Upon Marriage
and other
writings by Mary Astell

Edited and Introduced by
Bridget Hill

Gower/Maurice Temple Smith

Published by
Gower Publishing Company Limited,
Gower House,
Croft Road,
Aldershot,
Hants GU11 3HR
England

British Library Cataloguing in Publication Data

Astell, Mary
   The First English Feminist: Reflections upon
   marriage and other writings
   I. Title   II. Hill, Bridget
   828'.408   PR3316. A6/
   ISBN: 0 566 05090 0

Typeset in Great Britain by
Guildford Graphics Limited, Petworth, West Sussex.
Printed by in Great Britain at the University Press, Cambridge.

Contents

Preface   vii

Introduction   1

Mary Astell's published works   63

PART I   WOMEN, MEN AND MARRIAGE

Reflections upon Marriage, 1706   67

PART II   AN EDUCATION FOR WOMEN

A Serious Proposal to the Ladies, Part I, 1696   135

Excerpts from *A Serious Proposal to the Ladies*, Part II, 1697   173

PART III   LOVE AND FRIENDSHIP, FAITH AND REASON

Excerpts from *A Collection of Poems*, 1689   183

Excerpts from *Letters concerning the Love of God*, 1695   191

Excerpts from *The Christian Religion*, 1705   197

CONTENTS

PART IV   POLEMIC: RELIGIOUS AND POLITICAL

A Fair Way with the Dissenters, 1704   205

Excerpts from *Moderation Truly Stated*, 1704   225

Excerpts from *An Impartial Enquiry into the Causes of Rebellion
and Civil War*, 1704   229

PART V   EPILOGUE

Mary Astell's Preface to the *Embassy Letters* of Lady Mary
Wortley Montagu, 1724 & 1725   233

Preface

Mary Astell's writings are less well known than they deserve: even to university students her work is not always readily accessible. Many who have come across her as 'the first English feminist' have been anxious to find out more, but for the general reader there is virtually no access to her work. My purpose here is to make at least some of her writings available. My choice has been dictated by two considerations: firstly to present a comprehensive account of her ideas on marriage, women's role within and without it, and her proposal for meeting what she saw as the urgent need for the education of women; and secondly to present sufficient of her other writings to give an insight into the very varied beliefs she held, and so to see her as a whole character – complex and paradoxical though that may be.

There is unlikely to be agreement on the main influences on her work, nor on the relationship between her religious and political ideas and those on women and marriage. But at least the challenge she presents will be out in the open.

I am indebted to Patricia Crawford who made valuable suggestions – and corrections – on the Introduction. It was Ruth Perry, with whom I had interesting exchanges, who first drew my attention to Mary Astell's poems. I am deeply grateful to Jonathan Rée, who was responsible for identifying the Malebranche quotation on page 79. My main debt, however, is to my husband.

BH

Introduction

Today Mary Astell is better known in the U.S.A. than in her own country. Yet few works of social history on the period of her life fail to make some reference to her. Often she is labelled by the authors as an early – if not the first – English feminist. Such a claim is made on the basis of two of her works: *A Serious Proposal, Part I* and *Reflections upon Marriage,* her so-called 'feminist' writings.[1] In these two works she outlined her deeply pessimistic views of marriage and the bleak prospects for happiness that it offered. In her analysis the most biting sarcasm is reserved for the enemy – men. Her solution, or rather the only palliative she could see for women in this situation, was more education. She argued fiercely against the natural inferiority of women, maintaining that it was not to nature but to women's exclusion from the education enjoyed by men, that any inferiority was due.

At her best Mary Astell is very quotable. Her meaning is conveyed by the force of her words. She wrote in a highly combative, not to say bold, style. Her readers are immediately aware of the anger and passion behind her words – a passion that is sometimes barely contained.

If she had written nothing else besides these two works, Mary Astell would deserve far greater study than she has received so far. On the basis of these two works alone the powerful and independ-

1

ent intelligence of a remarkable woman is revealed. That both works ran to several editions in her lifetime suggests something of their popularity among her contemporaries.

Her reputation today continues to rest almost exclusively on these 'feminist' writings. With modern feminism in the process of discovering its roots this is not surprising. The search provides a powerful motivation behind all study of women's history, and a valid one. But in the case of Mary Astell such an approach leaves too much unexplained. If she is seen as the author of these two works alone, the historian's problem is simplified: Mary Astell can be neatly labelled as an early feminist expressing enlightened views on the education of women and wittily satirising the submissive role of women in marriage. Unfortunately such a view of her is inadequate. It distorts the real Mary Astell by ignoring her complexity, and by failing to see her contradictions and the paradoxes in her thinking. Whether or not she was a feminist, she was so many other things besides – a sincerely devout woman of high Anglican and Tory sympathies, a woman with sufficient familiarity with the scriptures and current theological debate to be equal to taking on some of the leading religious thinkers of her time. She was a passionate believer in the divine right of kings at a time when few were prepared to expound such an 'old-fashioned' doctrine. She joined swords with Daniel Defoe by savagely attacking dissenters at the time of the Occasional Conformity debate.[2] She was to attack Dr White Kennett's sermon on the fast of the martyrdom of Charles I because of its failure to analyse correctly the causes of the Civil War, and totally to absolve the King from any blame.[3]

Along with the great diversity of her writings and the seeming paradoxes they present, there is Mary Astell herself; one moment she addresses herself to 'Persons of Quality', and the next to the foundation of a charity school for the daughters of Chelsea pensioners. There is Mary Astell, the possessor of the sharpest of tongues, who could assassinate in words the characters of her enemies, and the writer of poetry on love and friendship. There is the malicious scorn she heaped on the heads of men and the unsparing admiration she expressed for her own sex.

It is this very complexity of her character, the conflicting and contradictory nature of her ideas, that makes her so intriguing and so worthy a subject of study.

In 1915 Florence Smith, a student at Columbia University, submitted a thesis for her Doctor of Philosophy degree. Its subject was Mary

Astell. The thesis was approved and published by the University press in 1916,[4] at which time little was known of Mary Astell, and indeed, very little interest was shown in either her or her work. Three articles on her had appeared in the 1890s – two of them, significantly, by women[5] – and later, in 1913, an article had portrayed her as one of a group of 'English Femmes Savantes' at the end of the seventeenth century.[6] But, as far as we know, the publication of Florence Smith's thesis aroused little contemporary interest, and it seems to have lain dormant for some years until, in the 1960s, sufficient demand for access to the work prompted the publishers to reprint it.

Florence Smith's concern with Mary Astell's writings began with an interest in women's education in late seventeenth and early eighteenth century England. In the event, the research contained in her thesis went way beyond such initial and limited interest and probed not only Mary Astell's writings on education but those on marriage and the relations between the sexes. Its analysis of her political and religious writings revealed her very diverse interests and, indeed, the wide knowledge she brought to bear on the major religious and political controversies of her time. The thesis remains an essential starting-point for anyone concerned with Mary Astell's life and work.

Our knowledge of her life is still tantalisingly scant. There are long periods when we have no trace of her existence. Innumerable questions that might contribute to a greater understanding of her must remain unanswered. Most would-be biographers have gone back to the work of George Ballard for the bare facts.[7] Unfortunately even these are often suspect, if not clearly in error. What is strange is that only 20 years after her death, although she was still read with interest and even enthusiasm, the facts about her life seem to have vanished nearly into obscurity. It was not that Ballard did not try. He wrote to all her surviving friends seeking information about her. Yet often he met with no success and, when this happened, he seems not to have been averse to relying on rumours. Since his writings, very little has been added to our knowledge of her. Other accounts of her life, particularly in the 50 or so years after Ballard, are nevertheless of interest for they do occasionally provide information about her not included by Ballard which suggests access to additional sources.[8]

Early Life

Mary Astell was born in Newcastle-upon-Tyne on 12 November 1666. Her parents, Peter and Mary Astell, had been married the previous year. The marriage united the families of the Astells and Erringtons, both of which had earlier played an important role in the history of the town. The Erringtons, like the Astells, were a merchant family associated with the Hostmen's Company.

Mary was one of three children. William had died in infancy; Peter was to become a lawyer, remain in Newcastle all his life, and die in 1711. Their father was enrolled as an apprentice in the Company of Hostmen in 1653 when he was described as the son of 'William Astell of Newcastle gentleman'.[9] This would seem to identify a former under-sheriff of Newcastle, who was a noted Royalist and who died in 1658.[10] Probably also in 1653, Peter Astell senior was made a Clerk of the Company, and continued to hold this position until his death.[11] In 1655 he was made responsible for the collection of duty on the export of all grindstones, whetstones, or rubstones – a privileged export right confined to members of the Hostmen. At the time, however, he was still serving his apprenticeship and was described as 'servant unto Mr George Dawson, Alderman.'[12] Clearly the Company had some difficulty collecting the fines imposed on its members, for the next mention of Peter Astell was in 1661 when he was named as one of those empowered to 'distreine the Goods' of those who had broken the Company's regulations.[13] He was only to become a member of the Company of Hostmen in 1674, just over four years before his death.[14] In the register of St John's Church, Newcastle, his burial is recorded on 21 March 1678–79 as 'Peter Astell Gent'.[15]

The Hostmen had enjoyed a virtual monopoly of coal and grindstone shipments since early in the sixteenth century but, under Elizabeth I, the Company was incorporated and their exclusive privileges confirmed. Before the Civil War the Company had exercised a dominant role in Newcastle political and economic life. Indeed the hold of a small élite of the Company over the town increased as the century advanced. During the Civil War control of the Company passed to new hands, particularly those of the Dawsons, a leading Puritan family, one of whom – Henry Dawson – had been largely responsible for the creation in the late 1630's of an unofficial lectureship in his house. In fact little was changed in the Company as a result of the war, and after 1659 control passed from the radicals back to the moderates. On the whole members of the Company tended to share the political conservatism, and often the catholicism, of the gentry of the north.[16]

The Astell family, then, in the second half of the seventeenth century, would seem to have been people of some substance, of conservative, perhaps Royalist, sympathies. Yet in passing, it might be remarked that Peter Astell served his apprenticeship under George Dawson, one of the leading Puritan family mentioned earlier, whose members were purged from the Corporation in 1643 when the Earl of Newcastle occupied the town for the King, and that one of the same group of Puritans was Anthony Errington, a warden of the Merchant Adventurers who in 1633 had been of the Reform party opposed to the oligarchical hold of the inner ring of the Hostmen's Company.

The most interesting member of the Astell family, apart from Mary, is Ralph Astell. He was an MA and became curate of St Nicholas's church, Newcastle, in 1667. In 1660 he had demonstrated his loyalty to the Crown by publishing *Vota Non Bella*, an exceedingly bad poem expressing pro-monarchist principles. Of course it proves nothing. Many former Parliamentarians in the same circumstances had been all too anxious to establish their loyalty to the King. In this respect Ralph Astell is not remarkable. There is one brief reference to him in the Gateshead Church Records of 1675–76: 'one pinte of sack when Mr. Astell preached, 1s.2d., six quarts of Wyne and sack for one Communion 6s.9d.'[17] But it is to John Brand, the antiquarian, we owe the additional and significant piece of information, apparently drawn from Bishop Cosin's register, that in 1667 Ralph Astell was 'suspended for bad behaviour'.[18] He was to die two years later. Had his demonstration of pro-monarchical zeal been unconvincing? We do not know, but what makes him of interest is that, according to Ballard, he was 'the uncle who was a clergyman' responsible for giving Mary Astell a good education.[19] Observing 'her aptitude for learning',[20] he is said to have instructed her in 'philosophy, mathematics and logic'.[21] He is also said to have taught her Latin and French. Yet later, in her correspondence with Henry Dodwell, the scholar and theologian, about his *A Case in View Considered*, (1705) in which the future relationship between non-jurors and the Church was reviewed, it emerged that 'she did not understand Latin, as Mr Dodwell, from her quoting ancient authors, thought she had, but she told him she read them in the French and other Translations'.[22]

Mary Pilkington emphasises her 'acuteness of understanding' as a child,[23] and George Ballard remarks on her having a 'piercing wit, a solid judgement, and tenacious memory'.[24] Yet if Ralph Astell was in fact her teacher she must have been a remarkably precocious child as he died when she was only thirteen!

How her important teenage years were spent we do not know. It is possible that she continued her education under another tutor, or she may have been sent to school, or, for at least part of this time, she may have been employed in nursing her mother who was to die in October 1684. It was almost certainly her mother who is referred to in the Hostmen Company records as 'old Mrs. Astell' who was given a pension of £3 6s 8d per annum 'during the Companies pleasure' after the death of their clerk.[25]

Mary was now eighteen and an orphan. Two years later, it is suggested, she left Newcastle for London. For a girl of twenty to set off for the metropolis, turning her back on her home and family, her friends and relations, seems extraordinary. It was certainly unusual. Was she alone? In her letter to Archbishop Sancroft, the non-juror, that prefaces the collection of poems she sent to him in 1689, she mentions how the Archbishop was 'pleased to receive a poor unknown, who hath no place to fly unto'.[26] In her biographical sketch of Mary Astell, Mary Pilkington tells us that her move to London was 'for the purpose of letting them [her own sex] benefit by the information she had gained'.[27]

In those early years in London, of which we know so little, Mary Hays was later to suggest that Mary Astell 'prosecuted her studies with diligence and success'. From her subsequent writings it seems certain she must have read widely in philosophy, politics, theology and history. The same writer also insists that in the period immediately following her arrival in London she devoted herself to scientific studies.[28]

There is no evidence of the exact date of her arrival in London. If as has been suggested, she came to London in her twentieth year she would have arrived three years before her collection of poems was sent to Archbishop Sancroft in 1689. The prefatory letter to that collection implies she had been there a little time before she wrote. The evidence contained in the earlier letter of approach to Sancroft on her first arrival in London, when help and advice had been given her, poses some unanswerable questions. How had she come to know the Archbishop? Or, if she did not know him, and had no introduction to him, how very extraordinary it was for a young girl to decide to write to him! Even more extraordinary was her subsequently sending him two volumes of her poems! It is tantalising to speculate on the significance of the words she used to describe to him her departure from Newcastle and arrival in London 'when even my kinsfolk had failed, and my familiar Friends had forgotten me'.[29]

We do not know where she lived on her first arrival in London. For a considerable period of her London life she lived in Chelsea. One writer has argued that she settled there 'to be near her friend and correspondent Bishop Atterbury'.[30] A nineteenth century account has her in a house 'in Swan Walk, opposite the Physic Garden,' from about 1715 to the time of her death in 1731.[31] It seems probable, however, that she had lived in Chelsea ever since the 1690s. Her friendship with Lady Catherine Jones, the daughter of the Earl of Ranelagh, and her dedication to Lady Catherine of *Letters Concerning the Love of God* published in 1695, would suggest she was already a near neighbour to Ranelagh House where Lady Catherine lived at the time. A letter she wrote to Henry Dodwell in March 1706 was written from Chelsea.[32] Ralph Thoresby went to visit a Chelsea friend in August, 1712, and on the way met 'Mr. Croft, the minister who introduced me to the celebrated Mrs Astell'.[33]

It was in those early years of her residence in London, when in her late 20s and 30s, that her major works were written. The period in which all but the last of her works appeared was relatively short – 1694 to 1705. After this there was a gap of four years before her final work appeared.

The London Years

When she was 27, Mary Astell embarked on a series of exchanges with John Norris (1657–1711), Rector of Bemerton, near Salisbury. Norris has been described as 'the last offshoot from the school of Cambridge Platonists',[34] a group that included Ralph Cudworth, father of Damaris Masham, Henry More, Benjamin Whichcote and John Smith. Norris had corresponded with Henry More in the early 1680s. By the time the correspondence between Norris and Mary Astell began, the school of Cambridge Platonists was already in decline.

As a student of Malebranche, Norris adopted the French philosopher's belief that we 'see all things in God'. God, he believed, should be the sole and not just the principal object of our love. 'We should collect and concentrate', he wrote, 'all the rays of our love into this one point, and lean towards God with the whole weight of our soul.'[35]

How she came to know Norris or whether she knew him apart from his writings we do not know, but their exchange of letters began in 1693. She raised with him the question of how, according to his theory, pain and sin could be explained. If Norris was right in seeing God as the source of all our sensations, then was God not to be seen as the author of pain as well as pleasure? And as the author of pain could He remain the object of our love or would He not rather become that of our aversion? Norris expressed some surprise that it was a *woman* who saw flaws in his argument, and hastened to argue his way out of the difficulty. God, he argued, was indeed the author of all our sensations, and therefore of pain as well as of pleasure. But, he went on, she had failed to distinguish between two kinds of good, that which arises from the pleasure we feel and that which is done to us by God. So pain is given us by God as the punishment for sin. It may lead us to fear Him but not to hate Him. She responded by arguing that just as there were different kinds of good, so were there different kinds of pain: physical pain given us for our good by God, and intellectual pain, or what she identified as sin, which could not originate in God. Norris denied such a distinction and insisted that all pain is caused by God. Pain, he agreed, was evil but becomes a relative good as it is a way of avoiding greater evil. But, he went on, if all pain originates in God, sin does not. The exchange went on to a discussion of the nature of divine love – a subject on which they found themselves more in agreement.

Today, although the discussion between them is of little but historic interest, the letters do have another interest for us. Mary Astell had expressed some difficulty in accepting Norris's idea of God as the sole object of her love. Later they were to discuss together the distinction between the love of God and the love of friends, but in Letter III what had earlier been only a suspicion becomes a certainty.[36] The whole tone of this letter is intensely personal. She desperately appeals for Norris's help to cure her 'disorder', a passionate friendship with another woman, confessing that she found it difficult 'to love at all, without something of Desire'. She was convinced by Norris's teaching but 'sensible Beauty does too often press upon my Heart, whilst Intelligible is disregarded'. Pathetically she attempts to depersonalise her dilemma by expressing her friendship for women in general but the pretence breaks down. She admits to 'an agreeable Movement in my soul towards her I love' and confesses to finding Norris's teaching 'that we may seek Creatures for our good, but not love them as our good' is 'too nice for common Practice'.

If she had hoped for a remedy, or even advice, from Norris she must have been disappointed. His only suggestion was more meditation!³⁷ Had he understood what she was trying to tell him? Might he have understood but decided to ignore it? In view of his later insistence on publishing the exchange it seems likely that he failed to appreciate her implicit confession of a passionate love for a woman.

If there was any doubt as to the object of her desire, it is soon dispelled when one looks at the letters exchanged between Norris and Mary Astell on the proposed publication of the correspondence. There was considerable reluctance on her part and it was only on Norris's insistence that she finally agreed. When she did it was on condition that her name should not be mentioned, and that the work should be dedicated to a lady she would name to him. The lady was Lady Catherine Jones, daughter of the Earl of Ranelagh, Paymaster General of the Navy. Lady Catherine was prominent in court circles and entertained George I at Ranelagh Gardens in 1715, when Handel's Water Music was played with the composer conducting an orchestra of 50 from one of the city barges.³⁸ The friendship between the two women seems to have begun soon after Mary Astell's move to London. If, as seems possible, Mary Astell settled in Chelsea soon after her arrival in London, Lady Catherine Jones would have been her near neighbour. The friendship was close, even passionate, but not, it appears, always a happy one. 'None ever loved more generously than I have done', Mary Astell wrote, 'yet perhaps never any met with more ungrateful Returns.'³⁹ Earlier she had written of friendship that:

No loss nor sickness causeth such a smart,
No racks nor tortures so severely rend,
As the unkindness of a darling Friend.

It is tempting to see Lady Catherine as the subject of this poem.

Although Mary had always 'propos'd the noblest end' of friendship, God had denied it to her.

> Thrice blessed be thy jealousie,
> Which would not part
> With one small corner of my heart,
> But has engross'd it all to thee.[40]

Isn't this much the same concern she attemped to communicate later to John Norris? If it is indeed a reference to Lady Catherine Jones it may date Mary Astell's residence in Chelsea from the 1680s.

When her father died in 1711 leaving large debts outstanding from the time he was Paymaster General, Lady Catherine and her two sisters petitioned Parliament for the right to sell their estate in order to settle the debt. Finally the petition was granted. Lady Catherine moved from the grandeur of Ranelagh Gardens to Jews Row – also in Chelsea.

According to Thomas Birch, writing to George Ballard in 1749, Mary Astell 'lived many years at Chelsea with Lady Catherine', but when exactly he does not say, and there is no confirmation of this suggestion.[41] Nevertheless Jews Row was very close to Mary Astell's house.

The dedication to Lady Catherine in Letters Concerning the Love of God is fulsome. She was, we read, of 'unfeigned goodness', 'eminent virtue', 'of so much sweetness and modesty' and 'a compleat and finished person'. She provided the author with 'a lively idea of Apostolical Piety'. When they prayed together Mary Astell could fancy herself 'in the neighbourhood of Seraphic Flames'. Finally, Mary Astell admits she loved her 'with the greatest tenderness'.

If Lady Catherine was Mary Astell's most intimate friend, she was by no means her only woman friend. Of those others of whom we are aware it is noticeable how many were titled ladies. Apart from Lady Catherine there was Lady Anne Coventry, Lady Elizabeth Hastings and Lady Mary Wortley Montagu. The exceptions were Elizabeth Elstob, that remarkable scholar of Anglo-Saxon who was later to become George Ballard's correspondent when he was compiling his Memoirs of Several Ladies of Great Britain, and for a time was Mary Astell's neighbour in Chelsea, and Katherine Atterbury, wife of Francis, Bishop of Rochester, a leading spokesman of the new High Church party.

Lady Elizabeth Hastings was the fourth daughter of Theophilus,

7th Earl of Huntingdon of Ledstone Hall, Yorkshire. She was an ardent churchgoer and a very devout woman. When, in 1705, she inherited the family estate and became extremely rich, she was determined that 'a wise and religious use was made of it'. She was to prove a generous benefactress. By all accounts she was a remarkably beautiful woman and much sought after by 'several of the nobility'[42] although she chose to remain unmarried. Her great fortune may have provided the reason, for she made clear that she regarded any marriage for money as a sure recipe for unhappiness. With Mary Astell she shared an interest in the expansion of education for women, and was one of those named as the would-be benefactress of Mary Astell's scheme for a 'religious retirement'. Later, in 1709, with Lady Catherine Jones and other women, she was responsible for the founding of a charity school for the daughters of the pensioners at the Chelsea Royal Hospital, in the planning of which Mary Astell was closely involved.

Perhaps the most remarkable of her woman friends was Lady Mary Wortley Montagu (1689–1762). Twenty years the younger, she was very far from conforming to the model of pious devotion that characterised many of Mary Astell's other close friends. She was however, a highly intelligent and gifted woman, and Mary Astell 'triumphed in Lady Mary's talents as proofs of ... the mental equality of the sexes, if not the superiority of women to men'.[43] She possessed one quality that Mary Astell particularly admired – a powerful independent spirit that rejected convention and custom – and also possessed the will to be her own person answerable to none. How the two women became acquainted we can only surmise. Possibly it was through their mutual friend and acquaintance, Lady Ranelagh, mother of Lady Catherine Jones, or through Lady Mary's aunt, Lady Cheyne who also lived in Chelsea. What is certain is that a copy of the first edition of *A Serious Proposal* was given to Lady Mary with an inscription in Mary Astell's hand (this copy is now in the British Library). This might suggest they were already friends in the 1690s when Lady Mary was still a child. Much later Lady Mary was to write to her daughter of how, at the age of 15, her desire had been 'to found an English monastery for ladies', and that had she then been 'mistress of an independent fortune', she would have carried out the project and 'elected myself lady abbess'.[44] This suggests that she took Mary Astell's proposal seriously.

In 1724 Lady Mary forwarded to Mary Astell the manuscript

copy of her *Embassy Letters*. After reading them Mary Astell was enthusiastic for their publication but the author insisted that they were not to be published during her lifetime. Yet in the copy she returned to Lady Mary, Mary Astell had inscribed a Preface which reflects 'that fond partiality which old people of ardent tempers sometime entertain for a rising genius in their own line'.[45]

It is through this friendship with Lady Mary that we have one of the most illuminating – and authentic – comments on Mary Astell. It comes from Lady Louisa Stuart, Lady Mary's grand-daughter, who included some introductory anecdotes when the *Letters and Works* of her grandmother were finally published. From her we learn that Mary Astell was 'a very pious, exemplary woman, and a profound scholar'. But far from the 'fair and elegant prefacer' described by the first editor of the letters, she was 'in outward form ... rather ill-favoured and forbidding' and, as her readers all too readily can believe, 'of a humour to have repulsed the compliment roughly, had it been paid her while she lived'.[46] Such a description of her appearance is borne out by Mary Astell's own view of herself as 'one to whom Nature has not been over liberal'.[47]

In this humorous and gently teasing comment on Mary Astell, there is also a genuine admiration. 'Whatever were her foibles and prejudices', Lady Louisa writes, 'her piety was genuine, fervent, and humble'.[48]

Since most of their lives were spent with those of their own sex it is not surprising that friendship between women assumed such importance. In many cases women saw far more of their female friends than they did of their husbands, or other men. Katherine Phillips, the 'matchless Orinda' had earlier remarked how 'men exclude women from friendship's vast capacity'.[49] For unmarried women friendship assumed an even greater importance, and this was certainly true for Mary Astell. 'Having by Nature a strong Propensity to friendly Love', she wrote, she was 'loath to abandon all Thoughts of Friendship'.[50] She considered that 'one considerable cause of the degeneracy' of her age was 'the little true Friendship that is to be found in it'.[51] She thought one of the main advantages of her 'Religious Retirement' was 'the opportunity of contracting the purest and noblest friendship'.[52]

When presenting her *Collection of Poems* to Archbishop Sancroft in 1689 Mary Astell had written that it was 'not without pain and reluctancy that I break from my beloved obscurity'.[53] Many of her biographers have presented her as a woman of great modesty. Ballard, for example, insists she was 'extremely fond of obscurity, which she courted and doted on beyond all earthly blessings; and was as ambitious to slide gently through the world, without so much as being seen or taken notice of, as others are to bustle and make a figure in it'.[54] This apparent lack of ambition is supported by her resistance to Norris's attempts to persuade her to publish the *Letters Concerning the Love of God*, and her final agreement only on condition that Norris should 'make no mention of my Name, no not so much as the initial Letters'.[55] When the *Letters* were published they were described as 'between the Author of The Proposal to the Ladies and Mr. John Norris'. In fact *A Serious Proposal to the Ladies* had appeared not under her name but as 'By a Lover of her Sex'. Nevertheless, there never seemed much doubt about her authorship and many freely acknowledged her authorship even though her name was never revealed. Indeed, she was ascribed authorship of two pamphlets that are clearly not hers at all; the anonymous *An Essay in Defence of the Female Sex* of 1696 and *The Case of Moderation and Occasional Communion* of 1705.[56]

In all her writings, but most particularly in her poetry, ambition is a recurring theme. In the poem, 'In Emulation of Mr Cowley', written in her early 20s, she wrote:

> What shall I do? not to be Rich or Great
> Not to be courted and admir'd,
> With Beauty blest, or Wit inspir'd,
> Alas! these merit not my care and sweat,
> These cannot my Ambition please.

If it was not for 'Fame's trumpet having, so short a breath' all would surely pursue ambition:

> Who wou'd not then, with all their might
> Study and strive to get themselves a name?[57]

Ambition then seems to have been something of a preoccupation with her. Yet the ambition she craved had nothing to do with personal fame or fortune. What she wanted was to make a mark in the world, and to make it as a *woman*. Her *Reflections upon Marriage* was first published anonymously in 1700, and only the third edition revealed, not her name, but her sex. So while she seemed reluctant to divulge her name as author, she was not so reluctant to reveal the author's sex. In her *A Serious Proposal to the Ladies* she called on women to 'exalt and establish' their 'Fame'.[58] But the 'fame' she wanted for them was the recognition of women's ability and achievement wherever they were revealed. It was this concern that led her to praise so wholeheartedly Lady Mary Wortley Montagu's *Letters* − 'pleas'd that a *Woman* Triumphs!'.[59]

Mary Astell remained unmarried as did so many of the outstanding women of the period − Elizabeth Elstob, Jane Barker who admitted to 'a secret disgust against matrimony', Celia Fiennes, Anne Killigrew, Bathsua Makin among others. The attitude of late seventeenth and early eighteenth century society to such women reflected the absence of what had formerly been one of the two alternatives open to unmarried daughters − to marry or to go into a nunnery. Lawrence Stone has estimated that the percentage of recorded daughters of the gentry reaching the age of 50 who had never married rose from 10 per cent in the sixteenth century to nearly 25 per cent between 1675 and 1799.[60] The problem for the propertied class of what to do with unmarried daughters became acute. Unequipped both socially and economically to earn their own living they were increasingly resented as a burden on their family or relatives.

Mary Astell's proposal for a 'Religious Retirement' recognised the particular problem facing spinsters in a society where 'all women are understood either married or to be married'.[61] If women were not to marry, the best alternative was something resembling a nunnery, a place of at least temporary withdrawal from the world. Given the powerful pressure on them to marry, few women could view spinsterhood as other than abject failure. 'Taught to think Marriage her only Preferment',[62] Mary Astell wrote, a woman never considered 'that she should have a higher Design than to get her a Husband.'[63] Many 'quite terrified with the dreadful Name of Old Maid', sought refuge in 'some dishonourable Match . . . to the disgrace of her Family and her own irreparable Ruin.'[64]

Given more education, Mary Astell believed that there were women who having considered 'the Good and Evil of a Married State'[65] would decide to reject it. Seeing the role wives were expected to play, some might well conclude it was 'not good for a woman to marry.'[66] Part of her intention in *Reflections* was to suggest spinsterhood as a real alternative to marriage, and one which might give women, or at least upper-class women, a degree of independence. Earlier in the century Thomas Middleton's *Roaring Girl* had observed that only by remaining chaste could she retain her independence. 'I have no humour to marry;' she said, 'I love to lie a' both sides a' the bed myself: and again, a' the other side, a wife, you know, ought to be obedient, but I fear I am too headstrong to obey; therefore I'll ne'er go about it ... I have the head now of myself, and I am man enough for a woman: marriage is but a chopping and changing, where a maiden loses one head, and has a worse i' the place.'[67]

After talking of how the responsibility in the family for educating children, 'a most necessary Employment, perhaps the chief of those who have any', fell on the mother and therefore how important her education was, Mary Astell hastened to reassure those without children. Knowledge, she told them, 'would not lie dead upon their hands' for 'the whole World is a single Lady's Family, her opportunities of doing good are not lessen'd but encreas'd by her being unconfin'd.'[68] It was a generous phrase in keeping with the generosity of her sympathy with women who remained unmarried.

For women like herself, lacking beauty and fortune, Mary Astell saw spinsterhood as offering a unique liberty:

> O how uneasy shou'd I be,
> If tied to Custom and formalitie,
> Those necessary evils of the Great,
> Which bind their hands and manacle their feet,
> Nor Beauty, Parts, nor Portion are expose
> My most beloved Liberty to lose.[69]

It was a revolutionary idea. Not all women were capable of supporting themselves, and even fewer could earn a living through writing. But where they were financially independent, spinsterhood offered the possibility of self-fulfilment. Such women, with Mary Astell, could thank heaven that:

> ... my time is all my own,
> I when I please can be alone;
> Nor Company, Nor Courtship steal away
> That treasure they can ne're repay.[70]

Those women who could view spinsterhood with equanimity were few. The same scorn with which spinsterhood was regarded was transferred to any woman aspiring to learning. 'A Learned Woman', as Bathsua Makin observed, 'is thought to be a Comet that bodes Mischief whenever it appears'.[71] Just as the spinster was seen as

15

unnatural and a freak, so was the 'learned lady' regarded as betraying unwomanly and masculine characteristics. If you were a woman of learning it might be better to conceal the fact! Indeed this was precisely the advice Lady Mary Wortley Montagu gave her granddaughter, for as she put it 'the parade of it can only serve to draw on her the envy, and consequently the most inveterate hatred'.[72]

Many women of intelligence, even the strongest and most confident, were inhibited from revealing their real abilities by the scorn for learning. Those women who wrote were reluctant to reveal their authorship of books. The first time that Susan Centlivre's play, *The Platonic Lady*, was performed in 1706, it ran for only four days. In the edition of the following year was a dedication 'to the generous encouragers of female ingenuity' of whom she hoped to find sufficient 'to protect her against the carping malice of the vulgar world, who think it a proof of their sense to dislike everything that is writ by women.'[73] Even Katherine Philips, the 'matchless Orinda', admitted that sometimes she thought the writing of poetry was 'a diversion so unfit for the sex to which I belong that I am about to resolve against it for ever.'[74] In the Epistle prefacing the Duchess of Newcastle's *Philosophical and Physical Opinions* in 1663, the Duke pinpointed the reasons for the doubt cast on her authorship since 'no lady could understand so many hard words.' 'Here's the crime', he wrote, 'a Lady writes them, and to intrench so much on the male prerogative is not to be forgiven.'[75]

Mary Astell was very conscious of the way in which anything from a female author was regarded. In John Norris's preface, *To the Reader*, in *Letters concerning the Love of God*, he acknowledged that after reading Mary Astell there might be 'a diffidence in some who from the excellency of these writings may be tempted to question whether my correspondent be a woman or not'.[76] In her first letter to Norris Mary Astell presumed 'to beg his attention a little to the impertinencies of a Woman's pen'.[77]

'Learned ladies' were the subject of numerous satires and Mary Astell's notion of a 'Religious Retirement' did not escape attention. In *The Tatler* Swift referred to her as 'a profess'd *Platonne*, the most unaccountable Creature of her Sex'. She was described as having 'run over *Norris*, and *Moor*, and *Milton*, and the whole Set of Intellectual Triflers'. She was cast in the role of Madonella, the head of a Protestant nunnery where, in association with her friend Lady Elizabeth Hastings and others described as 'this Order of Platonick

Ladies',[78] she led a staff consisting of Elizabeth Elstob and Mary
de la Rivière Manley – a wonderfully ill-assorted pair![79] Mary Astell's
'Religious Retirement' was described as a 'College for Young Damsels;
where instead of Scissors, Needles, and Samplers; Pens, Compasses,
Quadrants, Books, Manuscripts, Greek, Latin, and Hebrew are to take
up the whole Time'. Manley was to give the inmates 'at least a
superficial Tincture of the Ancient and Modern Amazonian Tacticks'![80]

In the plays of the period the 'learned lady' was a stock subject
for satire. Perhaps the most sympathetic of such learned ladies –
and the one closest to Mary Astell – was Valeria in Susan Centlivre's
The Bassett Table, first performed in 1705. Valeria, 'that little She-
Philosopher' as she is called by Ensign Lovely, her doting admirer,
is preoccupied with natural philosophy and is at present mad about
dissecting insects. One of the other female characters refers to learning
as 'ridiculous indeed for Women; Philosophy suits our Sex, as Jack
Boots would do'. 'Custom', replies Valeria, 'would bring them as
much in Fashion as Furbeloes, and Practice would make us as valiant
as e'er a Hero of them all: the Resolution is in the Mind – Nothing
can enslave that.' What most suggests that Susan Centlivre was thinking of Mary Astell is the mocking suggestion that Valeria might
found 'a College for the Study of Philosophy, where none but Women
should be admitted . . .' The response from Valeria was worthy of
Mary Astell. 'What you make jest of', she retorts, 'I'd execute, were
Fortune in my Power.' When Ensign Lovely fears the advances a
Captain Hearty is making to her, Valeria reassures him: 'If he was
a Whale, he might give you pain, for I should long to dissect him;
but as he is a Man, you have no reason to fear him!'[81]

Whenever in history women had achieved anything remarkable,
Mary Astell pointed out, men tended to dismiss it claiming 'that
women acted above their sex. By which we must suppose they wou'd
have their Readers understand, that they were not Women who
did those Great Actions, but that they were Men in Petticoats!'[82]

Of her later life we know little. Yet from the mere fragments
of information that exist we learn something of the austerity and
self-discipline of her character. According to one account 'ascetic habits
and physical suffering' prevented her writing after 1710, 'and she
gave herself up to devotion.'[83] Mary Pilkington related how although
'mild and merciful' to the faults of others, 'to errors committed by
herself she was much more severe; and when guilty of those slight
imperfections to which the most virtuous are liable, she wou'd punish

them with an abstinence scarcely to be endured'.[84] 'Abstinence', she is said to have insisted, 'was the best physic.'[85] Every Sunday, regardless of the weather, she would walk from her home in Chelsea to St Martin's Church to hear her favourite preacher. Ultimately she was to die of cancer. For some years, we are told, she concealed the disease from her friends and when finally she sought the advice of a surgeon it was too late. Her breast was removed, an operation she endured 'with a degree of fortitude which astonished the surgeon... and in spite of all arguments could not be persuaded to suffer her person to be held.'[86] That few of her friends knew of her condition is confirmed by Lady Louisa Stuart who describes a meeting between her grandmother and Mary a few weeks before she died. After 'a serious discussion of some religious subject, very eagerly pursued on Mrs. Astell's side', there occurred a pause and she confided to Lady Mary that she was dying. Then to demonstrate her friendship with Lady Mary she went on: 'if departed spirits be permitted to revisit those whom they have loved on earth, remember I make you a solemn promise that mine shall appear to you and confirm the truth of all I have been saying.'[87]

Of Mary's last few days we have the account sent in a letter from Lady Elizabeth Hastings to Bishop Wilson ten days after her death on 9th May 1731. She wrote how 'she was five days actually a-dying, Lady Catherine Jones was with her two days before her death; she then begged to see no more of her old acquaintance and friends, having done with the world and made her peace with God'.[88]

The historical background

The society at which Mary Astell directed her work on the education of women, the nature of the marriage contract and the submissive role women were expected to play as wives, was that of the 1690s and early 1700s. Looking back to the developments over the century exactly how, for better or worse, had the position of women changed? It is a complex question and one not easily answered.[89]

In a variety of ways the Civil War years and Interregnum had undermined traditional ideas of the family, marriage and women's role of obedience and submission to men. For women of both sides, and of all classes, the war had often meant the absence of husbands

and the need for wives to take increased responsibilities in running
the farm, the trade, or simply in coping with the day-to-day business
of looking after the house, the children and servants, and tending
the garden or smallholding that was the extent of their landed property. Such new responsibilities had led to an increased independence
among many women. Some Royalist wives had even had experience
of litigation in the attempt to get their husbands and their property
released.

For many women the period had meant unprecedented involvement
in political activity and, at least temporarily, the rejection of the
notion that politics were men's business. In the petitioning of Parliament of the 1640s and 1650s women are now known to have played
a significant role. Women petitioned for peace, against the evil effects
of the decline of trade, against Bishops and the Laudian innovations,
and for the release of their husbands from prison. They rioted against
enclosures and took a leading role in political demonstrations of
all kinds. There were many women Levellers – not least the wife
of John Lilburne – and many petitioned Parliament for the release
of the Leveller leaders in 1649. By their actions women seemed
to be laying claim to the Leveller belief that men and women were
born free and equal, and demonstrating their ability to speak and
act for themselves – quite independently of their husbands.

The period of the Civil War and Interregnum had seen the break-
down of Church courts and the relaxation of supervision over the
morals of men and women. Coupled with a greater social and physical
mobility it resulted in much greater sexual freedom for women.

However, it was above all the contribution made by the sects
– Baptists and, more particularly, Quakers and Ranters – which did
most to undermine the patriarchal view of the family and the women's
traditional role within it. Women apparently occupied a numerically
dominant position within the sects. In many, the belief in self-
government meant women played an increasing part in their organisation and management.

In the sects' insistence on individual conscience and the direct
relationship between the believer and God, the role of the educated
ministry and the authority of the Church was diminished. Above
all it was the belief in the spiritual equality of men and women
that contributed most to the part women played within the sects.
The belief that women had equal souls with men had been emphasised
earlier by Richard Bolton, but it was underlined by Samuel Torshell

in 1645 when he wrote 'The soul knows no difference of sex'. Some sects – the Baptists and, more particularly, the Quakers – taking such claims to their logical conclusion, allowed women to preach. As Fox was to ask: 'May not the spirit of Christ speak in the female as well as in the male?'[90] Even more than preach, women prophesied. The horror of the outcry against such preaching and prophesying women makes clear that some critics saw clearly the threat to the traditional role of women such activities represented.

If preaching and prophesying enabled women to achieve a self-expression hitherto denied them, new ideas (some of them expressed by women themselves) on marriage, the injustices of a commercial marriage market, and on divorce encouraged them in practices which weakened the marriage bond, tended to erode the role of the husband as spiritual and temporal head of the household, questioned the unequal education given to women and their whole role of submission and obedience to their husbands.

The idea of the spiritual equality of the sexes and the supreme importance of individual conscience freed women from spiritual dependence on their husbands. When it came to a question of loyalty to a husband or loyalty to religious conviction it was the latter that won out. Thus Mrs Chidley asked in 1641 'what authority [the] unbelieving husband hath over the conscience of his believing wife; it is true he hath authority over her in bodily and civil respects, but not to be a lord over her conscience.'[91] From the claim to religious independence for women it was but a short step to that of political and social independence. It was not just the unity of the Church that was threatened but the unity of the family.

So the 1640s and 1650s might seem to represent a great step in the emancipation of women; a permanent break with the past. But such a view of the influences at work in this period overlooks the extent and strength of the opposition which derived not just from Anglicans and Presbyterians but from the sects, or rather the male sectaries, themselves. They were usually all too anxious to make and maintain the distinction between the liberty of women to believe and worship as their consciences dictated, and the traditional role of obedience that women owed their husbands and fathers. And there were many who were not at all sure just how far women's liberty of conscience should be taken. With the Restoration and the sects' move towards less political objectives developed the trend towards more clearly defined institutional frameworks and a more traditional and conservative approach.

Of course there were other long-term tendencies that worked in the same direction – towards a return in emphasis to the traditional role of women. In the first place, the seventeenth century sees the beginning of a development that was to accelerate in the next century – the gradual decline in the economic opportunities for women, and even, as in the case of midwifery, brewing and printing, the exclusion of women from fields where hitherto they had been prominent. In agriculture farmers' wives who had enjoyed a role that was admittedly not one of equality, but at least approached an economic partnership with their husbands, were for reasons of choice as well as of developments in agriculture withdrawing from labour.

Another factor which mitigated against women was the changing sex ratio. Evidence suggests that although the sex ratio was lowest in towns, particularly London, the problem created by a surplus of women extended to many rural as well as urban areas. As Moll Flanders was to comment: 'The market is against our sex just now, the men play the game all into their own hands.'[92]

The advances in capitalist organisation in industry and agriculture seen in this century ensured the victory by its close of economic individualism over traditional and communal arrangements. So it was that the importance of the family and household declines with the increasing importance of the individual. At first sight this might seem to suggest the decline within the family of the authority of the father, the traditional head of the household. But the victory of individualism was a victory for property, and wives by their very legal definition were propertyless so that all the Puritan emphasis on the virtues of thrift, industry and discipline tended towards the reinforcement not the weakening of the authority of husband and father.

It was this that above all led to that 'crisis in marriage which bore particularly hard upon the feminine part of the population'.[93] It was not just that there seems to have been an increasing emphasis on mercenary motives for marriage but that, in conditions where it was becoming more difficult and far more expensive, to find a husband, the importance of marriage for women actually increased. This crisis existed long before the 1690s but, when in 1695 effective censorship ended, the pent-up frustrations of many women, not just Mary Astell, were released. In a way it was a defensive action. It was to fail and nearly a century was to pass before the effort was renewed.

After 1660 there was a concerted attempt to re-establish social order which involved efforts to reimpose the traditional role of women and children in relation to their husbands and fathers. It seems certain that at the Restoration, as Keith Thomas has suggested, 'the more radical views on the family went underground'.[94]

Look, for instance, at *The Ladies Calling* which appeared in 1673. At one time it was thought to be the work of Lady Pakington, a Royalist, but it is now recognised to be the work of Richard Allestree, a Royalist clergyman and author of that other best seller, *The Whole Duty of Man* (1658). It ran to eight editions before 1700, indicative of its influence. In it Allestree, while recognising the equality of women's souls with those of men, makes clear 'that in respect of their intellects they are below men'.[95] He stresses the importance in women of a 'will duly submissive to lawful Superiors' for the contrary was 'the spring and original of infinite confusions, a grand incendiary which sets Kingdoms, Churches, Families in combustion'.[96] It was the duty of wives to obey their husbands not because of their vow to do so but 'from an original of much older date, it being the mulct that was laid upon the Woman's disobedience to God, that she (and all deriv'd from her) should be subject to the Husband; so that the contending for superiority is an attempt to reverse the Fundamental Law, which is almost as ancient as the World'.[97]

He saw the leading feminine virtue as that of modesty which 'restrains all excessive talkativeness'. Almost the worst sin in women was that of boldness. And lest any should recall the women preachers of the Interregnum, and seek to emulate them, he reminds his readers that St Paul 'expressly enjoins women to keep silence in the church'.[98]

Two years later Hannah Woolley restated the role of women in marriage: 'Undoubtedly the Husband', she wrote, 'hath power over the Wife and the Wife ought to be subject to the Husband in all things.'[99]

Yet attempts to put the clock back in family relations, as in politics, encountered serious obstacles. If some employment opportunities had now been denied women, others had emerged which provided women with new forms of self-expression. The advent of actresses, for example, opened the way into a new and important profession. Indeed, it is not too fanciful to see a continuity between the female preachers and prophetesses of the 1640s and 1650s and the post-Restoration actresses. Acting represented a similar break with the notion that

22

women should be kept out of public life and that their place was in the privacy of the home. The arrival of women on the stage was an encouragement to the emergence of women playwrights. Together they contributed to the new focus on women and women's dilemma both in and out of marriage which is the subject of a great deal of Restoration theatre.

One of the things that distinguishes the post-Restoration period as far as women are concerned was the changed nature of the means by which articulate women expressed themselves. Women, admittedly mainly upper-class women, moved from a more private expression of their thoughts in spiritual diaries, letters and poetry, to a more public expression. Women playwrights opened the way for women novelists. Remarkably Aphra Behn combined both skills. But in other areas, where the existence of current debate ensured all contributions were in the public eye, women, if still only a few, now made their entry.

Religion was one area in which women had, for a long time, been more free to express themselves than in other fields, although one needs to acknowledge that there were still men who thought it was more important that women should keep to the religion in which they had been reared, or should adopt that of their husbands, than that they should be able to defend their faith. So Halifax, in his *Advice to a Daughter*, suggested the reason for a woman keeping to the faith in which she had been brought up 'is somewhat stronger for your sex than it will perhaps be allowed to be for ours; in respect that the voluminous inquiries into the truth, by reading, are less expected from you'.[100] Nevertheless religion and religious controversy had provided one area in which intelligent women could use their minds. Mary Astell was by no means alone among educated upper-class women in her knowledge of the Bible and her grasp of contemporary theological debate. Women of the sects had demonstrated their ability to play a major part in religious life and thought, and while the debt was seldom acknowledged, many upper-class women must have been aware of the precedents set.

It was not new to the post-Restoration period for women to express their views on education, particularly education for their own sex, but now far more women entered into the debate. Here again, Mary Astell in her *A Serious Proposal, Part I*, was not alone in expressing views on the inadequacy of educational provision for women and ideas for some solution to the problem. The same is true of works on such diverse subjects as cookery and midwifery.

Women artists that emerge in the period, with the notable exception of Mary Beale, are usually amateurs. They had no training. But, as Myra Reynolds suggests, the real incentive behind their painting – and there were many such amateur painters among women – was the 'inner demand for some form of self-expression'. It was this that made them welcome any 'opportunity for the free play of their own individuality'.[101]

Accompanying the venturing into print of many women playwrights, novelists and poets, there would seem to have been a marked increase in women readers. Of course female literacy everywhere lagged far behind that of men, but over the century as a whole there is evidence that, at least among the middle ranks of women, increased leisure led to a greater interest in literature. This tendency was greatest in towns, and above all in London. If the ability of women to read was related to their ability to sign their names, it would appear that the former increased sharply in London towards the end of the century and particularly in the 1690s, constituting 'an educational revolution ... among late Stuart and early Hanoverian women'.[102] One writer has talked of an 'advancing army of women readers' in this period.[103] Certainly the rise of a feminine readership would seem to be supported by the emergence of periodicals and newspapers specifically directed at a female audience. So, for example, the *Athenian Gazette*, later the *Athenian Mercury*, was started in 1690, with an eye on the woman reader.

The England of the post-Restoration period was very different from that of the 1640s but if the position of women had changed it was not solely on the debit side. One thing is certain. The memory of that earlier period was still fresh in men's and women's minds. Even for those like Mary Astell, who thoroughly disapproved of much of what had been done, said or written earlier, the awareness of the developments at that time remained and, whether consciously or not, influenced her thinking and that of other female contemporaries.

A Serious Proposal

The first of Mary Astell's published works was *A Serious Proposal to the Ladies for the Advancement of their True and Greatest Interest* which appeared in 1694.[104] By 1701 it had run to four editions, which suggests something of its reception. Indeed, it was read even if its ideas were unacceptable. Three years after its appearance a second part followed. There seems no evidence that this was contemplated at the time of the publication of Part I which stands on its own. Part I contains all the details of her 'proposal' and the reasons which prompted her to make it.

Her scheme was a simple one – the creation of a 'Religious Retirement' (p.150) where women could, temporarily, withdraw from the world. But it was to be not only a place of retreat but one where women could be equipped to re-enter society and become useful members of it. She constantly emphasised this 'double aspect' of her female 'monastery' and, as she explains to women, the employment of its inmates was to be not only 'to magnify God, to love one another', but 'to communicate that useful *knowledge*, which by due improvement of your time in Study and Contemplation you will obtain' (p.151).

Her use of the word 'Monastery' was unfortunate for it immediately conjured up those Catholic institutions which, in her own words, 'tho' innocent in themselves, have been abused by superstitious practices' (p.150) and it did little to recommend her proposal. In fact she made clear the distinction between her 'Religious Retirement' and a nunnery. In her scheme 'piety shall not be roughly impos'd, but wisely insinuated', nor were there to be 'Vows or irrevocable Obligations, not so much as the fear of Reproach to keep our Ladies here any longer than they desire' (p.158). In answer to those who saw her proposal as a rejection of this world, she stressed that it was to be but 'a convenient and blissful recess from the noise and hurry of the world' (p.150). There was no inherent contradiction, in her view, between a contemplative and active life. The temporary removal from the world would not hinder women 'from bettering and improving it' when they returned. Indeed, she saw her 'Retirement' as 'a Seminary to stock the kingdom with pious and prudent Ladies' (p.152) who would be an example to the rest of their sex.

If religion was seen as 'its ... main design' with the performance of daily devotions and the regular observance of Sundays, holy days and fasts, 'one great end of this Institution,' she wrote, 'shall be to expel that cloud of Ignorance which Custom has involv'd us in, to furnish our minds with a stock of solid and useful Knowledge' (p.152). Of what exactly that knowledge should consist we are left uncertain, but the importance of discussion and the exchange of ideas is suggested by her mention of 'instructive discourses' and 'ingenious conversation'. The emphasis was to be on the need to train minds rather than on the acquisition of knowledge. Languages were of value – not in themselves – but because they gave access to 'useful Authors' (p.153). The aim of the education women received must be, in a phrase reminiscent of Bacon, not 'in learning words but things' (p.152). It was better to read and thoroughly understand a few well-chosen and good books than to thumb through a vast number and the understanding of French which so many ladies included among their accomplishments could be put to good use by discovering the French philosophers, Descartes and Malebranche, and the works of Madame Dacier and Scudéry, rather than reading those 'idle Novels and Romances' (p.155). Among the 'harmless and ingenious Diversions' (p.157) positively encouraged for the inmates of her seminary, music was particularly emphasised.

Women in her 'Religious Retirement' when not engaged in religious devotions were to be 'employ'd in innocent, charitable, and useful Business: either in study in learning themselves or instructing others' for, as Mary Astell stresses, 'it is design'd that part of their Employment be the Education of those of their own Sex' (p.156). It is true that, at least in this work, she confined her concern about education to the upper classes. She envisaged her seminary sending back into the world a body of women trained to take over responsibility for the education of the children of 'Persons of Quality' (p.165), and, when their finances permitted, to extend their responsibility to the education of daughters of gentlemen 'who are fallen into decay' so that they might be 'put in a comfortable way of subsisting' (p.166) and, she adds significantly, despite their lack of dowry, made more marriageable.

Her proposed institution was to be run under a strict discipline but one imposed by 'friendly Admonitions, not magisterial Reproofs' (p.158). The standards of accommodation, dress and diet were to be determined by those who subscribed to the scheme, but its author was in no doubt that their choice would be guided by 'what Nature not Luxury requires' (p.157). There were to be no 'superfluities': the time to be spent by the inmates on their toilet, on sleeping and eating was to be 'no more than necessity requires' (p.157). Tuition would be undertaken by 'persons of irreproachable Lives, of a consummate Prudence, sincere Piety and unaffected Gravity' (p.158). The suggested annual fee was £500 to £600, a sum few but 'Persons of Quality' would have been able to afford.

According to George Ballard, a bishop intervened to prevent a prominent lady giving £10,000 towards the realisation of Mary Astell's scheme.[105] The lady concerned is thought to have been Princess Anne of Denmark which might help to explain why the second part of *A Serious Proposal* published in 1697 was dedicated to her and not, as was the first part, to ladies in general! The name of Lady Elizabeth Hastings was also put forward as the possible unknown benefactress, but there is some doubt whether the two were yet acquainted at this time. A letter dated 13 July 1738 from Elizabeth Elstob, the Anglo-Saxon scholar, to George Ballard after he had requested information about the name of the lady concerned produced no further evidence. Elizabeth Elstob had never 'heard Mrs. Astell mention the Good Lady's name', but the bishop who intervened to discourage the lady from donating such a sum was revealed by Mary Astell to be Bishop Burnet[106] who disliked what he saw as the Catholic overtones of her proposal. However, in view of this attitude, it seems curious that he was later to write in favour of 'something like Monasteries without Vows' where young women could acquire 'a due Measure of Knowledge and a serious Sense of Religion.'[107]

The idea of a place of 'Religious Retirement' to which women could withdraw and where they could continue their education was not new and can be traced from the time of Henry VIII's suppression of nunneries up to the second half of the eighteenth century. It is now generally agreed that nunneries had provided a solution to the gentry's problem of disposing of their unmarriageable daughters, and Milton was not alone in seeing them as 'a convenient stowage for their withered daughters'. But nunneries were more than that. Possibly under financial pressure in the years immediately before the Reformation, they appear increasingly to have opened their doors to paying pupils not merely of the well-to-do but from tradesmen and even yeomen. Given the state of girls' boarding schools at the time, it seems likely that the education they provided was quite as good as if not better than that they would have received either at home or at such schools. Certainly from the 1530s onwards there are cases of Protestants lamenting the passing of nunneries as useful places of education for women. In the mid-sixteenth century, for example, Thomas Becon begged that there be 'some consideration of this matter had among the rulers of the Christian Commonweal that the young maids might be Godly brought up.'[108] Later, John

Aubrey, Thomas Fuller and Richard Allestree among others were to express the same regret.

In the first half of the seventeenth century, Lettice, Lady Falkland, harboured the notion of a 'place for the education of young gentle-women and for the retirement of widows ... in several parts of the kingdom' but she had been discouraged from pursuing the idea by 'those evil times'.[109] The community at Little Gidding formed by Nicholas Ferrar and his nieces, had been a practical — and private — example of something similar to what later Mary Astell had in mind. As *A Serious Proposal* was being written, Mary and Anne Kemys at Naish Court in Glamorganshire were at the centre of a kind of Anglican sisterhood.

Perhaps the most interesting of the proposals that precede Mary Astell's was that put forward by Clement Barksdale — an intriguing character who consistently demonstrated his unfashionable interest in women's education. In 1659 he was responsible both for the transla-tion and publication of Anna Maria Schurman's *The Learned Maid, or Whether a Maid may be a Scholar* which had already aroused considerable interest on the Continent. In 1675 he wrote *A Letter Touching a Colledge of Maids, or a Virgin Society* in which he proposed the formation of a girl's college 'somewhat like the Halls of Commoners at *Oxford*', combining both religious and secular objects and with the declared purpose of improving 'ingenuous Maids in such qualities as best become their Sex, and may fit them both for a happy Life in this, and much more in the next world'. Unlike Anna Maria Schurman, Barksdale's proposal was not confined to daughters of the upper-class although his college acknowledged class differences. The daughters of the rich would be served and waited on by '*Maids* of meaner birth and estate' but both would be guided by governesses in 'a method of private Reading and Devotion'. The entrance fee would be £5 'more or less, according to the quality of the persons' and, although his broadly based curriculum included training in the traditional accomplishments of music, dancing, needlework and draw-ing, the library was to include 'choice Authors of *History, Poetry,* and especially of *Practical Divinity* and *Devotion*'. There were to be not only examples of English writers but of works of 'Learned, as well as Modern *Language*'.[110] The most able were to study both natural and moral philosophy. The girls could be taken away from the college by their fathers at any time, either for a few days or 'to dispose of them in marriage'.[111] While there was no suggestion of provision for wives, Barksdale's 'Virgin Society' resembles in design that put forward nearly twenty years later by Mary Astell.

After 1694, her idea of a 'Protestant nunnery' won support from, among others, John Evelyn, George Wheler, Robert Nelson and Lady Mary Wortley Montagu. The idea did not die. In the works of Thomas Amory, in Samuel Richardson's *Sir Charles Grandison*, and in the novels of Sarah Fielding and Sarah Scott among others, one can trace the recurrent theme of a 'Religious Retirement' for women.[112] Not all these authors were agreed on the details of what was required but all saw the desirability of a place of retirement from the world where women could go both for religious and secular education.

Three years after Mary Astell made her proposal, Daniel Defoe published his *An Essay upon Projects* in which he put forward his scheme for 'An Academy for Women'. While expressing his 'very great esteem' for 'what is proposed by that ingenious lady', he was at some pains to distinguish his proposals from her's. The 'Religious Retirement', he insisted, 'would be found impracticable' not only for the reason that 'nothing but the height of bigotry can keep up a nunnery', but because 'the levity' of the opposite sex would 'not bear the restraint'.[113] The difficulty in discerning important differences between the two proposals might lead one to conclude that Defoe was jealous of Mary Astell for having published her proposal first.

In his Essay there is a suggestion of just how much single women were the prey of those whom Mary Astell described as 'bold importunate and rapacious vultures'. To protect his Academy against infiltrators he demanded an Act of Parliament to 'make it felony without Clergy for any man to enter by Force or Fraud into the House, or to solicit any Woman though it were to marry, while she was in the House.'[114] It is a sinister comment on the nature of society at that time and makes clear why Mary Astell saw the need for a place of retreat for women.

What is new in Mary Astell's proposal is that it represents 'the first considered attempt to interest Englishwomen in the higher education of their sex'[115] – a notion that had not previously been made the subject of a general appeal to women nor been made so powerfully. What is interesting is that the idea re-emerges in the late seventeenth century – and not merely in the work of Mary Astell.

Roger Thompson saw Mary Astell's proposal as part of what he called 'a desperate rearguard action against a shocking decline of standards'.[116] His view is supported by evidence that the quality of education for women had not improved. Certainly there had been mounting criticism of existing boarding schools for girls as the century progressed. After the Restoration there seems to have been a further sharp decline in standards – possibly a reflection of the more general decline in public manners of these years.

Although *A Serious Proposal* was the first of Mary Astell's published works, in many ways it anticipates the conclusions she reached about the lives of women, whether single or married, that later found fuller expression particularly in her *Reflections upon Marriage* published in 1700. (In the texts that follow I have reversed the chronological order and made *Reflections upon Marriage* precede *A Serious Proposal*[117] for the latter presents the only solution she offered given the state of marriage as it was.) She saw more education as the only answer available to women in their existing circumstances, but would have been the first to acknowledge that it was by no means a complete answer. 'My earnest desire', she wrote, 'is that you Ladies would be as perfect and happy as 'tis possible to be in this imperfect state' (p.142). That more education was her only answer suggests perhaps just how 'imperfect' she saw this state as being.

Her argument starts from the basic premise that in so far as women are inferior to men it is the result not of nature but of education. She challenges those who 'deny us the improvement of our Intellectuals' either to take their stand on the old argument that women have no souls, which, she adds 'at this time a day when they are allow'd to Brutes, would be as unphilosophical as it is unmannerly, or else let them permit us to cultivate and improve them' (p.154).

She does not spare her audience. Far too often women were 'content to be Cyphers in the World, useless at the best, and in a little time a burden and nuisance to all about them' (p.143). Angrily she asks of women: 'Why are you so preposterously humble?' (p.141) The 'ill conduct of too many' had led them to 'pass for those little useless and impertinent Animals' (p.152). What, she demands of them 'stops your flight' and 'keeps you groveling here below, like Domitian catching Flies when you should be busied in obtaining Empires?' (p.143) Perhaps conscious of the severity of her censure she hastens to reassure her audience. Her aim, she insists, 'is not to expose, but to rectifie' (p.142) their failures.

One such failure was their wastage of time in slavishly following fashion, in endeavouring to excel in 'trifles', in seeking distinction in mere ornamental accomplishments – and to what purpose but that of winning 'Fustian Compliments and Fulsome Flatteries' (p.140) and 'to attract the Eyes of Men ... vain, insignificant men' (p.141)? Women had become slaves to 'that Tyrant Custom' (p.147) intent 'on doing as their neighbours do' lest they attract to themselves 'all the Scofs and Noises of the world' (p.162). She appeals to women to 'dare to break the enchanted Circle that custom has plac'd us in' (p.141).

Her scorn for how little men have to show for all the lavish care and time bestowed on their education is unbounded. She would offer them advice but 'they think themselves too wise to receive Instruction from a Woman's Pen'. Men, 'often guilty of greater faults' yet 'divert themselves with our Miscarriages' (p.142). Denying women the benefit of a liberal education, they then complain of the consequences when women are 'taught to be Proud and Petulant, Delicate and Fantastick, Humorous and Inconstant' (p.144). It is against men, the 'Enemy from without' (p.145), that her religious retirement offers a refuge: for 'Heiresses and Persons of Fortune' it offered a haven from 'the rude attempts of designing Men' (p.165). She expressed contempt for money and what money will buy, whether a marriage, 'a sounding Title or a great Estate' (p.139). Her 'retirement' represented for women who had 'more Money than Discretion' an escape from predatory men.

Reflections upon Marriage

Six years after *A Serious Proposal* was published there appeared *Some Reflections upon Marriage Occasion'd by the Duke and Dutchess of Mazarine's Case which is also considered*.[118] It ran through four editions by 1730 (1700, 1703, 1706, 1730). To the third edition of 1706 – (the one reproduced here) was added a Preface 'in answer to some Objections'.

The Duchess of Mazarine, a near-neighbour of Mary Astell's, had been forced into an unhappy marriage, one of the consequences of which was a scandal that reverberated around Europe. The case of the duchess served, Mary Astell wrote, 'as an unhappy shipwrack to point out the dangers of an ill Education and unequal Marriage' (p.90). Neither side escaped her censure but her sympathy was reserved for the duchess 'who being capable of everything must therefore suffer more'.

31

For such unhappy marriages entered into on ill-considered motives, there was no solution. The wives had to bear the consequences and Mary Astell did not underestimate them. 'To be yok'd for Life to a disagreeable Person and Temper; to have Folly and Ignorance tyrannise over Wit and Sense; to be contradicted in everything one does or says, and bore down not by Reason but Authority; to be denied ones most innocent desires, for no other cause but the Will and Pleasure of an absolute Lord and Master, whose Follies a Woman with all her Prudence cannot hide, and whose Commands she cannot but despise at the same time she obeys them; is a misery none can have a just idea of, but those who have felt it' (p.90). These words sum up Mary Astell's whole condemnation of so many upper class marriages.

Nevertheless, she saw marriage as 'too sacred to be treated with Disrespect'. Being the 'Institution of Heaven', it was not just 'the only Honourable way of continuing Mankind' (p.93), but provided 'the best that may be for Domestic Quiet and Content, and for the Education of Children' (pp.93–4). Happy marriages, she insisted, were possible but they required care – above all a choice based on reason with the chief inducement that of friendship. But if marriage was 'such a blessed State', why were there so few happy marriages? In large part the blame lay with men in their motives for entering into marriage and their ill-conduct within it. More often than not such motives were mercenary; 'What will she bring is the first enquiry? How many acres? Or how much ready Coin?' Such considerations were not unimportant, she acknowledged, for 'Marriage without a Competency' was 'no very comfortable Condition' (p.94) but it was not the main, and certainly not the only, consideration. Mercenary marriages were doomed. For the very best of women, as Mary Astell ironically suggested, they could become 'a very great Blessing' by giving her the 'opportunity to exercise her Virtue'. For, she continued 'Affliction' was 'the only useful school that Women were ever put to' for it 'rouses her understanding, opens her Eyes, fixes her Attention' (p.96). Such a wife 'was never truly a Happy Woman till she came in the Eye of the World to be reckon'd Miserable' (p.97). By no means all injured wives would react like this! Many, and who could blame them, would follow the example set by their husbands.

Marriages for love, if rarer, were no different. Equally irrational, men were 'govern'd by irregular Appetites' (p.97) or a man might think himself in love with a woman's wit but 'cannot hope to find a Woman whose Wit is of a size with his' (p.98), and when the occasion arises for a woman to turn her wit on him he might find it less agreeable! When you add those who 'Marry without any Thought at all, further than that it is the Custom of the World' (p.99) to those who marry for money, love or wit, there are very few marriages remaining.

Mary Astell would be the first to admit that it is not just men who are in the wrong, but as 'a Woman ... can't properly be said to Choose', as 'all that is allow'd her, is to Refuse or Accept what is offer'd' (p.99), women are more to be pitied than censured. If a man can anticipate no happiness from marriages for money, wit or beauty, how much less can a woman expect of them? Hers is by far 'the harder bargain' for 'if the Matrimonial Yoke be grievous, neither Law nor Custom afford her that redress which a Man obtains' (p.101). If she has the bad fortune to marry a man with a 'disagreeable Temper', she will be 'as unhappy as anything in this World can make her'. She cannot, like her husband, 'find entertainments abroad', she has not 'a hundred ways of relieving' herself, all she can do is stay at home and 'make her best on't' (p.103).

For women, then, the right marriage partner was of far greater importance than for men. No 'Woman of any tolerable Sense' should trust herself to a man who 'doats on a Face', who 'makes Money his Idol' or 'who is Charm'd with vain and empty Wit'. How could she love or honour such a 'trifle of a Man' and if she cannot either love or honour him she should never promise to obey him, for such obedience 'as is paid only to Authority, and not out of Love and a Sense of the Justice and Reasonableness of the Command, will be of uncertain Tenure'. If nevertheless a woman obeys, she must be 'endow'd with a Wisdom and Goodness much above what we suppose the Sex capable of, I fear much greater than e're a Man can pretend to' (pp.104–5)!

If this is what a woman who marries 'prudently' can expect, what of those who marry beneath them, who 'purchase a Lord and Master' and 'at the price of her Discretion'? Even more will he assert his authority and tend to overlook any obligations entered into before marriage. For every man expects a wife 'whom he can intirely Govern ... who must be his for Life, and therefore cannot quit his Service let him treat her how he will'. Even those who marry their social equals have 'no security but the Man's Honour and Good nature' (p.106). And what are those worth?

So what remains as the best guarantees of a happy marriage? 'A good understanding' and 'a Virtuous Mind' are the principal considerations in the choice of a marriage partner, and Mary Astell adds 'as much equality as may be' (p.108). But a wise choice of a partner was not sufficient to guarantee married happiness. The role of subjection that women were assigned was 'a bitter Cup' (p.109) and it would be easier for them to bear if it was not claimed 'oftner and more Imperiously than either Discretion or Good Manners will justifie'. The vows of marriage which involved a mutual agreement and a 'certain Civility and Respect' are quite 'as much the Woman's due as Love, Honour and Obedience are the Man's' (p.108). If, despite all a woman forfeits by marriage, there is not only no acknowledgement of a husband's obligations to her but even disrespect, a woman must be a saint if she continues to pay him the obedience he demands. But if men continue to regard women with contempt and women continue to suffer it, they cannot but become aware of 'their own real superiority' (p.112).

There is little here to suggest that marriage could be a 'blessing' for women. The most that is hoped for is that it should prove 'tolerable' (p.114). Of those who entertained great hopes of marriage, many would be disappointed, their only consolation being their reward in heaven. Marriage was their 'time of Tryal' (p.115).

Finally, and seemingly conclusively, Mary Astell argues that 'she then who Marrys ought to lay it down for an indisputable Maxim that her Husband must govern absolutely and intirely, and that she has nothing else to do but to Please and Obey'. If incapable of exercising 'Humility and Self-denial, Patience and Resignation' (p.116) then the role of wife is not for her.

However, Mary Astell cannot leave it there and she goes on to qualify the statement. No-one will convince a woman of the wisdom and goodness of her husband against all evidence to the contrary so, although she may submit, it will be from necessity not from reason. This is why, she argues, it is in men's interests for women to be good Christians. A Christian woman 'will freely leave him the quiet Dominion of this World whose Thoughts and Expectations are plac'd on the next', and by directing all their ambition heavenwards women will be sufficiently compensated 'for all the neglect and contempt the ill-grounded Customs of the World throw on her'. Thus the duty of obedience would be paid 'for God's sake' (p.128), and obedience to her husband was a woman's religious duty.

To survive the trials of marriage, women, Mary Astell argued, needed 'a strong Reason ... a truly Christian and well-temper'd Spirit' and 'all the Assistance the best Education can give her'. Little wonder that women married so hastily for if they stopped to consider 'they seldom would Marry at all' (p.131). More education would ensure that women 'marry more discreetly' or that they 'never consent to be a wife' (p.127).

The Preface which was added to the third edition of 1706 represents the best of her writing.[119] It appears to have been written at great speed and in passionate anger. If there is ambiguity – even apparent contradiction – in *Reflections*, the added Preface poses even greater problems for reaching any conclusions as to what exactly Mary Astell thought. Did she really believe, for example, that wives must obey their husbands and in all cases believe them 'Wise and Good and in all respects the best' (p.116)? Must a woman obey for no other reason than that there must be one seat of authority 'for Order's sake' (p.104) however lacking her husband might be in the qualities demanded in those that exert authority? In the Preface to the first edition she insists "Tis a very great Fault ... to submit to Authority, when we should only yield to Reason' (p.69). Was a man's right to govern forfeited when he abused his power as husband? Again the Preface suggests so when it argues that 'if Arbitrary Power is evil in itself, and an improper Method of govening Rational and Free Agents, it ought not to be Practis'd any where'. If marriage was a divinely ordained institution how was it that it ignored any idea of women's happiness? It is a curious choice of text that Mary Astell takes to head her preface to the third edition of *Reflections*: 'If a Virgin marry, she hath not sinned, nevertheless such shall have trouble.' Was marriage divinely ordained for men only? Must women be content with marriage as 'an excellent preparation for heaven' as it was their 'Duty to suffer everything without Complaint'? Yet in the Preface such an idea of women's role in marriage provoked that passionate response: 'If all Men are born free, how is it that all Women are born slaves?' (p.76). Women, she argued, were as yet 'too weak to dispute men's authority' and were 'not so well united as to form an Insurrection' (p.86) – but had they the right to challenge men's authority, and, when stronger and more united, to overthrow it? 'Far be it from her,' she insists, 'to stir up Sedition of any sort' (p.70), and yet she can ask 'can it be thought that an ignorant weak Woman shou'd have patience to bear a continual

Outrage and Insolence all the days of her Life?' (p.117)

Although it is tempting to try and resolve these questions, it would be a mistake. George Ballard, unable to accept the strong words in which she expressed her scorn for men, invented an unhappy love affair as explanation.[120] If we are to understand her we have to accept the ambiguities and contradictions of her writing. They were a part of her make-up and help to explain the tensions that inevitably developed in a woman of intelligence holding such diverse beliefs.

The year before *Reflections* was published, a sermon was preached by John Sprint at a wedding in Sherborne in Dorset. As his text he took 'But she that is married careth for the things of the world, how she may please her Husband'. On the grounds of being misrepresented by his female critics, 'my waspish accusers', Sprint decided to publish the sermon. He did so under the title *The Bride-Woman's Counsellor*. The duty of a wife in pleasing and comforting her husband was God's punishment for her role in the Fall as 'the Tempter's Agent'. To refuse that duty 'doth wickedly pervert the end of her Creation'. A good wife would never 'will or desire what she herself liked, but only what her Husband should approve and allow'. She must be like 'a mirror which hath no Image of its own, but receives its Stamp and Image from the Face that looks into it'. A wife should not address her husband by his Christian name – 'a Custom more Common than comely' – but as 'Lord and Master', a fitting address for 'one whom God hath appointed and ordained to be her Superior and Head'.[121]

Whether Mary Astell read the sermon we do not know, but it seems likely. Two works published in 1700 demonstrate the angry response it provoked among women. One was the poem, *The Ladies Defence: Or the Bride-Woman's Counsellor Answer'd*, by Lady Elizabeth Chudleigh, and the other *The Female Advocate; or, a Plea for the just liberty of the Tender Sex, and particularly of Married Women* that appeared under the pseudonym 'Eugenia'. The very response to the sermon might suggest that the views expressed in it were exceptional and not wholly representative of attitudes to the role of the wife in marriage. It is more difficult, however, to dismiss Lord Halifax's *The Lady's New Year Gift; Or, Advice to a Daughter* (1688)[122] written for his daughter Elizabeth – then twelve years old – to whom he was devoted. Significantly it was by far his most popular work, and over the following century ran to 25 editions. He admitted that at times he shrank 'as if struck at the prospect of danger to which a young woman must be exposed'. The institution of marriage was, he thought, 'too sacred to admit a liberty of objecting to it' (p.278). He explained to his daughter that one of the disadvantages of her sex is that 'young women are seldom permitted to make their own choice' of a husband. More often they are called on to accept the recommendations of their parents even if this goes against their inclinations. All they can do is to make the best of it and 'by a wise use of everything they may dislike in a husband turn that by degrees to be very supportable which, if neglected might in time beget an aversion'. The inequality between the sexes, the existence of which Halifax did not doubt, makes women 'better pre pared for the compliance that is necessary' (p.277). In order to help his daughter prepare herself for marriage he reviewed the type of husband with whom she might be forced into marriage. First was the adulterer or persistently unfaithful husband (and here Halifax acknowledged the double standard of a society which made 'that in the utmost degree criminal in the woman' which 'in a man passeth under a much gentler censure' (p.279)). Second was the drunkard 'and there is by too frequent examples evidence enough that such a thing may happen, and yet a wife may live too without being miserable' (p.280). Third was the choleric or ill-humoured man and 'there is a great deal of nice care requisite to deal with a man of this complexion' (p.282). A covetous husband is the fourth possibility, and although even he could be endured, 'a close-handed wretch', significantly, was the worst fate that Halifax could envisage for his daughter. Finally there was the feeble-minded husband – for whom there was a great deal to be said in Halifax's view, for 'if you will be more ashamed in some cases of such a husband, you will be less afraid than you would perhaps be of a wise one'! To have an idiot as a husband was the next best thing to having him dead 'in which case the wife hath right to administer' (p.285) so all the more important, warned Halifax, 'when your husband shall resolve to be an ass ... take care he may be *your* ass' (p.286).

Given such possibilities, Halifax suggested his daughter should 'pray for a wise husband, one that by knowing how to be a master for that very reason will not let you feel the weight of it' (p.286).

Earlier Hannah Woolley in *The Gentlewoman's Guide to the Female Sex* (1675) had emphasised a wife's duty 'to give honour, respect and reverence' to her 'lawful (though lording) husband' and stressed how she should endeavour 'to hide his faults and infirmities, and not detect them yourself, or suffer them to be discovered'.[123] As did Mary Astell, she warned of the consequences of marrying 'one you have either abhorrence or loathing to; for it is neither affluence of estate, potency of friends, nor highness of descent can alloy the insufferable grief of a loathed bed.'[124] Later in *The Queen-like Closet*, she issued a warning to all women who if they 'would consider the Policy of Men... might be generally happy; whereas now very few are so'. She had seen enough of them, she adds 'as it hath given me a sufficient Caution to beware of them.'[125] Yet here spoke a woman who, unlike Mary Astell was married twice, and happily, to 'two Worthy, Eminent, and brave Persons'.[126] Nevertheless, in the language she reserves for men in general she rivals Mary Astell.

Evidence suggests that Mary Astell was far from exaggerating the frequency of mercenary marriages among the upper class. It was, said Hannah Woolley, 'an ordinary thing, in these Late Times, for Gentlemen, when they hear of a Fortune, presently to make their Addresses to that Lady, a Gentlewoman, let her be as deformed or unhandsome a Creature as is imaginable'.[127] Although he believed 'Gentlemen in their Marriages ought to consider a great many things more than Fortune', Gilbert Burnet added, 'tho' generally speaking, that is the only thing sought for'.[128] Later Lady Mary Wortley Montagu was to make the same point when she commented bitterly that 'people in my way are sold like slaves; and I cannot tell what price my masters will put on me'.[129]

John Norris, in the course of his duties as adviser to the publishers of *The Athenian Mercury*, was asked whether friendship was possible between a man and his wife. After consideration he replied that Yes, there *could* be 'strict friendship between Man and Wife'. A husband, he wrote like 'the greatest Monarch in the World may find Opportunities to descend from the Throne of Majesty to the familiar Caresses of a dear Favourite: and unking himself a while for the more glorious Title of Friend.'[130] Norris, who appears to have been attractive to women, was married and had a large family. His answer serves not merely to remind us of just what women like Mary Astell were up against in even the most sympathetic of men, but of how deeply rooted was the particular analogy which he uses.

The king/subject analogy in marital relations

To many, the analogy between sovereign and subject relations and those of husband and wife must have seemed a dangerous one after 1660. A king had been removed by his subjects and the memory of that lost head was not to be forgotten in a hurry. The 1640s had seen a ferment of discussion in which traditional relationships between parents and children and husbands and wives had been subjected to a critical reappraisal. 'It is but too frequent a complaint',[131] wrote Robert South in 1679, 'that neither are men so good husbands, nor women so good wives, as they were before that *Accursed Rebellion* had made that fatal leading breach in the conjugal tie between the *best of Kings* and the *happiest of People*.' The anxiety to secure social order that accompanied the re-establishment of the monarchy was extended, not surprisingly, to a desire to redefine domestic relations along traditional lines.

The Ladies Calling of 1673 was an attempt to restate traditional views of marriage and the roles of husbands and wives. The view of marriage it expressed was a conservative one, but it is significant that it was specifically addressed to women, thus hinting at a degree of concern about women breaking away from custom and convention.

Far from diminishing, the problem presented by relations between sovereign and subject actually increased as the century ended. Tories in the reign of both Charles II and James II continued to emphasise the deification of kingship, while the leaders of the Church preached the doctrine of non-resistance to a hereditary monarch. These two beliefs were so fundamental to the leadership of the Church of England that to attack one was to attack both. With a religious theory of monarchical power went a religious explanation of the domestic submission of wives.

Although the characters of both Charles and James strained the idea of the spiritual leadership of the monarchy, the problem became acute after 1688 when William of Orange was invited to accept the Crown. Could he be accepted as the lawful King of England despite the fact that James was still alive? There was much heartsearching among high Churchmen but, in the event, only Archbishop Sancroft, six bishops and 400 clergy refused to take the Oath of Allegiance to William and Mary. They were deprived of their positions. Those who had failed to take the course of the non-jurors now had the problem of justifying their taking no action except that of expressing loyalty to William and Mary.

In January 1689 the Convention Parliament agreed that 'James the second, having endeavoured to subvert the constitution of the kingdom by breaking the original contract between king and people, and by the advice of Jesuits and other wicked persons having violated the fundamental laws and having withdrawn himself out of this kingdom, has abdicated the government and that the throne is thereby become vacant'.[132]

It would not have been surprising if some wives with adulterous and deserting husbands took the analogy to its logical conclusion and claimed legitimate grounds had been provided for divorce and remarriage. In fact, after 1697 although it became possible – if expensive – for an injured husband to get a divorce with permission to remarry, there was no such possiblity for an injured wife.

For Tories believing in hereditary succession, however, it was impossible for a throne to 'become vacant'. Some claimed that Mary was in fact James II's lawful hereditary heir, as James had not only deserted the kingdom but the son said to have been born to him in 1688 was not in fact his but had been planted in Queen Mary's bedchamber! Absurd as this story was, it also failed to provide a solution since William refused to be either Regent or Consort. When, finally, the possibility of William and Mary becoming joint sovereign seemed inevitable, some Tories began to argue that the Glorious Revolution could not have been resisted as it had been divinely ordained. Others argued along good Hobbesian lines, that obedience was due to any government that ensured the security and protection of society. A curious distinction was made between accepting William as the *de facto* King but continuing to recognise James as the *de iure* monarch. For the Whigs there was no such problem. Kingly government was the result of a contract between king and subjects. If the king proved tyrannical his subjects had the right to resist, and even, to 'abdicate' him.

Events after 1688 did not lessen the anxieties of the High Church Tories. So unpopular did William prove that Jacobitism continued to thrive throughout the 1690s. There had been no settlement of the question of the ultimate succession in 1688, and as William and Mary remained without children, the problem of their successor became crucial as their reign progressed.

Mary Astell was born six years after the Restoration. Her whole upbringing and what we know of her early life in London suggests

High Church and conservative influence. That extraordinary friendship with Archbishop Sancroft on her arrival in London suggests where her sympathies lay in 1689.

For anyone believing as she did in the natural hierarchy of society, it was difficult to ignore the analogy between king/subject and husband/wife relations: allusion to it abounded throughout the literature of the period. Thus, it was hardly necessary to be told that 'a Family, well Govern'd is like a Kingdom well Rul'd':[133] it was so much an unconscious assumption about political and domestic relationships. Mary Astell disapproved of play-going, but she cannot have remained unaware of how many dramatists were exploiting the analogy and even probing its ultimate logic. Many dramatists acknowledged that the position of women had changed. As Hilaria tells her uncle in Edward Ravenscroft's *The Careless Lovers* (1673), 'it is not now as it was in your young days, women then were poor sneaking, sheepish creatures. But in this Age, we know our own strength.'[134] In Thomas Otway's *The Atheist* (1685) Portia asks 'Do not our Fathers, Brothers and Kinsmen often upon pretence of it, bid fair for Rebellion against their Sovereign. And why ought not we, by their Example, to rebel as plausibly against them?'[135] 'When parents grow arbitrary', says Olivia in Aphra Behn's *The Younger Brother* (1696) ''tis time we look into our Rights and Privileges.'[136] The victim of an arranged and unhappy marriage, Lady Brute in Vanbrugh's *The Provok'd Wife* (1697) debates whether or not she is justified in taking a lover: 'Let me see — What opposes? — My matrimonial vow — Why, what did I vow? I think I promis'd to be true to my husband. Well; and he promis'd to be kind to me. But he han't kept his word. Why then I'm so absolv'd from mine. Aye that seems clear to me. The argument's good between the king and the people, why not between the husband and the wife?'[137]

Mary Astell uses the analogy frequently. A wife, she wrote, 'Elects a Monarch for Life' and 'gives him an Authority she cannot recall however he misapply it' (p.103).[138] Women should therefore be more careful in accepting a man for a husband. Whatever the pre-marital financial agreements 'Covenants betwixt Husband and Wife, like Laws in an Arbitrary Government, are of little Force, the Will of the Sovereign is all in all' (p.106). Husbands who lack the qualities necessary for exerting authority justly, are, 'Usurpers being always most desirous of Recognitions and busie in imposing Oaths, whereas a Lawful Prince contents himself with the usual Methods and Securities' (p.109). She talks here of husbands but she was thinking of William of Orange. Although 'the Order of the World requires an *Outward* Respect and Obedience from some to others', it will never 'be well either with those who Rule or those in Subjection, even from the Throne to every Private Family, till those in Authority look on themselves as plac'd in that Station for the good and improvement of their Subjects, and not for their own sakes'. Husbands like kings are 'the Representatives of God', and women 'shou'd respect their Governours as plac'd in God's stead' (p.110–11). If a wife 'cannot patiently submit even when Reason suffers with her, who does not practise Passive Obedience to the utmost', she will 'never be acceptable to such an absolute Sovereign as a Husband' (p.115).

Sometimes the analogy leads her into difficulties. If government is not based on 'a Superior Understanding' and rests on power alone, 'there can be no such thing as Usurpation; but a Highway-Man so long as he has strength to force, has also a Right to require our Obedience' (p.76). Yet elsewhere she insists, 'I love Justice too much to wish Success and continuance to Usurpations, which tho' submitted to out of Prudence, and for Quietness sake, yet leave every Body free to regain their lawful Right whenever they have Power and Opportunity'. Tyranny will lead the oppressed to 'throw off even a Lawful Yoke that sits too heavy'. She does not condone such action, but neither does she condemn it. Even when a woman has freely chosen her husband, if nevertheless he 'proves a Tyrant, the consideration that he was ones own Choice will not render [wives] more Submissive and Patient, but I fear more Refractory' (p.131).

Although she does not accept with Locke that a King who abuses his power forfeits, by that abuse, his right to govern, when it comes to relations between a tyrannical husband and a wife she is clearly less certain. She emphasises how much worse is arbitrary power in the family than in the kingdom 'by how much 100,000 Tyrants are worse than one' (p.76). In revealing 'the inconsistency of a double standard'[139] as between attitudes in national and domestic politics, she also reveals inconsistencies in her own thinking. It is not just for the sake of logic chopping – an attempt to score points against her adversaries, the Whigs – that she probes the analogy so deeply.[140] She wants to establish a logic in her own thinking and she encounters insurmountable obstacles. Irony is used both to confound her political enemies and also to confound men in general – and women who are 'Wise enough to Love their Chains' (p.86)! When she comes to what women must endure as wives the irony is still there but it does not disguise her profound sympathy with their lot. Even though a husband cannot legally deprive a 'Wife of Life', she writes bitterly, 'he may however do what is much more grievous to a generous Mind, render Life miserable, for which she has no Redress, scarce Pity which is afforded to every other Complainant. It being thought a Wife's Duty to suffer everything without Complaint' (p.76). 'It being thought' is rather different from 'I think' – it is a not insignificant qualification.

Reading her work one is constantly made aware of how her attachment to the divine right of kings and passive obedience opposes her reluctance to accept women's position as slaves to domestic tyranny. What is left to them but to submit 'unless they are Strong enough to break the Yoke, to Depose and Abdicate, which, I doubt', she adds ambiguously, 'would not be allow'd of here' (p.102). Many who shared her political and religious views saw the danger of taking the analogy too far, and rejected it. In contrast Mary Astell seems to deliberately explore it even when it produces contradictions in her own thinking.

The problem of dissent

The dilemma posed by 1688 for High Church Tories was exacerbated by the divisions that developed within the ranks of the Church of England. Its prestige and self-confidence had already been seriously undermined by the non-jurors' accusations that it had betrayed its own principles. Some of the leading divines of the Church, including the non-juror Archbishop Sancroft, with whom Mary Astell corresponded in the 1680s, favoured a far more comprehensive Church embracing dissenters, but on this aspect of his beliefs Mary Astell remained silent. Although a Comprehension Bill was drawn up alongside a Toleration Bill, the fear of losing their monopoly position within the Church made many Anglicans extremely hostile to any suggestions for a broad-based Church. The fact that William III was known to be sympathetic to such ideas did little to quieten such fears. Indeed, the idea that dissent was a dangerous threat to the authority of the Church was strengthened by the events of the 1690s.

The apparent increasing numerical strength of the dissenters alarmed

Anglicans. In fact, the number of dissenter meeting houses – particularly in London – did increase, but dissenters never constituted more than a small minority of the population so that the threat they offered to the Church seems to have been much exaggerated. Nevertheless, such a belief was strong and sincerely held by many Anglicans. Events in Scotland where Presbyterians had abolished episcopacy were seen as a warning of what might happen here. Then, while the Toleration Act reimposed many of the earlier restrictions on non-conformists, it did give them a legal status in the community, and, as we shall see, the growing practice of Occasional Conformity began to penetrate the Anglican monopoly of state office.

Increasingly, in the years following 1689, the whole intellectual atmosphere, particularly as manifested by a more rational attitude towards religion, seemed hostile to the Anglican Church. Even more alarming was the fact that ideas expressed by Locke in *The Reasonableness of Christianity* in 1695, and by the Deist, John Toland, in *Christianity not Mysterious* were seen to be shared by some of the most prominent of Anglicans. With the lapsing of the Licensing Act of 1695 there was nothing to prevent the free expression of such ideas. It was from the Latitudinarian wing that there emerged two voluntary societies, the Society for Promoting Christian Knowledge and the Society for the Propagation of the Gospel, in an effort to prove that the real strength of the Church lay within itself and was not dependent on the state.

Geoffrey Holmes has talked of 'the tortured state of the Established Church after the Settlement'[141] and the frenzied reaction of the 'Church in Danger' campaign launched in 1696 with the publication of Francis Atterbury's *A Letter to a Convocation Man*. Its intentions in the religious debate were paralleled in the political arena by the revived interest in the 'English Rebellion'. Clarendon's *History of the Rebellion*, although completed in the 1670s was only published in 1702–04 as, it would seem, a carefully planned part of the Tory campaign against dissent – and more particularly against Occasional Conformity.

When it became clear that Queen Mary was to bear no children and that therefore the successor to the throne was Anne, eldest daughter of James and strongly Anglican, the succession problem only diminished temporarily. Anne's health was known to be poor, and her only son, the Duke of Gloucester – also an Anglican – was to die in 1700. This did not prevent Tory Anglicans from having high hopes of support from Anne in their campaign to protect the

Church of England from the threat of dissent.

It is against this background that Mary Astell's political and religious writings are to be seen. They were concerned with precisely those issues that preoccupied High Church Tories. In 1704 she published three pamphlets: *A Fair Way with the Dissenters and their Patrons, Moderation Truly Stated,* and *An Impartial Enquiry into the Causes of Rebellion and Civil War in this kingdom.*

The practice of Occasional Conformity, by which non-conformists could attend an Anglican service once a year and thereby receive a certificate of attendance from the vicar that qualified them for public office, was not new. It was a device that had been used by some non-conformists to evade the restrictions on their occupation of public office by the Test and Corporation Acts. Exactly how many Occasional Conformists there were we do not know. What angered the Tories was that, in some corporations, dissenters had managed to infiltrate to such a degree as to enable them to influence parliamentary elections in the Whig interest. One or two barefaced demonstrations of Occasional Conformity at the end of the 1690s suddenly made it an explosive issue. In 1702 Henry Sacheverell, the principal High Church propagandist, preached a sermon on *The Political Union: A Discourse showing the Dependence of Government on Religion,* in which Occasional Conformity was denounced as 'a religious piece of hypocrisy as even no heathen government would have endured'.[142] The sermon was 'hysterical in its obsession with Dissent'[143] and put forward the urgent need for Church and state to stand together against this threat.

Daniel Defoe had no sympathy for Occasional Conformists. He regarded them as 'playing Bopeep with God Almighty',[144] but he was not prepared to accept Occasional Conformity being made an excuse for an all-out attack on dissent. He had already published one pamphlet on the subject but, in 1702, he wrote his *The Shortest Way with Dissenters or Proposals for the Establishment of the Church,* a parody of exactly the kind of propaganda the High Church Tories were using against dissenters. He recommended that a law be passed 'that whoever was found at a conventicle should be banished the nation and the preacher be hanged'.[145] His aim was to reveal the absurdity of the policy of intolerance but the irony was lost on many of those at whom it was aimed – an additional reason for their anger with Defoe when his real intentions were realised.

A furious debate was conducted over the next few years in which a host of pamphleteers joined. In 1703, the Rev James Owen, a dissenting minister, published a defence of Occasional Conformity in a pamphlet entitled *Moderation a Virtue; or the Occasional Conformists justified*. Meanwhile Defoe had followed up his attack with *More Short Ways with the Dissenters*, published in 1704. It was against these two pamphlets that Mary Astell directed two of her works of 1704 – *Moderation Truly Stated* and *A Fair Way with the Dissenters and their Patrons*, the latter being reproduced in this volume, in full as an example of her polemic. It demonstrates just how totally committed she was to the views of High Church Tories. Her aim, she wrote, was 'the total destruction of Dissenters as a Party',[146] for it was they who, as 'that dearest Spawn'[147] of the Church of Rome, were responsible for the Civil War, and it was they who were now intent on 'the Ruin of the Church'.[148] It is interesting to note the use she makes of Clarendon's *History* in accounting for the oubreak of the Civil War and the *'never to be forgotten 41'*.[149] The language is passionate and there is no question of her loyalty and sincere religious devotion, but the argument is less than convincing.

Her answer to Owen, *Moderation Truly Stated*, is prefaced by a reply to Dr Davenant's *Essays upon Peace at Home and War Abroad*[150] in which he argued for toleration and greater moderation towards dissenters. In her rejection of Davenant's argument for toleration she agrees with him that factions are to be avoided in government but argues that, if the king is sovereign and will 'let his own Prudence Govern and not the Artifice or Insolence of any of his Subjects', there should be none.[151] This part of her pamphlet takes the form of a dialogue between two fictitious characters – John Nokes and William Styles. Nokes represents Davenant and puts forward the argument against an Occasional Conformity Bill; Styles, representing Mary Astell's views, opposes it. Needless to say Styles' argument is by far the stronger. Davenant had mentioned women as constituting a not inconsiderable group within dissent, and Mary Astell makes this an excuse for introducing into the dialogue a discussion of the power of female dissent, and then introduces a woman speaker who takes Styles to task for underestimating women's abilities.

The final work of 1704 was *An Impartial Inquiry into the Cause of Rebellion and Civil War in the Kingdom* which was occasioned by the sermon delivered by Dr White Kennett, Archdeacon of Huntingdon, on 31 January 1704 – the day of the fast for the Martyrdom of Charles I. Kennett, a moderate churchman, had no sympathy with the High Church revival of the doctrine of divine right. He was passionately anti-Catholic and he saw the doctrine as closely related to catholicism and the absolutist governments of Europe.

In his sermon, later published under the title *A Compassionate Enquiry into the Causes of the Civil War*, he attempted to give an alternative to the Tory analysis of events leading up to the Civil War, which insisted that the central blame lay with the dissenting sects. For a man who had some sympathy for dissenters to preach the sermon at all showed courage if not foolhardiness. In his sermon he concentrated on the French alliance as the ultimate cause of the rebellion. It had led, he argued, to 'Fears of Popery' and to 'the Jealousies of Oppression and Illegal Power'.[152] Although he carefully avoided explicitly apportioning any blame to Charles I, he nevertheless makes clear his responsiblity for the civil war by implication. If he had thought such an explanation would prove acceptable he had reckoned without Mary Astell and others who found it wholly inadequate. The sermon produced a storm of protest and many pamphleteers rushed into the fray but 'the longest and weightiest contribution' was Mary Astell's.[153]

Drawing liberally on Clarendon's *History* and the work of Foulis[154] she argues in favour of the doctrines of divine right and passive obedience and totally absolves Charles I from any blame for the Civil War. The real cause was the doctrine of 'the *Presbyterians*, or *Whiggs*, or whatever you will call them ... who place the Supreme Power originally in the People' and reject 'the *Just* and *Legal* Rights of an English Monarch' as '*Arbitrary Power*'.[155] While both Mary Astell and White Kennett are apparently concerned with the events of the 1640s, it is clear that they were in fact thinking of contemporary politics.

It must have been particularly galling to Mary Astell when Daniel Defoe sprang to Kennett's defence in 1704 and, once again, gave his support to the dissenters' cause. It did nothing to abate the savagery of the abuse thrown at Kennett. When he published his history of England two years later, he argued not only against the Tory interpretation of events leading to the Civil War but suggested that Clarendon's *History* was 'far from serving any one Side only',[156] once again provoking a fierce response from those promoting the High Church case. The whole debate serves to remind us of just how much the events of the 1640s still rankled in the minds of many.

The cause of Occasional Conformity was lost by the Tories overplaying their hand. They had placed far too much reliance on Anne's support. After all was she not a devout Anglican? However, the three bills to prohibit the practice of Occasional Conformity proved deeply divisive of the nation. Three times the bills were passed in the Commons only to be thrown out by the Lords. The third bill was 'tacked' on to the Land Tax bill – a bill voting supplies for the pursuit of the War of the Spanish Succession which was being waged at the time. This proved too much for Anne. To divide the country into two warring factions at a time when unity was essential was one thing, but to threaten the whole war effort was another, and was putting the country to ransom. It also proved too much for many moderate Tories. There was a decisive rejection of the High Church demand, and by 1705 the cause seemed lost. It had done little to promote the 'Church in Danger' campaign.

After 1710 Mary Astell was to produce no further works but her intellectual activity continued. In 1714, Dr John Walker produced his massive work, *The Sufferings of the Clergy*, an analysis of those Church of England clergy, heads of colleges, Fellows, scholars etc., who had been excluded from their posts in the 1640s. It was an answer to Dr Calamy's[157] *Abridgement of the Life of Mr Baxter* which included a Chapter IX concerned with those 'silenced and ejected' as a result of refusing to comply with the requirements of the Act of Uniformity of 1662. It was started in the atmosphere generated by the issue of Occasional Conformity when the Tories were pressing for the revocation of the Toleration Act.

In the Preface Dr Walker acknowledged the help of many 'Reverend and Learned Persons' and listed them. At the end of his list was added the name of 'Ingenious Mrs. Astell', the only woman among them, who 'was pleas'd to procure for me some Considerable Papers and Informations'.[158] Among the clergy was included a John Squire, AM of St Leonard, Shoreditch. It is a lengthy entry and it ends by Walker acknowledging it as the work of Mary Astell 'to whom I beg Leave in this Place to pay my Thanks for that great Favour'.[159]

Her cooperation in this venture serves to underline the identification of Mary Astell's religious and political views with those of Dr Walker, a Tory High Churchman, who certainly shared Dr Henry Sacheverell's convictions about the identity of Church and state and reacted with the same feelings of horror and outrage to the murder of a 'divinely appointed king', and to what was seen as the growing threat to the Church from dissent. Like Dr Walker, Mary Astell's 'prejudices were violent'[160] and so too sometimes was the language in which she expressed them.

Some Conclusions

Many of those who have written about Mary Astell, and even those referring to her in passing, have attempted to label her. She has been variously described as a Platonist, a Cartesian rationalist, a Lockean feminist, an English Femme Savante, and 'the first major English feminist'.[161] If some of these labels are more relevant to her than others, there is not one that, by itself, adequately describes her ideas.

Not for nothing has John Norris been called 'the last of the Cambridge Platonists'.[162] By the end of the century the school was in decline and the ideas of Locke had taken over. It is true that Mary Astell was caricatured by Swift as 'a profess'd Platonne' but when his caricature proceeds to have her 'run over Norris' it is making an important point.[163] The reason she entered into correspondence with Norris was her disagreement with some of his arguments. On occasion, as we have seen, she found difficulty in accepting Norris's insistence that God was the only proper object of her love. She 'found it more easie to recognise his Right than to secure the Possession'.[164] In her last letters to Norris she was at some pains to reconcile his views with those of Locke, and particularly Locke's argument in *An Essay concerning Human Understanding* (1690). But Norris, in his reply to her, firmly rejected Locke's argument. What finally persuaded her that the two were irreconcilable was Locke's publication of *The Reasonableness of Christianity* (1695) which she saw as threatening to undermine the authority of the Anglican Church. By the time she wrote *The Christian Religion* in 1705 she had taken sides, if reluctantly, against Locke.

After *Letters Concerning the Love of God* she appears not to have pursued the debate. One who did was Damaris Masham (1658–1708), daughter of Ralph Cudworth, one of the most notable of the Cambridge Platonists, who was to become a close friend and disciple of Locke's. The object of Norris's *Reflections upon the Conduct of Human Life in a Letter to my Lady Masham* (1690), she pursued the debate begun by Mary Astell in *A Discourse Concerning the Love of God* (1696) which revealed how profoundly Locke had influenced her thinking, and just how far she had moved away from Norris's platonism.

That Mary Astell respected Locke 'that Great Master of good Sense'[165] there can be no doubt. She would have welcomed his notion that 'Reason must be our last judge and guide in all things'[166] although Locke had no monopoly of the idea. What she could not accept was the complete break with traditional authority that Locke's *Two Treatises of Civil Government* represented. She still clung to the idea of the sanctity of kingship which Locke was at such pains to discard, and was as far from accepting the idea of a contractual theory of government between king and subjects as she was from the idea of a voluntary compact in domestic relations. She rejected the idea that 'by the Miscarriage of those in Authority, it [Supreme Power] is forfeited.'[167] At the conclusion of her *Reflections upon Marriage* she makes it clear that she cannot go along with those who argue that 'if a Man has not these Qualifications [to govern] where is his Right? That if he misemploys it, he abuses it. And if he abuses, according to modern Deduction, he forfeits it.'[168]

Surprisingly she seems to have been unaware of Locke's *Thoughts on Education* (1693) which owed so much to the views of Fénelon, and to which Damaris Masham was deeply indebted. Indeed, if anyone fits the title of 'Lockean feminist' Damaris Masham might seem the best qualified.

If Locke's political ideas were not to Mary Astell's liking, neither was his theology. She was all in favour of women applying reason to their religious faith, and she would have accepted Locke's insistence that the scriptures were the only source of religious truth, but Locke's *The Reasonableness of Christianity* (1695) went too far for her in its rejection of the mysteries of Christianity and in its insistence that all could interpret the Gospels for themselves. It threatened to displace the clergy from their authoritative role within the Church. It is true that however, at the end of her exchange of letters with John Norris, she had attempted to reconcile their views. But Locke's work was only the beginning of a powerful movement within the Church in favour of a more reasonable Christianity. Archbishop Tillotson was to revolutionise preaching when he adopted a coolly reasoned and unemotional approach in his sermons. But, above all, it was John Toland, the Deist, who shocked High Anglicans with his *Christianity not Mysterious* (1696) and the host of pamphleteers that were released when the Licensing Act expired in 1695. They were seen as representing a dangerous trend towards scepticism and irreligion. When Mary

Astell's *Christian Religion* was published in 1705, it set out to attack Locke and Tillotson – but always in highly respectful language.

In *A Serious Proposal* Mary Astell had stressed the importance of women who had acquired a knowledge of the French language, using it to read not romances but for 'the study of Philosophy (as I hear the *French Ladies* do) *Descartes, Malebranche* and others'.[169] English women, she suggested, should emulate Madame Dacier, the classical scholar, and Madeleine de Scudéry. Curiously, although she admitted to a great admiration for Descartes and a commitment to his ideas, she does not appear to have ever read him in the original. All her references are to translations of popularisations of Descartes's work such as Francois Bayle's *The General System of Cartesian Philosophy* (1670) and Arnauld's *The Art of Thinking or the Port Royal Logic* (1685). It was the latter work that she used as the basis for the second part of *A Serious Proposal* – in which the influence of Descartes's method is clear. The confirmation that she is unlikely to have read Descartes in the original is found in one of her letters to John Norris, who had urged her to read Malebranche, where she admitted she was unable to read 'that ingenious Author in his own Language'.[170]

There is also no evidence that she read the work of the most influential of the French reformers, Poulain de la Barre, a radical Cartesian, translated from the French as *The Woman as good as the Man: or the Equality of both Sexes* in 1677. Nor does she make reference to other French writers who were concerned with women's education – with the exception of Madeleine de Scudéry. In her emphasis on the close relationship between the contempt in which women were held and their inadequate education as compared with men, Mary Astell seems to have followed Madeleine de Scudéry closely. But in the objects with which such education were to be pursued she differed fundamentally from that author. If Mlle de Scudéry believed in an expansion of educational provision for women it was not to be at the expense of any sacrifice of the ornamental accomplishments. Her aim was not to give women self-respect and intellectual independence but rather 'to produce women who could function agreeably in social situations'.[171] Of Madame de Maintenon, François Fénelon or Charles Perrault Mary Astell makes no mention, just as – even more surprising – she seems not to have read Anna Maria von Schurman's *A Learned Maid* (1641) which Clement Barksdale had translated into English in 1659.

Nevertheless French ideas, and more particularly the ideas of Descartes, greatly influenced Mary Astell as they did all English rational thought. The satires on 'learned ladies' in Restoration drama owed much to Molière's *Les Femmes Savantes*. It was to Aphra Behn that we owe the first translation of Fontenelle's *Conversations on the Plurality of Worlds* in 1686. The habit of compiling long lists of illustrious women from history or the Bible to make the point that men had no monopoly of glory, a habit Mary Astell shared with many others of both sexes writing on women at the end of the seventeenth and in the early eighteenth century, is also found in French writers on women. But Mary Astell was selective in what she absorbed of any influence. It seems that it was not so much the details of Cartesianism but the general principles that she adopted in her thinking. She remained very independent, taking only what she wanted from any writer. So the influence of Platonism, like the influence of Locke and Descartes was not allowed to exclude other, and often, contradictory influences.[172]

She read widely. In *Moderation Truly Stated* (1704) there are over 60 works published during the Interregnum and covering a remarkable range of opinion, to which she makes detailed reference, as well as a host of sermons.[173] In seeking to explain the sudden upsurge in interest in women's education and women's role in marriage of the 1690s, historians have perhaps underestimated the lasting effects of the period of the Civil War on women's consciousness. However opposed to the ideas of that period, Mary Astell was very familiar with its writings and must have been aware of its ideas about women and marriage.

The description of Mary Astell as 'the first major English feminist' is only one of several such labels: 'the founder of the feminist movement', 'undoubtedly a blue-stocking and a feminist', 'the first systematic feminist in England'.[174] Of course, much depends on what is meant by 'feminist'. Almost certainly there will be many modern feminists who will find it difficult to recognise Mary Astell as a forebear. Joan Kinnaird's concern to make what she sees as her very 'tame' feminism compatible with High Anglican Tory views has led her to suggest that 'our tendency to assume that there is necessarily a contradiction between feminism and conservatism' has led us astray.[175] On the contrary, she argues, Mary Astell's conservative views on marriage and women's education were fully in accord with her conservative views on religion and politics. Feminism, in the seventeenth century and early eighteenth century, it is concluded, was as much of conservative as radical origins. Yet surely this is to see Mary Astell as totally divorced from her historical context and to attempt to fit her into some preconceived idea of what late seventeenth and early eighteenth century feminism ought to have been. We need to remember that 'a feminist movement at that stage would have been inconceivable.'[176]

Mary Astell was not a freak in her religious and political views which bind her closely to the general intellectual atmosphere of her period and her class. She was by no means exceptional in combining traditional views on religion and politics with views on women's education and marriage, which, for her time, were remarkably enlightened. Aphra Behn and Mary de la Rivière Manley were both passionate Tory advocates despite their more liberated views on women. Lady Mary Chudleigh, the poetess who wrote *The Ladies Defence: Or The Bride-Woman's Counsellor Answer'd* (1700), shared Mary Astell's religious devotion and high Tory views. In the disputes and debates of the years following the Glorious Revolution there was, as Geoffrey Holmes has said 'no genuine 'radical' element'.[177] 'Feminism' or the kind of enlightened views on women that Mary Astell displayed are not conditional on the existence of a radical movement any more than they are dependent on 'conservative Anglican thought'.[178]

In another effort to explain Mary Astell, she is labelled as 'sexually odd' and 'a man-hating recluse'.[179] There is in her feminism, another writer claims, 'a rejection of physiological womanhood'.[180] Is there a hint here of precisely the same sort of contemporary accusations levelled at 'learned ladies', of being desexed, or of 'acting above their sex'?

In her writings it is true that her scorn for men is expressed with powerful directness. 'Their Vast Minds', she wrote, 'lay Kingdoms waste.'[181] The young men of her time were 'bold importunate and rapacious vultures'![182] Such comments led Francis Atterbury, Bishop of Rochester, to suggest she was vulgar and lacked breeding! 'She has not the most decent manner of insinuating what she means', he wrote, 'but is now and then a little offensive and shocking in her expressions.'[183] A more recent writer has found such expressions 'an unattractive feature of Mrs. Astell's personality'.[184] If her language is more powerful, is her scorn for men all that different from that expressed by other women at the time, and more particularly those who shared her idea that where women were found inferior to men it was the result of their exclusion from the educational opportunities enjoyed by men, and owed nothing to nature? Not surprisingly, having arrived at such a conclusion, women went on to analyse the causes of such exclusion. Who was to blame? The growing consciousness of the deprivation inflicted on them by men, of men's contemptuous attitude to them, of the humiliation of their assigned role, all led to the same answer. The expression of anti-male feeling should not surprise us. It is indeed a step in the direction of a demand for equality, and as such, a move towards 'feminist' expression.

'Her sympathy with the lives of women', wrote Ada Wallas, 'was broader than her social theories lead one to expect.'[185] It is a perceptive comment. If Mary Astell never flattered women and was not afraid to tell them their weaknesses in as direct a language as she employed for men's failings, her admiration and love for women is extended to those with whom she had little or nothing in common, and whose ideas often must have been alien to her. So she condemned novels and novel-reading but this did not prevent her reading, with admiration, Madeleine de Scudéry's novel concerned with women's education.[186] She was a sincere and devout Christian but this did nothing to prevent her close friendship with Lady Mary Wortley Montagu, 'the free-thinking Mary' as Lady Louisa Stuart called her. She thought the notorious Madame Mazarine's behaviour imprudent, childish and inexcusable, but this did not prevent her feeling real sympathy for her. It was that sympathy that led her to greet any achievement women made with unsparing admiration.

In her *Reflections* Mary Astell argued that the scriptures should not be used to prove the natural subjection of women to men. Relations between the sexes 'ought to be decided by natural Reason only.'[187] But if men were to play the game of using scriptures against women in proof of their inferiority, she was prepared to list carefully woman after woman from the Bible to prove the contrary. Glory was no monopoly of the opposite sex. 'The Bible is for, not against us', she bravely insisted, 'and cannot without great violence done to it, be urg'd to our Prejudice.'[188]

'To plead for the Oppress'd and to defend the Weak', she wrote, 'seem'd to me a generous undertaking.'[189] It was – even if her idea of the 'Oppress'd' and 'Weak' was mainly confined to the upper classes. In the interest of such pleading and defence she was prepared to forget her own, sometimes passionately held, beliefs.

After her publications of 1704–05, four works in all, Mary Astell was to produce one more work in 1709. *Bart'lemy Fair or an Enquiry after Wit* was an answer to a pamphlet, *Letter concerning Enthusiasm* (1708) written by Lord Shaftesbury, but which Mary Astell wrongly attributed to a member of the Whig Kit-Kat club – and almost certainly Swift. Shaftesbury had argued for a moderate religion free from enthusiasm and based firmly on reason. Such a true religion need have no fear of ridicule or raillery. A rational religion could only emerge strengthened. He argued strongly against any attempt to straightjacket the beliefs of those within the Church. Riled by the recent satires on her and her 'protestant nunnery' in *The Tatler* Mary Astell was all too ready to assume the author was the same and she launched out in an attack on the Whig Kit-Kat club. Disillusioned by the failures of the High Church cause in 1705 the pamphlet is a bitter attack on the influence of Deism and what she saw as the increasing irreligion of her day.

Apart from her preface to the letters of Lady Mary Wortley Montagu, she was to write no more. Contemporary accounts suggest that, disappointed by the failures of the causes into which she had put all her energies, she occupied herself in her religious devotions and good works. She became more of an eccentric and adopted a very simple, not to say frugal, way of life.

After 1705 she must have experienced a great sense of defeat as one after another of the causes she had fought for failed. The High Anglican party, although enjoying a temporary recovery, was in decline and the particular brand of Toryism with which it was associated was to be overtaken by the Whig ascendancy. Her beloved Church was torn by dissension and she was to find herself on the losing side. Cambridge Platonism was virtually dead. What remained was her faith – in religion and in women and to these she devoted the remainder of her life.

No-one, I think, would have resisted sympathy so much as Mary Astell yet she presents a not untragic figure. The fight over the particular issues of her time to which she had devoted so much of her energy had found her on the losing side. Those issues are now of no more than historical interest yet they were fought with all the passion involved when traditional ideas and values are under attack. Perhaps we have underestimated the tension of those years between 1689 and 1714, which for Mary Astell must have been acute. As has been suggested, it was precisely because in all but her ideas on women's education and the nature of marriage she was such a traditionalist, that she was so remarkable. It made her call to women to reject 'that Tyrant Custom' all the more courageous. And if, as she told women 'there is a sort of Bravery and Greatness of Soul, which ... consists in living up to the dignity of our Natures',[190] who could have demonstrated it better?

Notes

1   Mary Astell, *A Serious Proposal to the Ladies For the Advancement of their True and Greatest Interest. By a Lover of her Sex.* London, 1694. (Hereafter *A Serious Proposal I*); and Mary Astell, *Some Reflections upon Marriage Occasion'd by the Duke and Dutchess of Mazarine's Case which is also consider'd.* London, 1700. (Hereafter *Reflections*)

2   Mary Astell, *A Fair Way with the Dissenters and their Patrons* London, 1704.

3   Mary Astell, *An Impartial Enquiry into the Causes of the Rebellion and Civil War in this Kingdom*, 1704.

4   Florence M. Smith, *Mary Astell*, Columbia University Press, New York, 1916.

5   Karl D. Bulbring, 'Mary Astell an Advocate of Women's Rights Two Hundred Years Ago', *Journal of Education*, April 1891
     Katherine S. Pattinson, 'Mary Astell', *The Pall Mall Magazine*, June 1893.
     Harriet M'Ilquham, 'Mary Astell: A Seventeenth Century Women's Advocate', *The Westminster Review*, vol. 149, no. 4, April 1898.

6   A.H. Upham, 'English Femmes Savantes at the end of the Seventeenth Century', *Journal of English and Germanic Philology*, XII (1913).

7   George Ballard (1706–55), a learned antiquarian with a sympathetic appreciation of women's abilities, was the author of *Memoirs of Several Ladies of Great Britain, who have been Celebrated for their Writings or Skill in the Learned Arts and Sciences*, 1752.

8   For example, Mary Hays, *Female Biography*, 1803. See below p.6

9   *Extracts from the Records of the Company of Hostmen of Newcastle-on-Tyne*, Publications of the Surtees Society, vol.CV, 1901, p.286.

10   Part of his epitaph read:

     ... whose heart bled
     When rebel feet cut off his head.
     And great good Shepherd humbly lay
     To his mad flock a bleeding prey.

     Quoted Richard Welford, *Men of Mark 'Twixt Tyne and Tweed*, 1895, p.122

11   *Records of the Company of Hostmen*, p.248, but on the same page there is a reference to a 'Mr. Austell, Clearke' in January 1647 which may well indicate Peter Astell.

12   Ibid, pp.105–6, 249.

13   Ibid, p.121

14   Ibid, p.271

15   Welford, op. cit., p.122.

16   Roger Howell, *Newcastle upon Tyne and the Puritan Revolution*, 1967, particularly Chapters I, II and V.

17 *Memoirs of the Life of Mr. Ambrose Barnes*, Publications of the Surtees Society, vol.L, 1867, p.414.

18 John Brand, *History and Antiquities of the Town and County of Newcastle on Tyne*, 2 vols., vol. I., 1789, p.317 footnote.

19 Ballard, op.cit., p.445.

20 Welford, op.cit., p.123.

21 Ballard, op.cit., p.445.

22 *Remarks and Collections of Thomas Hearne*, Ed. Rev. H.E. Salter, 1915, vol.X, p.426. (On her knowledge of French see p.51 suggesting any knowledge she had of French was acquired much later in her life.) See also Mary Astell, *The Christian Religion as Profess'd by a Daughter of the Church of England*, 1705, p.139.

23 Mrs Mary Pilkington, *Memoirs of Celebrated Female Characters*, (1804), 1811, p.33.

24 Ballard, op.cit., p.445.

25 *Records of the Company of Hostmen*, p.251.

26 *A Collection of Poems humbly presented and Dedicated to the most Reverend Father in God William by Divine Providence Lord Archbishop of Canterbury*, 1689, Rawlinson MSS poet. 154:50.

27 Mrs Mary Pilkington, op.cit., pp.33–4.

28 Mary Hays, *Female Biography*, vol.I, 1803, pp.213, 216. This suggestion could explain her interest in science and her belief that women were as capable of scientific speculation as men (see below p.201). Such an interest would seem to be confirmed by her letter to Sir Hans Sloane, the physician, of 25 April, 1724 (see Sloane MS. 4047:163) expressing a wish to call on him in order to see his 'noble Repository'. It also suggests that Susan Cent-livre's character of Valeria in *The Bassett Table* was inspired by Mary Astell.

29 *A Collection of Poems*, 1689, prefatory letter.

30 George Paston, *Lady Mary Wortley Montagu and her Times*, 1907, note pp.12–13.

31 Reginald Blunt, *Paradise Row*, 1906, pp.65, 67.

32 Rawlinson MSS.D198:91–99.

33 *Diary of Ralph Thoresby*, ed. Rev. Joseph Hunter, vol.II, 1830, p.161.

34 James Sutherland, *English Literature of the Late Seventeenth Century*, 1969, p.348

35 John Norris, *A Collection of Miscellanies*, 1717, p.228.

36 *Letters concerning the Love of God, between the Author of The Proposal to the Ladies and Mr. John Norris*, 1695, Letter III from Mary Astell to John Norris.

37 In his reply to her he wrote 'I must needs acknowledge that this (as all our other Duties) is more intelligible than practicable, though to render it so I know of no other Way than by long and constant Meditation . . .'.

38 Reginald Blunt, *The Wonderful Village*, 1918, p.86.

39 *Letters Concerning the Love of God*, 1695, See below p.195.

40 *A Collection of Poems*, 1689, from Stanza III of an untitled poem; see below p.189.

41 Ms Ballard 37:49.

42 Thomas Barnard, *An Historical Character relating to the Holy and Exemplary Life of the Rt. Honourable the Lady Elizabeth Hastings*, 1742, p.13.

43 Lady Louisa Stuart, granddaughter of Lady Mary, in her introductory anec-

dotes to: *Letters and Works of Lady Mary Wortley Montagu*, ed. Lord Wharn-cliffe, vol.I, 1893, p.85.

44   From a Letter to the Countess of Bute dated 20 October 1752, in: *The Works of the Right Honourable Lady Mary Wortley Montagu*, vol.IV, 1817, p.184.

45   Lady Louisa Stuart, op.cit., p.85.

46   *Letters and Works of Lady Mary Wortley Montagu*, vol.I, p.84.

47   *Letters Concerning the Love of God*, Preface.

48   *Letters and Works of Lady Mary Wortley Montagu*, vol.I, p.86.

49   Quoted Fidelis Morgan, *The Female Wits*, 1981, p.6.

50   *Letters Concerning the Love of God*; see below p.195.

51   *A Serious Proposal I*; see below p.163.

52   Ibid.

53   *A Collection of Poems*, 1689, preface.

54   Ballard, op.cit. p.447.

55   *Letters concerning the Love of God*, preface.

56   For a discussion of the authorship of the former work see Florence Smith, *Mary Astell*, 1916, Appendix II. The Bodleian Catalogue includes the latter work under Mary Astell's name. Dr George Hickes would seem to suggest her as the author in a letter to the Master of University College, dated 9 December 1704. See Ballard MSS 62:85.

57   *A Collection of Poems*, 1689; see below p.185.

58   *A Serious Proposal I*; see below p.140.

59   *Letters of the Right Honourable Lady M---y W---y M---e*, Preface; see below p.235.

60   Lawrence Stone, *The Family, Sex and Marriage in England 1500–1800*, 1977, p.44.

61   *The Lawes Resolutions of Women's Rights*, 1632, p.6.

62   *Reflections*; see below p.114.

63   Ibid. p.119.

64   *A Serious Proposal I*; see below p.169.

65   *Reflections*; see below p.127.

66   Ibid. p.130.

67   Thomas Middleton, *The Roaring Girl*, II.ii, 1611.

68   Mary Astell, *A Serious Proposal to the Ladies*, Part II, 1697; see below p.178.

69   *A Collection of Poems*, 1689; see below pp.188–9.

70   Ibid.

71   Bathsua Makin, *An Essay to Revive the Ancient Education of Gentlewomen in Religion, Arts and Tongues*, 1673, p.26.

72   *Letters and Works of Lady Mary Wortley Montagu*, vol.II, p.225.

73   See Fidelis Morgan, *The Female Wits*, 1981, p.54.

74   Ibid. p.9.

75   Myra Reynolds, *The Learned Lady in England 1650–1760*, 1920, pp.49, 50.

76   *Letters concerning the Love of God*; see below p.191.

77   Ibid. p.193.

78   *The Tatler*, no.32, from Tuesday 21 June to Thursday 23 June, 1709.

79   Elizabeth Elstob (1683–1756), the Anglo-Saxon scholar, believed women had an equal right to learning as men. Mary de la Rivière Manley (1663?–1724),

playwright and novelist, after being deceived into a bigamous marriage with her cousin, was deserted by him and supported herself by writing. The most well known of her works is *Secret Memoirs and Manners of Several Persons of Quality of both Sexes. From the New Atlantis*, 1709, in which she sought to discredit the Whigs by relating the more scandalous adventures of many prominent figures. She wrote as one very aware of most women's economic dependence and its consequences for their oppression.

80   *The Tatler*, no.63, from Thursday 1 September to Saturday 3 September 1709.

81   *The Works of the Celebrated Mrs Centlivre*, 3 vols. 1761, pp.210, 217, 218, 228.

82   Mary Astell, *The Christian Religion as Profess'd by a Daughter of the Church of England*, 1705; see below p.201.

83   Welford, op.cit., p.126.

84   Mrs Mary Pilkington, op.cit., p.34.

85   Mary Hays, op.cit., p.220.

86   Mrs Mary Pilkington, op.cit., p.34.

87   *Letters and Works of Lady Mary Wortley Montagu*, p.86.

88   C.E. Medhurst, *Life and Work of Lady Elizabeth Hastings*, 1914, pp.230–1.

89   Throughout the section that follows I am indebted to the following: Alice Clark, *The Working Life of Women in the Seventeenth Century*, 1919; Roger Thompson, *Women in Stuart England and America*, 1974; K.V. Thomas, 'Women and the Civil War Sects', *Past and Present*, no.13, April 1958; Patricia Higgins, 'The Reactions of Women, with special reference to women petitioners', from *Politics, Religion and the English Civil War*, ed. Brian Manning, 1973; Phyllis Mack, 'Women as Prophets during the English Civil War', from *The Origins of Anglo-American Radicalism*, ed. M. Jacob and J. Jacob, 1984, pp.214–230; Christopher Hill, *The World Turned Upside Down*, 1975, particularly Chapter 15.

90   Christopher Hill, *The World Turned Upside Down*, Penguin Books, 1975, p.311.

91   Quoted from Keith Thomas, op.cit. p.52.

92   Daniel Defoe, *Moll Flanders*, (1721), 1924, p.12.

93   Ian Watt, *The Rise of the Novel*, 1957, p.154.

94   Keith Thomas, op.cit., p.55.

95   *The Ladies Calling*, 1673, The Preface.

96   Ibid. p.16.

97   Ibid., p.70.

98   Ibid., pp.3–4.

99   Hannah Woolley, *The Gentlewoman's Companion: or a Guide to the Female Sex*, 1675, p.104.

100   George Savile, Marquis of Halifax, *The Lady's New Year Gift; or, Advice to a Daughter*, (1688), in *Complete Works*, Penguin, 1969, p.276.

101   Myra Reynolds, op.cit. p.88.

102   David Cressy, *Literacy and the Social Order*, 1980, p.147.

103   J.E. Gagen, *The New Woman*, 1954, p.100.

104   *A Serious Proposal I*. Numbers in brackets following quotes from this work refer to pages in this book.

105   Ballard, op.cit. p.446.

106   Ballard MSS 43:29 (Bodleian Library).

107   Gilbert Burnet, *History of His Own Time*, vol.II, 1734, p.653.

108   *The Catechism of Thomas Becon*, ed. for the Parker Society, 1844, p.377.

109   John Duncan, *Lady Lettice, Vi-Countess Falkland*, ed. M.F. Howard, 1968, p.92.

110   Clement Barksdale, *A Letter Touching a Colledge of Maids, or a Virgin Society*, written 12 August 1675, Sig Av, A2, A2v.

111   Ibid. Sig A2v.

112   John Evelyn, *Numismata*, 1697, p.265; George Wheler, *A Protestant Monastery*, 1698 Chapter IV; Robert Nelson, *An Address to Persons of Quality and Estate*, 1715, p.213; Robert Halsband, *The Life of Mary Wortley Montagu*, 1956, p.7; Thomas Amory, *Memoirs Containing the Lives of Several Ladies of Great Britain*, 1755; Thomas Amory, *The Life of John Buncle, Esq.*, vol.I, 1756, vol.II, 1766; Samuel Richardson, *Sir Charles Grandison*, in 7 volumes, vol.VI, letter IV, 1811; Sarah Fielding, *History of the Countess of Dellwyn*, 1759; Sarah Scott, *Millenium Hall*, 1762.

113   Daniel Defoe, *An Essay on Projects*, (1697) from *The Earlier Life and the Chief Earlier Works of Daniel Defoe*, ed. Henry Morley, 1889, pp.145–6.

114   Ibid., p.148.

115   Ada Wallas, *Before the Bluestockings*, 1929, p.111.

116   Roger Thompson, *Women in Stuart England and America*, 1974, p.201.

117   *A Serious Proposal I*, Numbers in brackets following quotes refer to pages in this book.

118   *Reflections*, Numbers in brackets following quotes refer to pages in this book.

119   *Reflections*, Numbers in brackets after quotes refer to pages in this book.

120   See Ballard, op.cit. p.450, footnote.

121   John Sprint, *The Bride-Woman's Counsellor*. Being a Sermon preach'd at a Wedding May the 11th, 1699, at Sherborne in Dorset, pp.2, 6, 7, 12–13.

122   Halifax, op.cit. All references included in brackets.

123   Hannah Woolley, *The Gentlewoman's Companion*, 1675, pp.2, 106, 107.

124   Ibid., p.89.

125   Hannah Woolley, *The Queen-like Closet*, Supplement, 1684, p.127.

126   Ibid. p.99.

127   Ibid. p.126.

128   Gilbert Burnet, *History of His Own Time*, vol.II, 1734, p.652.

129   *The Works of the Rt. Honourable Lady Mary Wortley Montagu*, vol.I, 1817, p.217.

130   John Norris, *A Collection of Miscellanies*, 1717, pp.311–14.

131   Robert South, *Sermons Preached upon Several Occasions*, (1679), in 6 volumes, vol.V, 1737, p.8.

132   *Commons' Journals*, X, p.14.

133   *The Husband's Instruction to his Family, or, Household Observations, Fit to be Observed by Wife, Children, and Servants*, 1685.

134   Edward Ravenscroft, *The Careless Lovers*, III, 1673, p.33 (but pagination in error).

135   Thomas Otway, *The Atheist*, 1685 in *Works*, ed. J.C. Ghosh, vol.II, 1968, p.379.

136   Aphra Behn, *The Younger Brother*, 1696, Ii.

137   Sir John Vanbrugh, *The Provok'd Wife*, 1697, Ii.

138 *Reflections.* All numbers in brackets following quotes refer to pages in this book.

139 Joan K. Kinnaird, 'Mary Astell and the Conservative Contribution to English Feminism', *The Journal of British Studies,* XIX, 1979, pp.68–9.

140 Although this is certainly an element in her pursuit of the analogy. As Susan Staves has pointed out: 'as political theory became more Whiggish, men did not necessarily wish to pursue the implications of the analogies and impute to their wives and children rights like those they themselves claimed as subjects.' (*Players' Scepters,* 1979, p.116.)

141 Geoffrey Holmes, *Religion and Party in Late Stuart England,* Historical Association, 1975, p.6.

142 Quoted in J.P. Kenyon, *Revolution Principles, The Politics of Party 1689–1720,* p.93.

143 Geoffrey Holmes, op.cit., p.11.

144 Daniel Defoe, *An Enquiry into the Occasional Conformity of Dissenters,* 1698.

145 Daniel Defoe, *The Shortest Way with Dissenters,* (1702) from *The Earlier Life and the Chief Earlier Works of Daniel Defoe,* ed. Henry Morley, 1889, p.238.

146 *A Fair Way with the Dissenters,* see below p.209.

147 Ibid., p.219.

148 Ibid., p.212.

149 *A Fair Way with the Dissenters,* See below p.222.

150 Charles Davenant, *Essays upon Peace at Home and War Abroad,* 1704.

151 *Moderation Truly Stated; or a Review of a Late Pamphlet entitl'd Moderation a Vertue with a Prefatory Discourse to Dr. D'Avenant concerning his Late Essays on Peace and War,* 1704, p.x.

152 White Kennett, *A Compassionate Enquiry into the Causes of the Civil War,* 1704, p.6.

153 G.V. Bennett, *White Kennett 1660–1728,* 1957, p.93.

154 Henry Foulis, *The History of the Wicked Plots and Conspiracies of our Pretended Saints,* in 3 books, 1662.

155 *An Impartial Inquiry,* 1704, See below p.229.

156 White Kennett, *The Compleat History of England,* (1706), 1719, preface.

157 Edmund Calamy (1671–1732), the biographer of non-conformity whose *Abridgement* of 1702 was his most popular and best-known work.

158 Dr John Walker, *The Sufferings of the Clergy,* 1714, Preface p.xxvi.

159 Ibid. Part II, p.177a.

160 A.G. Matthews, *Walker Revised,* 1948, Introduction p.xi.

161 Kinnaird, op.cit., p.55.

162 Sutherland, op.cit. p.348.

163 *The Tatler,* no.32, 1709.

164 *Letters Concerning the Love of God;* see below p.195.

165 Mary Astell, *Christian Religion,* p.256.

166 John Locke, *Essay Concerning Human Understanding,* 1690, Bk IV from *The Works of John Locke,* in 9 vols., vol.II, 1824, p.280.

167 John Locke, *Two Treatises of Government,* ed. Peter Laslett, Second Treatise, 1967, p.243.

168 *Reflections,* see below p.132.

169 *A Serious Proposal I,* See below p.155.

170   *Letters Concerning the Love of God*, 1695, p.149.

171   Carolyn C. Lougée, *Le Paradis des Femmes: Women, Salons and Social Stratification in 17th century France*, 1976, p.29.

172   So while, like John Norris, she was a disciple of Nicolas Malebranche in his belief that we 'see all things in God', she must also have been familiar with Malebranche's theory that women's inferiority was the result of their possessing more sensitive brain fibres (*La Recherche de la Vérité*, 1674, which was frequently translated into English).

173   Among the 60 works were: John Goodwin's *Theomachia* (1644); John Milton's *Eikonoklastes* (1649); Peter Sterry's *England's Deliverance from the Northern Presbytery* (1651); Thomas Edwards's *Gangraena* I, II & III (1646); John Lilburne's *England's Birthright Justified*, (1645); Henry Burton's *Conformity's Deformity (1646)*; John Saltmarsh's *The End of one Controversy* (1646); Sir Edward Coke's *Institutes* II (1643); Samuel Rutherford's *Free Disputation against Pretended liberty of Conscience* (1648); John Bastwick's *Independency not God's Ordinance* (1645); and Richard Baxter's *Christian Concord* (1653). In addition, she makes reference to Clarendon's *History of the Great Rebellion* and Calamy's *Abridgement of Baxter's Life*.

174   Kinnaird, op.cit., p.55; Robert Halsband, *The Life of Lady Mary Wortley Montagu*, 1956, p.117; Beatrice Scott, 'Lady Elizabeth Hastings', *Yorkshire Archaeological Journal*, vol.55, 1983, p.99; Katharine M. Rogers, *Feminism in Eighteenth Century England*, 1982, p.71.

175   Kinnaird, op.cit. p.66.

176   Sheila Rowbottom, *Women, Resistance and Revolution*, 1972, p.31.

177   *Britain after the Glorious Revolution, 1689–1714*, ed. Geoffrey Holmes, 1969, p.13.

178   Kinnaird, op.cit., p.75.

179   Roger Thompson, op.cit., p.12.

180   Ruth Perry, 'The Veil of Chastity: Mary Astell's Feminism', *Studies in Eighteenth Century Culture*, vol.9, 1979, p.25.

181   *Reflections*, See below p.115.

182   *A Serious Proposal I*, See below p.165.

183   Folkestone Williams, *Memoirs and Correspondence of Francis Atterbury, D.D., Bishop of Rochester*, 1869, vol.I, p.170.

184   Kinnaird, op.cit., p.67.

185   Ada Wallas, op.cit., p.128

186   Madeleine de Scudéry, *Artamène ou Le Grand Cyrus*, Paris, 1649–53.

187   Astell, *Reflections*, See below p.74.

188   Ibid. p.84

189   Ibid. p.131

190   *A Serious Proposal I*, See below p.171.

Mary Astell's published works

A Serious Proposal to the Ladies, for the Advancement of Their True and Greatest Interest. By a Lover of her Sex, 1694; 2nd ed. corrected 1695; 3rd ed. corrected 1696.

A Serious Proposal to the Ladies, Part II: wherein a method is offer'd for the improvement of their minds, 1697.

A Serious Proposal to the Ladies, in 2 parts. By a Lover of her Sex, 1697.

Some Reflections upon Marriage, Occasion'd by the Duke and Dutchess of Mazarine's Case; which is also consider'd, 1700; in the third ed., this became *Reflections upon Marriage,* To which is added a preface to answer to some objections, 1706; fourth ed., 1730.

Letters Concerning the Love of God Between the Author of the Proposal to the Ladies and Mr. John Norris, wherein his Discourse shewing That it ought to be entire and exclusive of all other Loves is further cleared and justified, 1695; 2nd ed., 1705, Corrected by the author and with some few things added; 4th ed., 1730.

Moderation Truly Stated: Or a Review of a Late Pamphlet entitl'd Moderation a Vertue with a Prefatory Discourse to Dr. D'Avenant concerning his late Essays on Peace and War, 1704.

A Fair Way with the Dissenters and their Patrons. Not writ by Mr. L---y, or any other Furious Jacobite whether Clergyman or Layman; but by a very moderate person and dutiful subject to the Queen, 1704.

An Impartial Enquiry into the Causes of Rebellion and Civil War in this Kingdom. In an examination of Dr. Kennett's Sermon Jan. 31, 1703–4 and Vindication of the Royal Martyr, 1704.

The Christian Religion as Profess'd by a Daughter of the Church of England, 1705.

Bartlemy Fair or an Enquiry after Wit in which due Respect is had to a Letter Concerning Enthusiasm. To my Lord XXX by Mr. Wotton, 1709; A Later Edn. of 1722 appeared under the title *An Enquiry after Wit* wherein the Trifling Arguing and Impious Raillery of the Late Earl of Shaftesbury in his letter concerning Enthusiasm and other Profane Writers are fully answered, and justly exposed.

A note on texts

Reflections upon Marriage is printed in full. *A Fair Way with Dissenters* apart from the omission of the Postscript is also printed in full. In the case of *A Serious Proposal Part I,* I have slightly cut the original where there was repetition, but not in a way to affect the argument. Matter omitted is indicated by ellipsis. . . . Where a whole paragraph has been omitted (p.163) this is indicated within the text.

The Preface from Lady Mary Wortley Montagu's *Turkish Letters* is printed in full. Other texts are excerpts from the original.

Wherever it has been possible to identify allusions in the texts, I have done so.

PART I
WOMEN, MEN AND MARRIAGE

REFLECTIONS
upon
MARRIAGE

The Third Edition

To which is Added

A PREFACE, IN ANSWER TO SOME OBJECTIONS.

If a Virgin Marry, she hath not sinned; nevertheless such shall have trouble.

The Wife is bound by the Law so long as her Husband liveth, but if her Husband be dead she is at liberty to be Married to whom she will, only in the Lord. But she is happier if she so abide after my Judgment. I Cor. 7. 28, 39, 40.

LONDON:

Printed for R. Wilkin, at the King's Head in St Paul's Church Yard, 1706.

The Preface

These Reflections being made in the Country, where the Book that occasion'd them came but late to Hand, the *Reader* is desir'd to excuse their Unseasonableness as well as other Faults; and to believe that they have no other Design than to Correct some Abuses, which are not the less because Power and Prescription seem to Authorize them. If any are so needlessly curious as to enquire from what Hand they come, they may please to know, that it is not good Manners to ask, since the Title-Page does not tell them: We are all of us sufficiently Vain, and without doubt the Celebrated Name of *Author*, which most are so fond of, had not been avoided but for very good Reasons: To name but one; *Who will care to pull upon themselves an Hornet's Nest?* 'Tis a very great Fault to regard rather who it is that Speaks, than what is Spoken; and either to submit to Authority, when we should only yield to Reason; or if Reason press too hard, to think to ward it off by Personal Objections and Reflections. Bold Truths may pass while the Speaker is Incognito, but are not endur'd when he is known; few Minds being strong enough to bear what Contradicts their Principles and Practices without Recriminating when they can. And tho' to tell the Truth be the most Friendly Office, yet whosoever is so hardy as to venture at it, shall be counted an Enemy for so doing.

Thus far the old Advertisement, when the Reflections first appear'd, A.D. 1700.

But the *Reflector*, who hopes *Reflector* is not bad English, now Governor is happily of the feminine Gender, had as good or better have said nothing; For People by being forbid, are only excited to a more curious Enquiry. A certain Ingenuous Gentleman (as she is inform'd) had the Good-Nature to own these Reflections, so far as to affirm that he had the Original M.S. in his Closet, a Proof she is not able to produce;[1] and so to make himself responsible for all their Faults, for which she returns him all due Acknowledgment. However, the Generality being of Opinion, that a Man would have had more Prudence and Manners than to have Publish'd such unseasonable Truths, or to have betray'd the *Arcana Imperii* of his Sex, she humbly confesses, that the Contrivance and Execution of this Design, which is unfortunately accus'd of being so destructive to the Government, of the Men I mean, is entirely her own. She neither advis'd with Friends, nor turn'd over Antient or Modern Authors, nor prudently submitted to the Correction of such as are, or such as *think* they are good Judges, but with an *English* Spirit and Genius, set out upon the Forlorn Hope, meaning no hurt to any body, nor designing any thing but the Publick Good, and to retrieve, if possible, the Native Liberty, the Rights and Privileges of the Subject.

Far be it from her to stir up Sedition of any sort, none can abhor it more; and she heartily wishes that our Masters wou'd pay their Civil and Ecclesiastical Governors the same Submission, which they themselves extract from their Domestic Subjects. Nor can she imagine how she any way undermines the Masculine Empire, or blows the Trumpet of Rebellion to the Moiety of Mankind. Is it by exhorting Women, not to expect to have their own Will in any thing, but to be entirely Submissive, when once they have made choice of a Lord and Master, tho' he happen not to be so Wise, so Kind, or even so Just a Governor as was expected? She did not indeed advise them to think his Folly Wisdom, nor his Brutality that Love and Worship he promised in his Matrimonial Oath, for this required a Flight of Wit and Sense much above her poor Ability, and proper only to Masculine Understandings. However she did not in any manner prompt them to Resist, or to Abdicate the Perjur'd Spouse, tho' the Laws of GOD and the Land make special Provision for

1   Alas, Mary Astell never revealed the identity of this 'Ingenuous Gentleman'.

it, in a case wherein, as is to be fear'd, few Men can truly plead Not Guilty.

Tis true, thro' Want of Learning, and of that Superior Genius which Men as Men lay claim to, she was ignorant of the *Natural Inferiority* of our Sex, which our Masters lay down as a Self-Evident and Fundamental Truth.[1] She saw nothing in the Reason of Things, to make this either a Principle or a Conclusion, but much to the contrary; it being Sedition at least, if not Treason to assert it in this Reign. For if by the Natural Superiority of their Sex, they mean that every Man is by Nature superior to every Woman, which is the obvious meaning, and that which must be stuck to if they would speak Sense, it wou'd be a Sin in *any* Woman to have Dominion over *any* Man, and the greatest Queen ought not to command but to obey her Footman, because no Municipal Laws can supersede or change the Law of Nature; so that if the Dominion of the Men be such, the *Salique Law*, as unjust as *English Men* have ever thought it, ought to take place over all the Earth, and the most glorious Reigns in the *English, Danish, Castilian,* and other Annals, were wicked Violations of the Law of Nature!

If they mean that *some* Men are superior to *some* Women, this is no great Discovery; had they turn'd the Tables they might have seen that *some* Women are Superior to *some* Men. Or had they been pleased to remember their Oaths of Allegiance and Supremacy, they might have known that *One* Woman is superior to *All* the Men in these Nations, or else they have sworn to very little purpose. And it must not be suppos'd, that their Reason and Religion wou'd suffer them to take Oaths, contrary to the Law of Nature and Reason of things.

By all which it appears, that our Reflector's Ignorance is very pitiable, it may be her Misfortune but not her Crime, especially since she is willing to be better inform'd, and hopes she shall never be so obstinate as to shut her Eyes against the Light of Truth, which is not to be charg'd with Novelty, how late soever we may be bless'd with the Discovery. Nor can Error, be it as Antient as it may, ever plead Prescription against Truth. And since the only way

---

1 Possibly a reference to William Nichols, D.D., *The Duty of Inferiours Towards their Superiours in Five Practical Discourses*, 1701, in which he argued that man possesses 'a higher state of natural perfection and dignity, and thereupon puts in a just claim of superiority, which everything which is of more worth has a right to, over that which has less' (pp.87–8).

to remove all Doubts, to answer all Objections, and to give the Mind entire Satisfaction, is not by *Affirming*, but by *Proving*, so that every one may see with their *own* Eyes, and Judge according to the best of their *own* Understandings, She hopes it is no Presumption to insist on this Natural Right of Judging for her self, and the rather, because by quitting it, we give up all the Means of Rational Conviction. Allow us then as many Glasses as you please to help our Sight, and as many good Arguments as you can afford to Convince our Understandings: But don't exact of us we beseech you, to affirm that we see such things as are only the Discovery of Men who have quicker Senses; or that we understand and Know what we have by Hearsay only, for to be so excessively Complaisant, is neither to see nor to understand.

That the Custom of the World has put Women, generally speaking, into a State of Subjection, is not deny'd; but the Right can no more be prov'd from the Fact, than the Predominancy of Vice can justifie it. A certain great Man has endeavour'd to prove by Reasons not contemptible, that in the Original State of things the Woman was the Superior, and that her Subjection to the Man is an Effect of the Fall, and the Punishment of her Sin. And that Ingenious Theorist Mr *Whiston*[1] asserts, That before the Fall there was a greater equality between the two Sexes. However this be 'tis certainly no Arrogance in a Woman to conclude, that she was made for the Service of GOD, and that this is her End. Because GOD made all Things for Himself, and a Rational Mind is too noble a Being to be Made for the Sake and Service of any Creature. The Service she at any time becomes oblig'd to pay to a Man, is only a Business by the Bye. Just as it may be any Man's Business and Duty to keep Hogs; he was not Made for this, but if he hires himself out to such an Employment, he ought conscientiously to perform it. Nor can anything be concluded to the contrary from St. *Paul's* Argument, *I Cor. II.* For he argues only for Decency and Order, according to the present Custom and State of things. Taking his Words strictly and literally, they prove too much, in that *Praying and Prophecying in the Church* are allow'd the Women, provided they do it with their Head Cover'd, as well as the Men; and no inequality can be inferr'd from hence,

1 William Whiston (1667–1752), divine, mathematician and Newtonian. Author of many works including *A New Theory of the Earth* (1696). He succeeded Newton as the Lucasian Professor and did much to popularise Newton's ideas. In 1710 he was deprived of his chair for casting doubt on the doctrine of the Trinity.

neither from the Gradation the Apostle there uses, that *the Head of every Man is Christ, and that the Head of the Woman is the Man, and the Head of Christ is GOD*; It being evident from the Form of Baptism, that there is no natural Inferiority among the Divine Persons, but that they are in all things Coequal. The Apostle indeed adds, that *the Man is the Glory of God, and the Woman the Glory of the Man*, Etc. But what does he infer from hence? he says not a word of Inequality, or natural Inferiority, but concludes, that a Woman ought to Cover her head, and a Man ought not to cover his, and that *even Nature itself, teaches* us, that *if a Man have long hair it is a shame unto him*. Whatever the Apostle's Argument proves in this place, nothing can be plainer, than that there is much more said against the present Fashion of Men's wearing long Hair, than for that Supremacy they lay claim to. For by all that appears in the Text, it is not so much a Law of Nature, that Women shou'd Obey Men, as that Men shou'd not wear long Hair. Now how can a Christian Nation allow Fashions contrary to the Law of Nature, forbidden by an Apostle, and declared by him to be a shame to Men? Or if Custom may make an alteration in one Case it may in another, but what then becomes of the Nature and Reason of things? Besides, the Conclusion the Apostle draws from his Argument concerning Women, *viz.* that they *shou'd have power on their heads because of the Angels*, is so very obscure a Text, That that Ingenious Paraphrast[1] who pleads so much for the *Natural Subjection* of Women, Ingenuously confesses, that he does not understand it. Probably it refers to some Custom among the *Corinthians*, which being well known to them the Apostle only hints at it, but which we are ignorant of, and therefore apt to mistake him. 'Tis like that the False Apostle whom St *Paul* writes against, had led *Captive* some of their Rich and Powerful but *silly Women*,[2] who having as mean an Opinion of the Reason GOD had given them, as any Deceiver cou'd desire, did not like the noble minded *Bereans, search the Scriptures whether those things were so*,[3] but lazily took up with having Men's Persons in admiration, and follow'd their Leaders Blindfold, the certain Rout to Destruction. And it is also probable, that the same cunning Seducer, imploy'd these Women to carry on his own Designs, and putting them upon what he might not think fit to appear in himself, made

1   William Nichols.
2   See II Tim. 3,6.
3   See Acts 17,11.

them guilty of Indecent Behaviour in the Church of *Corinth*. And therefore St *Paul* thought it necessary to reprove them so severely in order to humble them, but this being done, he takes care in the Conclusion to set the matter on a right Foot, placing the two Sexes on a Level, to keep Men as much as might be, from taking those advantages which People who have strength in their hands, are apt to assume over those who can't contend with them. For, says he, *Nevertheless*, or notwithstanding the former Argument, *the Man is not without the Woman, nor the Woman without the Man, but all things of GOD.*[1] The Relation between the two Sexes is mutual, and the Dependance Reciprocal, both of them Depending intirely upon GOD, and upon Him only; which one wou'd think is no great Argument of the natural Inferiority of either Sex.

Our *Reflector* is of Opinion that Disputes of this kind, extending to Human Nature in general, and not peculiar to those to whom the Word of GOD has been reveal'd, ought to be decided by natural Reason only. And that the Holy Scriptures shou'd not be Interested in the present Controversy, in which it determines nothing, any more than it does between the *Copernican* and *Ptolomean* Systems. The Design of those Holy Books being to make us excellent Moralists and Perfect Christians, not great Philosophers. And being writ for the Vulgar as well as for the Learned, they are accommodated to the common way of Speech and the Usage of the World; in which we have but a short Probation, so that it matters not much what part we Act, whether of Governing or Obeying, provided we perform it well with respect to the World to come.

One does not wonder indeed, that when an Adversary is drove to a Nonplus and Reason declares against him, he flies to Authority, especially to Divine, which is infallible, and therefore ought not to be disputed. But Scripture is not always on their side who make parade of it, and thro' their skill in Languages and the Tricks of the Schools, wrest it from its genuine sense to their own Inventions. And Supposing, not granting, that it were apparently to the Women's Disadvantage, no fair and generous Adversary but wou'd be asham'd to urge this advantage. Because Women without their own Fault, are kept in Ignorance of the Original, wanting Languages and other helps to Criticise on the Sacred Text, of which they know no more, than Men are pleas'd to impart in their Translations. In short, they shew their desire to maintain their Hypotheses, but by no means

1 I. Cor. 11,11–12.

their Reverence to the Sacred Oracles who engage them in such Disputes. And therefore the blame be theirs, who have unnecessarily introduc'd them in the present Subject, and who by saying that the *Reflections* were not agreeable to Scripture, oblige the Reflector to shew that those who affirm it must either mistake her Meaning, or the Sense of Holy Scripture, or both, if they think what they say, and do not find fault merely because they resolve to do so. For had she ever writ any thing contrary to those sacred Truths, she wou'd be the first in pronouncing its Condemnation.

But what says the Holy Scripture? It speaks of Women as in a State of Subjection, and so it does of the *Jews* and *Christians* when under the Dominion of the *Chaldeans* and *Romans*, requiring of the one as well as of the other a quiet submission to them under whose Power they liv'd. But will any one say that these had a *Natural Superiority* and Right to Dominion? that they had a superior Understanding, or any Pre-eminence, except what their greater Strength acquir'd? Or that the other were subjected to their Adversaries for any other Reason but the Punishment of their sins, and in order to their Reformation? Or for the Exercise of their Vertue, and because the Order of the World and the Good of Society requir'd it?

If Mankind had never sinn'd, Reason wou'd always have been obey'd, there wou'd have been no struggle for Dominion, and Brutal Power wou'd not have prevail'd. But in the laps'd State of Mankind, and now that Men will not be guided by their Reason but by their Appetites, and do not what they *ought* but what they *can*, the Reason, or that which stands for it, the Will and Pleasure of the Governor is to be the Reason of those who will not be guided by their own, and must take place for Order's sake, altho' it shou'd not be conformable to right Reason. Nor can there be any Society great or little, from Empires down to private Families, without a last Resort, to determine the Affairs of that Society by an irresistible Sentence. Now unless this Supremacy be fix'd somewhere, there will be a perpetual Contention about it, such is the love of Dominion, and let the Reason of things be what it may, those who have least Force, or Cunning to supply its will have the Disadvantage. So that since Women are acknowledg'd to have least Bodily strength, their being commanded to obey is in pure kindness to them and for their Quiet and Security, as well as for the Exercise of their Vertue. But does it follow that Domestic Governors have more Sense than their Subjects, any more than that other Governors have? We do not find that any Man thinks the worse of his own Understanding because another has superior Power; or concludes himself less capable of a Post of Honour and Authority, because he is not Prefer'd to it. How much time wou'd lie on Men's hands, how empty wou'd the Places of Concourse be, and how silent most Companies, did Men forbear to Censure their Governors, that is in effect to think themselves Wiser. Indeed Government wou'd be much more desirable than it is, did it invest the Possessor with a superior Understanding as well as Power. And if mere Power gives a Right to Rule, there can be no such thing as Usurpation; but a Highway-Man so long as he has strength to force, has also a Right to require our Obedience.

Again, if Absolute Sovereignty be not necessary in a State, how comes it to be so in a Family? or if in a Family why not in a State; since no Reason can be alledg'd for the one that will not hold more strongly for the other? If the Authority of the Husband so far as it extends, is sacred and inalienable, why not of the Prince? The Domestic Sovereign is without Dispute Elected, and the Stipulations and Contract are mutual, is it not then partial in Men to the last degree, to contend for, and practise that Arbitrary Dominion in their Families, which they abhor and exclaim against in the State? For if Arbitrary Power is evil in itself, and an improper Method of Governing Rational and Free Agents, it ought not to be Practis'd any where; Nor is it less, but rather more mischievous in Families than in Kingdoms, by how much 100000 Tyrants are worse than one. What tho' a Husband can't deprive a Wife of Life without being responsible to the Law, he may however do what is much more grievous to a generous Mind, render Life miserable, for which she has no Redress, scarce Pity which is afforded to every other Complainant. It being thought a Wife's Duty to suffer everything without Complaint. *If all Men are born free*, how is it that all Women are born slaves? as they must be if the being subjected to the *inconstant, uncertain, unknown, arbitrary Will* of Men, be the *perfect Condition of Slavery*? and if the Essence of Freedom consists, as our Masters say it does, in having a *standing Rule to live by*? And why is Slavery so much condemn'd and strove against in one Case, and so highly applauded, and held so necessary and so sacred in another?

Tis true that GOD told *Eve* after the Fall that *her Husband shou'd Rule over her*:[1] And so it is that he told *Esau* by the mouth of

1 Gen. 3,16.

Isaac his Father, that he shou'd serve his *younger Brother*, and shou'd in time, and when he was strong enough to do it, *break the Yoke from off his Neck.*[1] Now why one Text shou'd be a Command any more than the other, and not both of them be Predictions only; or why the former shou'd prove *Adam's* natural Right to Rule, and much less every Man's, any more than the latter is a Proof of *Jacob's* Right to Rule, and of *Esau's* to Rebel, one is yet to learn? The Text in both Cases foretelling what wou'd be; but, in neither of them determining what ought to be

But the Scripture commands *Wives* to *submit themselves to their own Husbands.* True; for which St. *Paul* gives a Mystical Reason (Eph 5.22, etc) and St *Peter* a Prudential and Charitable one (I St. Pet. 3.) but neither of them derive that Subjection from the Law of Nature. Nay St *Paul*, as if he foresaw and meant to prevent this Plea, giving directions for their Conduct to Women in general, I *Tim.* 2, when he comes to speak of *Subjection*, he changes his Phrase from *Women* which denotes the whole Sex, to *Woman* which in the New Testament is appropriated to a Wife.

As for his not suffering Women to speak in the Church, no sober Person that I know of pretends to it. That Learned Paraphrast indeed, who lays so much stress on the *Natural Subjection*, provided this Prerogative be secur'd, is willing to give up the other.[2] For he endeavours to prove that Inspir'd Women as well as Men us'd to speak in the Church, and that St. Paul does not forbid it, but only takes care that the Women shou'd signifie their Subjection by wearing a Veil. But the Apostle is his own best Expositor, let us therefore compare his Precepts with his Practice, for he was all of a piece, and did not contradict himself. Now by this Comparison we find, that tho' he forbids Women to teach in the Church, and this for several Prudential Reasons, like those he introduces with an *I give my Opinion, and now speak I not the Lord*, and not because of any Law of Nature, or Positive Divine Precept, for that the words *they are Commanded* (I Cor. 14.24.)[3] are not in the Original, appears from the *Italic* Character, yet he did not found this Prohibition on any suppos'd want of Understanding in Woman, or of ability to Teach; neither does he confine them at all times to *learn in silence.* For

1   Gen. 27,40.
2   William Nichols.
3   In fact I Cor. 14,34.

the Eloquent *Apollos* who was himself a Teacher, was instructed by *Priscilla* as well as by her Husband *Aquila*, and was improv'd by them both in the Christian Faith.[1] Nor does St. *Paul* blame her for this, or suppose that she *Usurp'd Authority* over that great *Man*, so far from this, that as she is always honourably mention'd in Holy Scripture, so our Apostle in his Salutations, *Rom 16.* places her in the Front, even before her Husband, giving to her as well as to him, the Noble Title of his *Helper in Christ Jesus*, and of one *to whom all the Churches of the Gentiles* had great Obligations.[2]

But it will be said perhaps, that in I *Tim.* 2. 13, etc. St *Paul* argues for the Woman's subjection from the Reason of things. To this I answer, that it must be confess'd that this (according to the vulgar Interpretation) is a very obscure place, and I shou'd be glad to see a Natural, and not a Forc'd Interpretation given of it by those who take it Literally. Whereas if it be taken Allegorically, with respect to the Mystical Union between Christ and his Church, to which St. *Paul* frequently accommodates the Matrimonial Relation, the difficulties vanish. For the Earthly *Adam's* being *Form'd* before *Eve*, seems as little to prove her Natural Subjection to him, as the Living Creatures, Fishes, Birds and Beasts being Form'd before them both, proves that Mankind must be subject to these Animals. Nor can the Apostle mean that *Eve* only sinned; or that she only was *Deceiv'd*, for if *Adam* sinn'd wilfully and knowingly, he became the greater Transgressor. But it is very true that the Second *Adam*, the Man Christ Jesus, *was first form'd*, and then his Spouse the Church. He was not in any respect *Deceiv'd*, nor does she pretend to Infallibility. And from this second *Adam*, promis'd to *Eve* in the Day of our first Parent's Transgression, and from Him only, do all their Race, Men as well as Women, derive their Hopes of Salvation. Nor is it promis'd to either Sex on any other Terms besides Perseverance in *Faith, Charity, Holiness and Sobriety*.

If the Learned will not admit of this Interpretation, I know not how to contend with them. For Sense is a Portion that GOD Himself has been pleas'd to distribute to both Sexes with an Impartial Hand, but Learning is what Men have engross'd to themselves, and one can't but admire their great Improvements! For after doubting whether there was such a thing as Truth, and after many hundred years

---

1   Acts 18, 24 & 26.
2   Rom. 16,3–4.

Disputes about it, in the last Century an extraordinary Genius arose,[1] (whom yet some are pleas'd to call a Visionary) enquir'd after it, and laid down the best Method of finding it. Not to the general liking of the Men of Letters, perhaps, because it was wrote in a vulgar Language, and was so natural and easy as to debase Truth to Common Understandings, shewing too plainly that Learning and true Knowledge are two very different things. "For it often happens (says that Author) that Women and Children acknowledge the Falsehood of those Prejudices we contend with, because they do not dare to judge without examination, and they bring all the attention they are capable of to what they reade. Whereas on the contrary, the Learned continue wedded to their own Opinions, because they will not take the trouble of examining what is contrary to their receiv'd Doctrines."

Sciences indeed have been invented and taught long ago, and, as Men grew better advis'd, new Modell'd. So that it is become a considerable piece of Learning to give an account of the Rise and Progress of the Sciences, and of the various Opinions of Men concerning them. But Certainty and Demonstration are much pretended to in this present Age, and being obtain'd in many things, 'tis hop'd Men will never Dispute them away in that which is of greatest Importance, the Way of Salvation. And because there is not any thing more certain than what is delivered in the Oracles of GOD, we come now to consider what they offer in favour of our Sex.

Let it be premis'd, (according to the Reasoning of a very Ingenious Person in a like Case) that One Text for us, is more to be regarded than many against us. Because that *One* being different from what Custom has establish'd, ought to be taken with Philosophical Strictness; whereas the *Many* being express'd according to the vulgar Mode of Speech, ought to have no greater stress laid on them, than that evident Condescension will bear. One place then were sufficient, but we have many Instances wherein Holy Scripture considers Women

---

1   Nicolas Malebranche. The quotation that follows comes from *La Recherche de la Vérité* (see Geneviève Lewis, Ed., *Malebranche*: De la Recherche de la Vérité, 3 Vols. (1675–8), Paris, Urin, 1946, Vol.3, Preface p.v). A translation into English by T. Taylor was published in 1694 and another edition in 1700. In fact Mary Astell's version is a somewhat free rendering of Taylor or else comes from another, perhaps even her own, translation.

very differently from what they appear in the common Prejudices of Mankind.

The World will hardly allow a Woman to say any thing well, unless as she borrows it from Men, or is assisted by them: But GOD Himself allows that the Daughters of *Zelophehad spake right*, and passes their Request into a Law.[1] Considering how much the Tyranny shall I say, or the superior Force of Men, keeps Women from Acting in the World, or doing any thing considerable, and remembring withal the conciseness of the Sacred Story, no small part of it is bestow'd in transmitting the History of Women famous in their Generations: Two of the Canonical Books bearing the Names of those great Women whose Vertues and Actions are there recorded. *Ruth* being call'd from among the *Gentiles* to be an Ancestor of the Messiah, and *Esther* being rais'd up by GOD to be the great Instrument of the Deliverance and Prosperity of the Jewish Church.

The Character of *Isaac*, tho' one of the most blameless Men taken notice of in the Old Testament, must give place to *Rebecca's*, whose Affections are more Reasonably plac'd than his, her Favourite Son being the same who was GOD's Favourite. Nor was the Blessing bestow'd according to his but to her Desire; so that if you will not allow, that her Command to *Jacob* superseded *Isaac's* to *Esau*, his desire to give the Blessing to this Son, being evidently an effect of his Partiality: You must at least grant that she paid greater deference to the Divine Revelation, and for this Reason at least, had a Right to oppose her Husband's Design; which it seems *Isaac* was sensible of, when upon his Disappointment he *trembled so exceedingly*.[2] And so much notice is taken even of *Rebecca's* Nurse, that we have an account where she Died and where she was Buried.[3]

GOD is pleas'd to record it among His Favours to the Ingrateful Jews, that He sent before them His Servants *Moses*, *Aaron*, and *MIRIAM*; who was also a Prophetess, and Instructed the Women how to bear their part with *Moses* in his Triumphal Hymn. Is she to be blam'd for her Ambition? and is not the High Priest *Aaron* also? who has his share in the Reproof as well as in the Crime; nor cou'd she have mov'd Sedition if she had not been a considerable Person, which appears also by the Respect the People paid her, in

---

1 Numbers 27,2.
2 Gen. Chaps. 25, 26, 27.
3 Gen. 24,59 & 35,8.

deferring their Journey till she was ready.[1]

Where shall we find a nobler piece of Poetry than *Deborah's* Song? or a better and greater Ruler than that Renowned Woman whose Government so much excell'd that of the former Judges? And tho' she had a Husband, she her self Judg'd *Israel* and consequently was his Sovereign, of whom we know no more than the Name.[2] Which Instance, as I humbly suppose, overthrows the pretence of *Natural Inferiority*. For it is not the bare Relation of a Fact, by which none ought to be concluded, unless it is conformable to a Rule, and to the Reason of things: But *Deborah's* Government was confer'd on her by GOD Himself. Consequently the Sovereignty of a Woman is not contrary to the Law of Nature; for the Law of Nature is the Law of GOD, who cannot contradict Himself; and yet it was GOD who Inspir'd and Approv'd that great Woman, raising her up to Judge and to Deliver His People *Israel*.

Not to insist on the Courage of that valiant Woman who deliver'd *Thebez* by slaying the Assailant;[3] nor upon the preference which GOD thought fit to give to *Sampson's* Mother, in sending the Angel to her, and not to her Husband, whose vulgar Fear she so prudently answer'd, as plainly shews her superior Understanding:[4] To pass over *Abigail's* wise conduct, whereby she preserv'd her Family and deserv'd *David's* acknowledgments, for restraining him from doing a Rash and unjustifiable Action; the Holy Penman giving her the Character of a *Woman of good Understanding*, whilst her Husband has that of a Churlish and Foolish Person, and a Son of *Belial*:[5] To say nothing of the wise Woman (as the Text calls her) of *Tekoah*;[6] or of her of *Abel* who has the same Epithet, and who by her Prudence deliver'd the City and appeas'd a dangerous Rebellion:[7] Nor of the Queen of *Sheba* whose Journey to hear the Wisdom of *Solomon*, shews her own good Judgment and great share in that excellent Endowment.[8] *Solomon* does not think himself too Wise to be Instructed by his Mother, nor too great to Record her Lessons, which if he had follow'd he might have spar'd the trouble of Repentance, and been deliver'd from a great deal of that Vanity he so deeply Regrets.[9]

What Reason can be assign'd why the Mothers of the Kings of *Judah*, are so frequently noted in those very short accounts that

1 Numbers 12.	4 Judges 13.	7 II Sam. 20, 16–22.
2 Judges 4 & 5.	5 I Sam. 25.	8 I Kings 10.
3 Judges 9, 53.	6 II Sam. 14.	9 I Kings 2.

are given of their Reigns, but the great Respect paid them, or perhaps their Influence on the Government, and share in the Administrations. This is not improbable, since the wicked *Athaliah* had power to carry on her Intrigues so far as to get possession of the Throne, and to keep it for some Years.[1] Neither was there any necessity for *Asa's* removing his Mother (or Grandmother) from being Queen, if this were merely Titular, and did not carry Power and Authority along with it.[2] And we find what Influence *Jezabel* had in *Israel*, indeed to her Husband's and her own Destruction.[3]

It was a *Widow Woman* whom GOD made choice of to sustain his Prophet *Elijah* at *Zarephah*.[4] And the History of the *Shunamite* is a noble Instance of the Account that is made of Women in Holy Scripture. For whether it was not the Custom in *Shunem* for the Husband to Dictate, or whether her's was conscious of her superior Vertue, or whatever was the Reason, we find it is she who Governs, dwelling with great Honour and Satisfaction *among her own People*. Which Happiness she understood so well, and was so far from a troublesome Ambition, that she desires no Recommendation to *the King or Captain of the Host* when the Prophet offer'd it, being already greater than they cou'd make her. The Text calls her a *Great Woman*, whilst her Husband is hardly taken notice of, and this no otherwise than as performing the Office of a Bailiff. It is *her* Piety and Hospitality that are Recorded, *She* invites the Prophet to *her House*; who converses with and is entertain'd by *her*. She gives her Husband no account of *her* Affairs any further than to tell him *her* Designs that he may see them Executed. And when he desires to know the reason of her Conduct, all the Answer she affords is, *Well*, or as the Margin has it from the Hebrew, *Peace*.[5] Nor can this be thought assuming, since it is no more than what the Prophet encourages, for all his Addresses are to *her*, he takes no Notice of her Husband. His Benefits are confer'd on *her*, 'tis *she* and *her Household* whom he warns of a Famine, and 'tis *she* who appeals to the King for the Restitution of *her House* and *Land*.[6] I wou'd not infer from hence that Women generally speaking, ought to govern in their Families when they have a Husband, but I think this Instance and Example is a sufficient Proof, that if by Custom or Contract, or the Laws of the Country, or Birth-right (as in the Case of Sovereign Princesses) they have

---

1   II Kings 11,1–3.   3   I Kings 16,31–33; 18,4; 19,2; 21.   5   II Kings 4.
2   I Kings 15,13.   4   I Kings 17,9.   6   II Kings 8,1–6.

the supreme Authority, it is no Usurpation, nor do they Act contrary to Holy Scripture, nor consequently to the Law of Nature. For they are no where that I know of forbidden to claim their Just Right: The Apostle 'tis true wou'd not have them *usurp* Authority where Custom and the Law of the strongest had brought them into Subjection, as it has in these parts of the World. Tho' in remoter Regions, if Travellers rightly inform us, the Succession to the Crown is entail'd on the Female Line.

GOD Himself who *is no Respecter of Persons, with whom there is neither Bond nor Free, Male nor Female, but* they *are all one in Christ Jesus,* did not deny Women that Divine Gift the Spirit of Prophecy, neither under the Jewish nor Christian Dispensation. We have nam'd two great Prophetesses already, *Miriam* and *Deborah,* and besides other Instances, *Huldah* the Prophetess was such an Oracle that the good King *Josiah,* that great Pattern of Vertue, sends even the High Priest himself to consult her, and to receive directions from her in the most arduous Affairs.[1] *It shall come to pass,* saith the Lord, *that I will pour out my Spirit upon all Flesh, and your Sons and your Daughters shall Prophesy,*[2] which was accordingly fulfill'd by the Mission of the Holy Ghost on the day of *Pentecost,* as St. *Peter* tells us. And besides others, there is mention of four Daughters of *Philip,* Virgins who did Prophesy.[3] For as in the Old, so in the New Testament, Women make a considerable Figure; the Holy Virgin receiving the greatest Honour that Human Nature is capable of, when the Son of GOD vouchsafed to be her Son and to derive his Humanity from her only. And if it is a greater Blessing *to hear the Word of GOD and keep it,* who are more considerable for their Assiduity in this than the Female Disciples of our Lord? *Mary* being Exemplary, and receiving a noble Encomium from Him, for her Choice of the better Part.

It wou'd be thought tedious to enumerate all the excellent Women mention'd in the New Testament, whose humble Penitence and ardent Love, as *Magdalen's;* their lively Faith and holy Importunity, as the *Syrophenician's;* extraordinary Piety and Uprightness, as *Elizabeth's;* Hospitality, Charity and Diligence, as *Martha's, Tabitha's;* etc. (see St. *Luc.* 8)[4] frequent and assiduous Devotions and Austerities, as

1   II Kings, 22,14.   2   Joel 2,28.   3   Acts 21,9.
4   Mary Astell's reference should read Luke 8,2; Mark 7,25–30; Luke 1, 5–57; Luke 10, 38 & 40; Acts 9,36.

Anna's;[1] Constancy and Courage, Perseverance and ardent Zeal, as that of the Holy Women who attended our Lord to His Cross, when His Disciples generally forsook, and the most Courageous had deny'd, Him; are Recorded for our Example. Their Love was stronger than Death, it follow'd our Saviour into the Grave. And as a Reward, both the Angel and even the Lord Himself appears first to them, and sends them to Preach the great Article of the Resurrection to the very Apostles, who being as yet under the Power of the Prejudices of their Sex, esteem'd the Holy Women's *Words as idle Tales and believed them not.*[2]

Some Men will have it, that the Reason of our Lord's appearing first to the Women, was their being least able to keep a Secret; a Witty and Masculine Remarque, and wonderfully Reverent! But not to dispute whether those Women were Blabs or no, there are many Instances in Holy Scripture of Women who did not betray the Confidence repos'd in them. Thus *Rahab* tho' formerly an ill Woman, being Converted by the *Report* of those Miracles, which tho' the *Israelites saw*, yet they *believ'd not in GOD, nor put their Trust in his Word*, She acknowledges the GOD of Heaven, and as a Reward of her faithful Service in concealing *Joshua's* Spies, is with her Family exempted from the Ruine of her Country, and also has the Honor of being nam'd in the Messiah's Genealogy.[3] *Michal* to save *David's* Life exposes her self to the Fury of a Jealous and Tyrannical Prince.[4] A Girl was trusted by *David's* Grave Councellors to convey him Intelligence in his Son's Rebellion; and when a Lad had found it out and blab'd it to *Absalom*, the King's Friends confiding in the Prudence and Fidelity of a Woman were secur'd by her.[5] When our Lord escap'd from the Jews, he trusted Himself in the hands of *Martha* and *Mary*.[6] So does St. *Peter* with another *Mary* when the Angel deliver'd him from *Herod*, the Damsel *Rhoda* too was acquainted with the Secret.[7] More might be said, but one wou'd think here is enough to shew, that whatever other Great and Wise Reasons Men may have for despising Women, and keeping them in Ignorance and Slavery, it can't be from their having learnt to do so in Holy Scripture. The Bible is for, and not against us, and cannot without great violence done to it, be urg'd to our Prejudice.

However, there are strong and prevalent Reasons which demon-

1 Luke 2,36–8.	4 II Sam. 3.	6 Luke 10,38 & 39.
2 Luke 24,11.	5 II Sam. 17,17–20.	7 Acts 12,12–14.
3 Josh. 2 and 6,22–25.		

strate the Superiority and Pre-eminence of the Men. For in the first place, Boys have much Time and Pains, Care and Cost bestow'd on their Education, Girls have little or none. The former are early initiated in the Sciences, are made acquainted with Antient and Modern Discoveries, they Study Books and Men, have all imaginable encouragement; not only Fame, a dry Reward now adays, but also Title, Authority, Power, and Riches themselves which purchase all things, are the Reward of their Improvement. The latter are restrain'd, frown'd upon, and beat, not *for* but *from* the Muses; Laughter and Ridicule that never-failing Scare-Crow is set up to drive them from the Tree of Knowledge. But if in spite of all Difficulties Nature prevails, and they can't be kept so ignorant as their Masters wou'd have them, they are star'd upon as Monsters, Censur'd, Envy'd, and every way Discourag'd, or at the best they have the Fate the Proverb assigns them, *Vertue is prais'd and starv'd*. And therefore since the coursest Materials need the most Curing, as every Workman can inform you, and the worst Ground the most elaborate Culture, it undeniably follows, that Men's Understandings are superior to Women's, for after many Years Study and Experience they become Wise and Learned, and Women are not Born so!

Again, Men are possess'd of all Places of Power, Trust and Profit, they make Laws and exercise the Magistracy, not only the sharpest Sword, but even all the Swords and Blunderbusses are theirs, which by the strongest Logic in the World, gives them the best Title to every thing they please to claim as their Prerogative; who shall contend with them? Immemorial Prescription is on their side in these parts of the World, Antient Tradition and Modern Usage! Our Fathers have all along both Taught and Practis'd Superiority over the weaker Sex, and consequently Women are by Nature inferior to Men, as was to be Demonstrated. An Argument which must be acknowledg'd unanswerable, for as well as I love my Sex, I will not pretend a Reply to *such* Demonstration!

Only let me beg to be inform'd, to whom we poor Fatherless Maids, and Widows who have lost their Masters, owe Subjection? It can't be to all Men in general, unless all Men were agreed to give the same Commands; do we then fall as Strays to the first who finds us? By the Maxims of some Men, and the Conduct of some Women one wou'd think so. But whoever he be that thus happens to become our Master, if he allows us to be Reasonable Creatures, and does not merely Compliment us with that Title, since no Man denies our Readiness to use our Tongues, it wou'd tend, I shou'd think, to our Master's advantage, and therefore he may be please to be advis'd to teach us to improve our Reason. But if Reason is only allow'd us by way of Raillery, and the secret Maxim is that we have none, or little more than Brutes, 'tis the best way to confine us with Chain and Block to the Chimney-Corner, which probably might save the Estates of some Families and the Honor of others.

I do not propose this to prevent a Rebellion, for Women are not so well united as to form an Insurrection. They are for the most part Wise enough to Love their Chains, and to discern how very becomingly they set. They think as humbly of themselves as their Masters can wish, with respect to the other Sex, but in regard to their own, they have a Spice of Masculine Ambition, every one wou'd Lead, and none will Follow. Both Sexes being too apt to Envy, and too backward in Emulating, and take more delight in detracting from their Neighbour's Vertue than in improving their own. And therefore as to those Women who find themselves born for Slavery and are so sensible of their own Meanness as to conclude it impossible to attain to any thing excellent, since they are, or ought to be best acquainted with their own Strength and Genius, She's a Fool who wou'd attempt their Deliverance or Improvement. No, let them enjoy the great Honor and Felicity of their Tame, Submissive and Depending Temper! Let the Men applaud, and let them Glory in, this wonderful Humility! Let them receive the Flatteries and Grimaces of the other Sex, live unenvy'd by their own, and be as much Belov'd as one such Woman can afford to Love another! Let them enjoy the Glory of treading in the Footsteps of their Predecessors, and of having the Prudence to avoid that audacious attempt of soaring beyond their Sphere! Let them Huswife or Play, Dress and be pretty entertaining Company! Or which is better, relieve the Poor to ease their own Compassions, reade Pious Books, say their Prayers and go to Church, because they have been Taught and Us'd to do so, without being able to give a better Reason for their Faith and Practice! Let them not by any means aspire at being Women of Understanding, because no Man can endure a Woman of Superior Sense, or wou'd treat a reasonable Woman civilly, but that he thinks he stands on higher ground, and that she is so Wise as to make exceptions in his Favour, and to take her Measures by his Directions; they may pretend to Sense indeed, since mere

Pretences only render one the more Ridiculous! Let them in short be what is call'd very Women, for this is most acceptable to all sorts of Men; or let them aim at the Title of *Good Devout* Women, since some Men can bear with this; but let them not Judge of the Sex by their own Scantling. For the great Author of Nature and Fountain of all Perfection, never design'd that the Mean and Imperfect, but that the most Compleat and Excellent of His Creatures in every Kind, shou'd be the Standard to the rest.

To conclude, if that GREAT QUEEN who has subdu'd the Proud, and made the pretended Invincible more than once fly before her; who has Rescu'd an Empire, Reduc'd a Kingdom, Conquer'd Provinces in as little time almost as one can Travel them, and seems to have Chain'd Victory to her Standard; who disposes of Crowns, gives Laws and Liberty to *Europe*, and is the chief Instrument in the Hand of the Almighty to pull down and to set up the Great Men of the Earth; who Conquers everywhere for others, and no where for her self but in the Hearts of the Conquer'd, who are of the number of those who reap the benefit of her Triumphs; whilst she only reaps for her self the Lawrels of Disinteressed Glory, and the Royal Pleasure of doing Heroically; if this Glory of her own Sex and Envy of the other, will not think we need, or does not hold us worthy of, the Protection of her ever Victorious Arms, and Men have not the Gratitude for her sake at least, to do Justice to her Sex, who has been such a universal Benefactress to theirs: Adieu to the Liberties not of this or that Nation or Region only, but of the Moiety of Mankind! To all the great things that Women might perform, Inspir'd by her Example, Encourag'd by her Smiles, and supported by her Power! To their Discovery of New Worlds for the Exercise of her Goodness, New Sciences to publish her Fame, and reducing Nature itself to a Subjection to her Empire! To their destroying those worst of Tyrants Impiety and Immorality, which dare to stalk about even in her own Dominions, and to devour Souls almost within view of her Throne, leaving a stench behind them scarce to be corrected even by the Incense of her Devotions! To the Women's tracing a new Path to Honor, in which none shall walk but such as scorn to Cringe in order to Rise, and who are Proof both against giving and receiving Flattery! In a word, to those Halcyon, or if you will *Millennium* Days, in which the Wolf and the Lamb shall feed together, and a Tyrannous Domination which Nature never meant, shall no longer render useless if not hurtful, the Industry and Understandings of half Mankind!

Some Reflections upon Marriage

Curiosity, which is sometimes an occasion of Good, and too frequently
of Mischief, by disturbing either our Own, or our Neighbour's Repose,
having put me upon reading the *Duke and Dutchess* of Mazarine's
Case;[1] I thought an Afternoon wou'd not be quite thrown away
in pursuing some Reflections that it occasion'd. The Name of *Mazarine*
is considerable enough to draw the Eyes of the Curious, and when
one remembers what a noise it once made in *Europe*, what Politick
Schemes have been laid, what vast Designs brought about by the
Cardinal that bore it; how well his measures were concerted for
the Grandeur of that Nation into which he was transplanted, and
that he wanted neither Power nor Inclination to establish his own
Family and make it as considerable as any Subject's could possible
be, and what Honours and Riches he had heap'd together in order
to this; one cannot but enquire how it comes about that he should
be so defeated in this last design? and that those to whom he intrusted
his Name and Treasure, should make a figure so very different from
what might have been expected from them? And tho' one had not
Piety enough to make a Religious Reflection, yet Civil Prudence
would almost enforce them to say, that *Man being in Honour has*

1 *Memoirs of the Dutchess of Mazarine.* Written in her name by The Abbott of
St. Réal, with a Letter Containing a True Character of Her Person and Conversation, 1713.

no Understanding, but is compar'd unto the Beasts that perish. He Blesseth his Soul, and thinks himself a happy Man, imagining his House will endure for ever, and that he has establish'd his Name and Family. But how wise soever he may be in other respects, in this he acts no better than the Ignorant and Foolish. For as he carries nothing away with him when he dies, so neither will his Pomp and Glory descend as he intended. Generous and Worthy Actions only can secure him from Oblivion, or what is worse, being remembred with Contempt; so little reason have we to Envy any Man's Wealth and Greatness, but much to Emulate his Wisdom and Vertue.

The Dutchess of *Mazarine's* Name has spread perhaps as far as her Uncle's and one can't help wishing that so much Wit and Beauty, so much Politeness and Address, has been accompany'd and supported by more valuable and lasting Qualities; one cannot but desire that her Advocate instead of recriminating had clear'd the imputations laid on her, and that she her self, who says enough in her Memoirs to shew she was unfortunate, had said more to prove her self discreet. They must be highly ill-natur'd who do not pity her ill Fortune at the same time that they must blame her Conduct, and regret that such a Treasure should fall into his hands who was not worthy of it, nor knew how to value and improve it; that she who was capable of being a great Ornament to her Family and Blessing to the Age she liv'd in, should only serve (to say no worse) as an unhappy Shipwrack to point out the dangers of an ill Education and unequal Marriage.

Monsieur *Mazarine* is not to be justified, nor Madam his Spouse excus'd. It is no question which is most Criminal, the having no Sense, or the abuse of a liberal Portion; nor any hard matter to determine who is most to be pity'd, he whom Nature never qualify'd for great things, who therefore can't be very sensible of great Misfortunes; or she, who being capable of every thing must therefore suffer more and be the more lamented. To be yok'd for Life to a disagreeable Person and Temper; to have Folly and Ignorance tyrannize over Wit and Sense; to be contradicted in every thing one does or says, and bore down not by Reason but Authority; to be denied ones most innocent desires, for no other cause but the Will and Pleasure of an absolute Lord and Master, whose Follies a Woman with all her Prudence cannot hide, and whose Commands she cannot but despise at the same time she obeys them; is a misery none can have a just Idea of, but those who have felt it.

These are great Provocations, but nothing can justify the revenging the Injuries we receive from others, upon our selves: The *Italian* Proverb shews a much better way; *If you would be reveng'd of your Enemies, live well.* Had *Madam Mazarine's* Education made a right Improvement of her Wit and Sense, we should not have found her seeking Relief by such imprudent, not to say scandalous Methods, as the running away in Disguise with a spruce Cavalier, and rambling to so many Courts and Places, nor diverting her self with such Childish, Ridiculous, or Ill-natur'd Amusements, as the greatest part of the Adventures in her Memoirs are made up of. True Wit consists not meerly in doing or saying what is out of the way, but in such surprizing things as are fit and becoming the person from whom they come. That which stirs us up to Laughter most commonly excites our Contempt; to please and to make Merry are two very different Talents. But what Remedies can be administred, what Relief expected, when Devotion, the only true Support in Distress, is turn'd into Ridicule? Unhappy is that Grandeur which makes us too great to be good; and that Wit which sets us at a distance from true Wisdom. Even Bigotry it self, as contemptible as it is, is preferable to Prophane Wit; for *that* only requires our Pity, but *this* deserves our Abhorrence.

A Woman who seeks Consolation under Domestic troubles from the Gaieties of a Court, from Gaming and Courtship, from Rambling and odd Adventures, and the Amusements mixt Company affords, may Plaister up the Sore, but will never heal it; nay, which is worse, she makes it Fester beyond a possibility of Cure. She justifies the Injury her Husband has done her, by shewing that whatever other good Qualities she may have, Discretion, one of the Principal, is wanting. She may be Innocent, but she can never prove she is so, all that Charity can do for her when she's Censur'd is only to be silent, it can make no Apologies for suspicious Actions. An ill Husband may deprive a Wife of the comfort and quiet of her Life; may give her occasion of exercising her Virtue, may try her Patience and Forti-tude to the utmost, but that's all he can do: 'tis her self only can accomplish her Ruin. Had Madam *Mazarine's* Reserve been what it ought to be, Monsieur *Herard*[1] needed not to have warded off so carefully, the nice Subject of the Lady's Honour, nor her Advocate

1 *The arguments of Mons. Herard for the Duke of Mazarin against the dutchess, his spouse, and the factum for the dutchess by Mons. St. Evremont,* trans. from French, 1699.

have strain'd so hard for Colours to excuse such Actions as will hardly bear 'em; a Man indeed shews the best side of his Wit, tho' the worst of his Integrity, when he has an ill Cause to manage. Truth is bold and vehement; she depends upon her own strength, and so she be plac'd in a true Light, thinks it not necessary to use Artifice and Address as a Recommendation; but the prejudices of Men have made them necessary: their Imagination gets the better of their Understanding, and more judge according to Appearances, than search after the Truth of Things.

What an ill Figure does a Woman make with all the Charms of her Beauty and Sprightliness of her Wit, with all her good Humour and insinuating Address; tho' she be the best Economist in the World, the most entertaining Conversation; if she remit her Guard, abate in the Severity of her Caution and Strictness of her Vertue, and neglect those Methods which are necessary to keep her not only from a Crime, but from the very suspicion of one.

Are the being forbid having Comedies in her House, an ill natur'd Jest, dismissing of a Servant, imposing Domestics, or frequent changing them, sufficient Reasons to Authorize a Woman's leaving her Husband and breaking from the strongest Bands, exposing her self to Temptations and Injuries from the Bad, to the contempt, or at the best to the pity of the Good, and the just Censure of all? A Woman of sense one would think should take little satisfaction in the Cringes and Courtship of her Adorers, even when she is single; but it is Criminal in a Wife to admit them: interested Persons may call it Gallantry, but with the modest and discreet it is like to have a harder Name, or else Gallantry will pass for a scandalous thing, not to be allow'd among Vertuous Persons.

But Madam *Mazarine* is dead, may her Faults die with her; may there be no more occasion given for the like Adventures, or if there is, may the Ladies be more Wise and Good than to take it! Let us see then from whence the mischief proceeds, and try if it can be prevented; for certainly Men may be very happy in a Married State; tis their own fault if they are at any time otherwise. The wise Institutor of Matrimony never did any thing in vain; we are the Sots and Fools if what he design'd for our Good, be to us an occasion of falling. For Marriage, notwithstanding all the loose talk of the Town, the Satyrs of Ancient or Modern pretenders to Wit, will never lose its due praise from judicious Persons. Tho' much may be said against this or that Match, tho' the Ridiculousness of some, the Wickedness of others and Imprudence of too many, too often provoke our wonder or scorn, our indignation or pity, yet Marriage in general is too sacred to be treated with Disrespect, too venerable to be the subject of Raillery and Buffonery. It is the Institution of Heaven, the only Honourable way of continuing Mankind, and far be it from us to think there could have been a better than infinite Wisdom has found out for us.

But upon what are the Satyrs against Marriage grounded? Not upon the State itself, if they are just, but upon the ill Choice, or foolish Conduct of those who are in it, and what has Marriage, considered in its self, to do with these? Let every Man bear his own Burden: If through inordinate Passion, Rashness, Humour, Pride, Covetousness, or any the like Folly, a Man makes an Imprudent Choice, Why should Marriage be exclaim'd against? Let him blame himself for entring into an unequal Yoke, and making Choice of one who perhaps may prove a Burthen, a Disgrace and Plague, instead of a Help and Comfort to him. Could there be no such thing as an happy Marriage, Arguments against Marriage would hold good, but since the thing is not only possible, but even very probable, provided we take but competent Care, Act like Wise Men and Christians, and acquit our selves as we ought, all we have to say against it serves only to shew the Levity or Impiety of our own Minds; we only make some flourishes of Wit, tho' scarce without Injustice; and tho' we talk prettily it is but very little to the purpose.

Is it the being ty'd to *One* that offends us? Why this ought rather to recommend Marriage to us, and would really do so, were we guided by Reason, and not by Humour or brutish Passion. He who does not make Friendship the chief inducement to his Choice, and prefer it before any other consideration, does not deserve a good Wife, and therefore should not complain if he goes without one. Now we can never grow weary of our Friends; the longer we have had them the more they are endear'd to us; and if we have One well assur'd, we need seek no further, but are sufficiently happy in Her. The love of Variety in this and in other cases, shews only the ill Temper of our own Minds, in that we seek for *settled* Happiness in this present World, where it is not to be found, instead of being Content with a competent share, chearfully enjoying and being thankful for the Good that is afforded us, and patiently bearing with the Inconveniences that attend it.

The Christian Institution of Marriage provides the best that may be for Domestic Quiet and Content, and for the Education of Children; so that if we were not under the tye of Religion, even the Good of Society and civil Duty would oblige us to what that requires at our Hands. And since the very best of us are but poor frail Creatures, full of Ignorance and Infirmity, so that in Justice we ought to tolerate each other, and exercise that Patience towards our Companions to Day, which we shall give them occasion to shew towards us to Morrow, the more we are accustom'd to any one's Conversation, the better shall we understand their Humour, be more able to comply with their Weakness and less offended at it. For he who would have every one submit to his Humours and will not in his turn comply with them, tho' we should suppose him always in the Right, whereas a Man of this temper very seldom is so, he's not fit for a Husband, scarce fit for Society, but ought to be turn'd out of the Herd to live by himself.

There may indeed be inconveniences in a Married Life; but is there any Condition without them? And he who lives single that he may indulge Licentiousness and give up himself to the conduct of wild and ungovern'd Desires, or indeed out of any other inducement, than the Glory of GOD and the Good of his Soul, through the prospect he has of doing more Good, or because his frame and disposition of Mind are fitted for it, may rail as he pleases against Matrimony, but can never justifie his own Conduct, nor clear it from the imputation of Wickedness and Folly.

But if Marriage be such a blessed State, how comes it, may you say, that there are so few happy Marriages? Now in answer to this, it is not to be wonder'd that so few succeed, we should rather be surpriz'd to find so many do, considering how imprudently Men engage, the Motives they act by, and the very strange Conduct they observe throughout.

For pray, what do Men propose to themselves in Marriage? What Qualifications do they look after in a Spouse? What will she bring is the first enquiry? How many Acres? Or how much ready Coin? Not that this is altogether an unnecessary Question, for Marriage without a Competency, that is, not only a bare Subsistence, but even a handsome and plentiful Provision, according to the Quality and Circumstances of the Parties, is no very comfortable Condition. They who marry for Love as they call it, find time enough to repent their rash Folly, and are not long in being convinc'd, that whatever fine Speeches might be made in the heat of Passion, there could

94

be no *real Kindness* between those who can agree to make each other miserable. But as an Estate is to be consider'd, so it should not be the *Main,* much less the *Only* consideration, for Happiness does not depend on Wealth, *that* may be wanting, and too often is, where *this* abounds. He who Marries himself to a Fortune only, must expect no other satisfaction than that can bring him, but let him not say that Marriage but that his own Covetous or Prodigal Temper, has made him unhappy. What Joy has that Man in all his Plenty, who must either run from home to possess it, contrary to all the Rules of Justice, to the Laws of GOD and Man, nay, even in opposition to Good nature, and Good breeding too, which some Men make more account of than all the rest; or else be forc'd to share it with a Woman whose Person or Temper is disagreeable, whose presence is sufficient to sour all his Enjoyments, so that if he has any remains of Religion, or Good manners, he must suffer the uneasiness of a continual watch, to force himself to a constrain'd Civility!

Few Men have so much Goodness as to bring themselves to a liking of what they loath'd, meerly because it is their Duty to like; on the contrary, when they Marry with an indifferency, to please their Friends or encrease their Fortune, the indifferency proceeds to an aversion, and perhaps even the kindness and complaisance of the poor abus'd Wife shall only serve to encrease it. What follows then? There is no content at home, so it is sought elsewhere, and the Fortune so unjustly got, is as carelessly squander'd. The Man takes a loose, what shou'd hinder him? He has all in his hands, and Custom has almost taken off that small Restraint Reputation us'd to lay. The Wife finds too late what was the Idol the Man adored which her Vanity perhaps, or it may be the Commands and importunities of Relations, wou'd not let her see before; and now he has got *that* into his possession, she must make court to him for a little sorry Alimony out of her own Estate. If Discretion and Piety prevails upon her Passions she sits down quietly, contented with her lot, seeks no Consolation in the Multitude of Adorers, since he whom only she desir'd to please, because it was her duty to do so, will take no delight in her Wit or Beauty: She follows no Diversion to allay her Grief, uses no Cordials to support her Spirit, that may sully her Vertue or bring a Cloud upon her Reputation, she makes no appeals to the mis-judging Croud, hardly mentions her Misfortunes to her most intimate Acquaintance, nor lays a load on her Husband to ease her self, but wou'd if it were possible conceal his Crimes, tho' her Prudence and Vertue give him a thousand Reproaches without her Intention or knowledge; and retiring from the World, she seeks a more solid Comfort than it can give her, taking care to do nothing that Censoriousness or even Malice itself can misconstrue to her prejudice. Now she puts on all her Reserves, and thinks even innocent Liberties scarce allowable in her Disconsolate State; she has other Business to mind: Nor does she in her Retirements reflect so much upon the hand that administers this bitter Cup, as consider what is the best use she can make of it. And thus indeed Marriage, however unfortunate in other respects, becomes a very great Blessing to her. She might have been exposed to all the Temptations of a plentiful Fortune, have given up her self to Sloth and Luxury, and gone on at the common rate even of the better sort, in doing no hurt, and as little good: But now her kind Husband obliges her to *Consider*, and gives opportunity to exercise her Vertue; he makes it necessary to withdraw from those Gaities and Pleasures of Life, which do more mischief under the Shew of Innocency, than they cou'd if they appear'd attended with a Crime, discomposing and dissolving the Mind, and making it uncapable of any manner of good, to be sure of any thing Great and Excellent. Silence and Solitude, the being forc'd from the ordinary Entertainments of her Station, may perhaps seem a desolate condition at first, and we may allow her, poor weak Woman! to be somewhat shock'd at it, since even a wise and courageous Man perhaps would not keep his ground. We would conceal if we could for the Honour of the Sex, Men's being baffled and dispirited by a smaller Matter, were not the Instances too frequent and too notorious.

But a little time wears off all the uneasiness, and puts her in possession of Pleasures, which till now she has unkindly been kept a stranger to. Affliction, the sincerest Friend, the frankest Monitor, the best Instructer, and indeed the only useful School that Women are ever put to, rouses her understanding, opens her Eyes, fixes her Attention, and diffuses such a Light, such a Joy into her Mind, as not only Informs her better, but Entertains her more than ever her *Ruel*[1] did tho' crouded by the Men of Wit. She now distinguishes between Truth and Appearances, between solid and apparent Good; has found out the instability of all Earthly Things, and won't any

1 A morning reception or salon such as was held by women of the French aristocracy in the seventeenth and eighteenth century.

more be deceiv'd by relying on them; can discern who are the Flatterers of her Fortune, and who the Admirers and Encouragers of her Vertue; accounting it no little blessing to be rid of those Leeches, who only hung upon her for their own Advantage. Now sober Thoughts succeed to hurry and impertinence, to Forms and Ceremony, she can secure her Time, and knows how to Improve it; never truly a Happy Woman till she came in the Eye of the World to be reckon'd Miserable.

Thus the Husband's Vices may become an occasion of the Wife's Vertues, and his Neglect do her a more real Good than his Kindness could. But all injur'd Wives don't behave themselves after this Fashion, nor can their Husbands justly expert it. With what Face can he blame her for following his Example, and being as extravagant on the one Hand, as he is on the other? Tho' she cannot justifie her Excesses to GOD, to the World, nor to her self, yet surely in respect of him they may admit of an excuse. For to all the rest of his Absurdities, (for Vice is always unreasonable,) he adds one more, who expects that Vertue from another which he won't practise himself.

But suppose a Man does not Marry for Money, tho' for one that does not, perhaps there are thousands that do; let him Marry for Love, an Heroick Action, which makes a mighty noise in the World, partly because of its rarity, and partly in regard of its extravagancy, and what does his Marrying for Love amount to? There's no great odds between his Marrying for the Love of Money, or for the Love of Beauty, the Man does not act according to Reason in either Case, but is govern'd by irregular Appetites. But he loves her Wit perhaps, and this you'll say is more Spiritual, more refin'd; not at all if you examine it to the Bottom. For what is that which now adays passes under the name of Wit? A bitter and ill-natur'd Raillery, a pert Repartee, or a confident talking at all, and in such a multitude of Words, it's odds if something or other does not pass that is surprizing, tho' every thing that surprizes does not please; some things being wonder'd at for their Ugliness, as well as others for their Beauty. True Wit, durst one venture to describe it, is quite another thing, it consists in such a Sprightliness of Imagination, such a reach and turn of thought, so properly exprest, as strikes and pleases a judicious Tast. For tho' as one says of Beauty, 'tis in no Face but in the Lover's Mind, so it may be said of some sort of Wit, it is not in him that speaks, but in the Imagination of his Hearer, yet doubtless there is a true Standard-Wit, which must be allow'd for such by every one who understands the Terms, I don't say that they shall *equally* like it; and it is this Standard-Wit that always pleases, the Spurious does so only for a Season.

Now what is it that strikes a judicious Tast? Not that to be sure which injures the absent, or provokes the Company, which poisons the Mind under pretence of entertaining it, proceeding from or giving Countenance to false Ideas, to dangerous and immoral Principles. Wit indeed is distinct from Judgment, but it is not contrary to it; 'tis rather its Handmaid, serving to awaken and fix the Attention, that so we may Judge rightly. Whatever Charms, does so because of its Regularity and Proportion; otherwise, tho' it is extraordinary and out of the way, it will only be star'd on as a Monster, but can never be lik'd. And tho a thought is ever so fine and new, ever so well exprest, if it suits not with Decorum and good manners, it is not just and fit, and therefore offends our Reason, and consequently has no Charms, nor should afford us any entertainment.

But it must not be suppos'd that Women's Wit approaches those heights which Men arrive at, or that they indulge those Liberties the other take. Decency lays greater restraints on them, their timorousness does them this one, and perhaps this only piece of Service, it keeps them from breaking thro' those restraints, and following their Masters and Guides in many of their daring and masculine Crimes. As the World goes, your Witty Men are usually distinguish'd by the Liberty they take with Religion, good Manners, or their Neighbour's Reputation: But, GOD be thank'd, it is not yet so bad, as that Women should form Cabals to propagate Atheism and Irreligion. A Man then cannot hope to find a Woman whose Wit is of a size with his, but when he doats on Wit it is to be imagin'd he makes choice of that which comes the nearest to his own.

Thus, whether it be Wit or Beauty that a Man's in Love with, there's no great hopes of a lasting Happiness; Beauty with all the helps of Art is of no long date, the more it is help'd the sooner it decays, and he who only or chiefly chose for Beauty, will in a little time find the same reason for another Choice. Nor is that sort of Wit which he prefers of a more sure tenure, or allowing it to last, it will not always please. For that which has not a real excellency and value in it self, entertains no longer than the giddy Humour which recommended it to us holds; and when we can like on no just, or on very little Ground, tis certain a dislike will arise, as lightly and as unaccountably. And it is not improbable that such a Husband may in a little time by ill usage provoke such a Wife to exercise her Wit, that is, her Spleen on him, and then it is not hard to guess how very agreeable it will be to him.

In a word, when we have reckon'd up how many look no further than the making of their Fortune, as they call it; who don't so much as propose to themselves any satisfaction in the Woman to whom they Plight their Faith, seeking only to be Masters of her Estate, that so they may have Money enough to indulge all their irregular Appetites; who think they are as good as can be expected, if they are but according to the fashionable Term, *Civil Husbands;* when we have taken the number of your giddy Lovers, who are not more violent in their Passion than they are certain to Repent of it; when to these you have added such as Marry without any Thought at all, further than that it is the Custom of the World, what others have done before them, that the Family must be kept up, the ancient Race preserv'd, and therefore their kind Parents and Guardians chuse as they think convenient, without ever consulting the Young ones Inclinations, who must be satisfied or pretend so at least, upon pain of their displeasure, and that heavy consequence of it, forfeiture of their Estate: These set aside, I fear there will be but a small remainder to Marry out of better considerations, and even amongst the few that do, not one in a hundred takes care to deserve his Choice.

But do the Women never chuse amiss? Are the Men only in fault? that is not pretended; for he who will be just, must be forc'd to acknowledge, that neither Sex are always in the right. A Woman indeed can't properly be said to Choose, all that is allow'd her, is to Refuse or Accept what is offer'd. And when we have made such reasonable allowances as are due to the Sex, perhaps they may not appear so much in fault as one would at first imagine, and a generous Spirit will find more occasion to pity, than to reprove. But sure I transgress — it must not be suppos'd that the Ladies can do amiss! he is but an ill-bred Fellow who pretends that they need amendment! They are no doubt on't always in the right, and most of all when they take pity on distressed Lovers! whatever they *say* carries an Authority that no Reason can resist, and all that they *do* must needs be Exemplary! This is the Modish Language, nor is there a Man of Honour amongst the whole Tribe that would not venture his Life, nay and his Salvation too in their Defence, if any but himself attempts to injure them. But I must ask pardon if I can't come up to these heights, nor flatter them with the having no faults, which is only a malicious way of continuing and encreasing their Mistakes.

Women, it's true, ought to be treated with Civility; for since a little Ceremony and out-side Respect is all their Guard, all the privilege that's allow'd them, it were barbarous to deprive them of it; and because I would treat them civilly, I would not express my Civility at the usual rate. I would not under pretence of honouring and paying a mighty Deference to the Ladies, call them fools to their faces; for what are all the fine Speeches and Submissions that are made, but an abusing them in a well-bred way? She must be a Fool with a witness, who can believe a Man, Proud and Vain as he is, will lay his boasted Authority, the Dignity and Prerogative of his Sex, one Moment at her Feet, but in prospect of taking it up again to more advantage; he may call himself her Slave a few days, but it is only in order to make her his all the rest of his Life.

Indeed that mistaken Self-Love that reigns in the most of us, both Men and Women, that over-good Opinion we have of our selves, and desire that others should have of us, makes us swallow every thing that looks like Respect, without examining how wide it is from what it appears to be. For nothing is in truth a greater outrage than Flattery and feign'd Submissions, the plain English of which is this, 'I have a very mean Opinion both of your Understanding and Vertue, you are weak enough to be impos'd on, and vain enough to snatch at the Bait I throw; there's no danger of your finding out my meaning, or disappointing me of my Ends. I offer you *Incense* 'tis true, but you are like to pay for't, and to make me a Recompence for your Folly in Imagining I would give my self this trouble, did I not hope, nay were I not sure, to find my own account in it. If for nothing else, you'll serve at least as an exercise of my Wit, and how much soever you swell with my Breath, 'tis I deserve the Praise for talking so well on so poor a Subject. We who make the Idols, are the greater Deities; and as we set you up, so it is in our power to reduce you to your first obscurity, or to somewhat worse, to Contempt; you are therefore only on your good behaviour, and are like to be no more than what we please to make you.' This is the Flatterer's Language aside, this is the true sense of his heart, whatever his Grimace may be before the Company.

Not but that 'tis possible, and sometimes matter of Fact, to express our selves beyond the Truth in praise of a Person, and yet not be guilty of Flattery; but then we must Think what we Say, and Mean what we Profess. We may be so blinded by some Passion or other, especially Love, which in Civil and Goodnatur'd Persons is apt to exceed, as to believe some Persons more deserving than really they are, and to pay them greater Respect and Kindness than is in strictness due to them. But this is not the present Case, for our fine Speech-makers doat too much on themselves to have any great passion for another, their Eyes are too much fixt on their own Excellencies, to view another's good Qualities through a magnifying Glass; or at least, if ever they turn that end of their Perspective towards their Neighbours, 'tis only in respect and reference to themselves. They are their own Centres, they find a disproportion in every line that does not tend thither, and in the next visit they make, you shall hear all the fine things they had said repeated to the new Object, and nothing remembred of the former but her Vanity, or something else as Ridiculous, which serves for a foil, or a whet to Discourse. For let there be ever so many Wits in the Company, Conversation would languish, and they would be at a loss, did not a little Censoriousness come in at a need to help them.

Let us then treat the Ladies as Civilly as may be, but let us not do it by Flattering them, but by endeavouring to make them such as may truly deserve our hearty Esteem and Kindness. Men ought really for their own sakes to do what in them lies to make Women Wise and Good, and then it might be hoped they themselves would effectually Study and Practise that Wisdom and Vertue they recommend to others. But so long as Men have base and unworthy Ends to serve, it is not to be expected that they should consent to such Methods as would certainly disappoint them. They would have their own Relations do well, it is their Interest; but it sometimes happens to be for their turn that another Man's should not, and then their Generosity fails them, and no Man is apter to find fault with another's dishonourable Actions, than he who is ready to do, or perhaps has done the same himself.

And as Men have little reason to expect Happiness when they Marry only for the Love of Money, Wit or Beauty, as has been already shewn, so much less can a Woman expect a tolerable life, when she goes upon these Considerations. Let the business be carried as Prudently as it can be on the Woman's side, a reasonable Man can't deny that she has by much the harder bargain. Because she puts her self entirely into her Husband's Power, and if the Matrimonial Yoke be grievous, neither Law nor Custom afford her that redress which a Man obtains. He who has Sovereign Power does not value the Provocations of a Rebellious Subject, but knows how to subdue him with ease, and will make himself obey'd; but Patience and Submission are the only Comforts that are left to a poor People, who groan under Tyranny, unless they are Strong enough to break the Yoke, to Depose and Abdicate, which I doubt wou'd not be allow'd of here. For whatever may be said against Passive-Obedience in another case, I suppose there's no Man but likes it very well in this; how much soever Arbitrary Power may be dislik'd on a Throne, not *Milton* himself wou'd cry up Liberty to poor *Female Slaves*, or plead for the Lawfulness of Resisting a Private Tyranny.

If there be a disagreeableness of Humours, this in my mind is harder to be born than greater faults, as being a continual Plague, and for the most part incurable; other Vices a Man may grow weary of, or may be convinced of the evil of them, he may forsake them, or they him, but his Humour and Temper are seldom, if ever put off, Ill-nature sticks to him from his Youth to his grey Hairs, and a Boy that's Humorous and Proud, makes a Peevish, Positive and Insolent Old Man. Now if this be the case, and the Husband be full of himself, obstinately bent on his own way with or without Reason, if he be one who must be always Admir'd, always Humour'd, and yet scarce knows what will please him, if he has Prosperity enough to keep him from considering, and to furnish him with a train of Flatterers and obsequious Admirers; and Learning and Sense enough to make him a Fop in Perfection; for a Man can never be a complete Coxcomb, unless he has a considerable share of these to value himself upon; what can the poor Woman do? the Husband is too wise to be Advis'd, too good to be Reform'd, she must follow all his Paces, and tread in all his unreasonable steps, or there is no Peace, no Quiet for her, she must obey with the greatest exactness, 'tis in vain to expect any manner of Compliance on his side, and the more she complies the more she may; his fantastical humours grow with her desire to gratifie them, for Age encreases Opiniatry in some, as well as it does Experience in others. Of such sort of folks as these it was that *Solomon spake,* when he said, *Seest thou a Man wise in his own conceit, there is more hope of a Fool than of him;* That is, the profligate Sinner, such a one being always a Fool in *Solomon's* Language, is in a fairer way of being convinc'd of his Folly, and brought to Reason, than the Proud Conceited Man. That Man indeed can never be good at heart, who is full of himself and his own Endowments.

Not that it is necessary, because it is not possible for one to be totally ignorant of his own good Qualities. I had almost said he *ought* to have a Modest sense of 'em, otherwise he can't be duly thankful, nor make the use of them that is required, to the Glory of God, and the good of Mankind; but he views them in a wrong light, if he discerns any thing that may exalt him above his Neighbours, make him over-look their Merit, or treat them with Neglect or Contempt. He ought to behold his Advantages with fear and trembling, as Talents which he has freely receiv'd, and for which he is highly Accountable, and therefore they shou'd not excite his Pride, but his Care and Industry.

And if Pride and Self-conceit keep a Man who has some good Qualities, and is not so bad as the most of his Neighbours, from growing better, it for certain confirms and hardens the Wicked in his Crimes, it sets him up for a Wit, that is, according to Modern acceptation, one who rallies all that is serious, a Contemner of the Priests first, and then of the Deity Himself. For Penitence and Self-condemnation are what his Haughtiness cannot bear, and since his Crimes have brought upon him the reproaches of his own Mind, since he will not take the regular way to be rid of them, which is by Humbling himself and making his Peace with Heaven, he bids defiance to it, and wou'd if he could believe there is no future State, no after Retribution, because he knows that a heavy lot is in justice due to him.

If therefore it is a Woman's hard Fate to meet with a disagreeable Temper, and of all others the Haughty, Imperious and Self-conceited are the most so, she is as unhappy as any thing in this World can make her. For when a Wife's Temper does not please, if she makes her Husband uneasie, he can find entertainments abroad, he has a hundred ways of relieving himself, but neither Prudence nor Duty will allow a Woman to fly out, her Business and Entertainment are at home, and tho' he makes it ever so uneasie to her she must be content and make her best on't. She who Elects a Monarch for Life, who gives him an Authority she cannot recall however he mis-apply it, who puts her Fortune and Person entirely in his Powers; nay even the very desires of her Heart according to some learned Casuists, so as that it is not lawful to Will or Desire any thing but what he approves and allows; had need be very sure that she does not make a Fool her Head, nor a Vicious Man her Guide and Pattern, she had best stay till she can meet with one who has the Government of his own Passions, and has duly regulated his own desires, since he is to have such an absolute Power over hers. But he who doats on a Face, he who makes Money his Idol, he who is Charm'd with vain and empty Wit, gives no such Evidence, either of Wisdom or Goodness, that a Woman of any tolerable Sense shou'd care to venture her self to his Conduct.

Indeed, your fine Gentleman's Actions are now adays such, that did not Custom and the Dignity of his Sex give Weight and Authority to them, a Woman that thinks twice might bless her self, and say, is this the Lord and Master to whom I am to promise Love, Honour and Obedience? What can be the object of Love but amiable Qualities, the Image of the Deity impress'd upon a generous and God-like Mind, a Mind that is above this World, to be sure above all the Vices, the Tricks and Baseness of it; a Mind that is not full of it self, nor contracted to little private Interests, but which in Imitation of that glorious Pattern it endeavours to Copy after, expands and diffuses it self to its utmost capacity in doing Good? But this fine Gentleman is quite of another Strain, he is the reverse of this in every Instance. He is I confess very fond of his own Dear Person, he sees very much in it to admire; his Air and Mien, his Words and Actions, every Motion he makes declares it; but they must have a Judgment of his size, every whit as Shallow, and a Partiality as great as his own, who can be of his Mind. How then can I Love? And if not Love, much less Honour. Love may arise from Pity or a generous Desire to make that Lovely which as yet is not so, when we see any hopes of Success in our Endeavours of improving it; but Honour supposes some excellent Qualities already, something worth our Esteem, and alas there is nothing more contemptible than this trifle of a Man, this meer Out-side, whose Mind is as base and Mean as his external Pomp is Glittering. His Office or Title apart, to which some Ceremonious Observance must be paid for Order's sake, there's nothing in him that can command our Respect. Strip him of Equipage and Fortune, and such things as only dazle our Eyes and Imaginations, but don't in any measure affect our Reason, or cause a Reverence in our Hearts, and the poor Creature sinks beneath our Notice, because not supported by real Worth. And if a Woman can neither Love nor Honour, she does ill in promising to Obey, since she is like to have but a crooked Rule to regulate her Actions.

A meer Obedience, such as is paid only to Authority, and not out of Love and a sense of the Justice and Reasonableness of the Command, will be of an uncertain Tenure. As it can't but be uneasie to the Person who pays it, so he who is to receive it will be sometimes disappointed when he expects to find it; for that Woman must be endow'd with a Wisdom and Goodness much above what we suppose the Sex capable of, I fear much greater than e're a Man can pretend to, who can so constantly conquer her Passions, and divest herself even of Innocent Self-Love, as to give up the Cause when she is in the right, and to submit her enlightned Reason, to the Imperious Dictates of a blind Will, and wild Imagination, even when she clearly perceives the ill Consequences of it, the Imprudence, nay Folly and Madness of such a Conduct.

And if a Woman runs such a Risque when she Marries Prudently according to the Opinion of the World, that is, when she permits her self to be dispos'd of to a Man equal to her in Birth, Education and Fortune, and as good as the most of his Neighbours, (for if none were to Marry, but Men of strict Vertue and Honour, I doubt the World would be but thinly peopled) if at the very best her Lot is hard, what can she expect who is Sold, or any otherwise betray'd into mercenary Hands, to one who is in all, or most respects unequal to her? A Lover who comes upon what is call'd equal Terms, makes no very advantageous Proposal to the Lady he Courts, and to whom he seems to be an humble Servant. For under many sounding Compliments, Words that have nothing in them, this is his true meaning, he wants one to manage his Family, an House-keeper, a necessary Evil, one whose Interest it will be not to wrong him, and in whom therefore he can put greater confidence than in any he can hire for Money. One who may breed his Children, taking all the care and trouble of their Education, to preserve his Name and Family. One whose Beauty, Wit, or good Humour and agreeable Conversation, will entertain him at Home when he has been contradicted and disappointed abroad; who will do him that Justice the ill-natur'd World denies him, that is, in any one's Language but his own, sooth his Pride and Flatter his Vanity, by having always so much good Sense as to be on his side, to conclude him in the right, when others are so Ignorant, or so rude as to deny it. Who will not be Blind to his Merit nor contradict his Will and Pleasure, but make it her Business, her very Ambition to content him; whose softness and gentle Compliance will calm his Passions, to whom he may safely disclose his troublesome Thoughts, and in her Breast discharge his Cares; whose Duty, Submission and Observance, will heal those Wounds other Peoples opposition or neglect have given him. In a word, one whom he can intirely Govern, and consequently may form her to his will and liking, who must be his for Life, and therefore cannot quit his Service let him treat her how he will.

And if this be what every Man expects, the Sum of his violent Love and Courtship, when it is put into Sense and rendred Intelligible, to what a fine pass does she bring her self who purchases a Lord and Master, not only with her Money, but with what is of greater Value, at the price of her Discretion? Who has not so much as that poor Excuse, Precedent and Example; or if she has, they are only such as all the World condemns? She will not find him less a Governor because she was once his Superior, on the contrary the scum of the People are most Tyrannical when they get the Power, and treat their Betters with the greatest Insolence. For as the wise Man long since observ'd, a Servant when he Reigns is one of those things for which the Earth is disquieted, and which no body is able to bear.

It is the hardest thing in the World for a Woman to know that a Man is not Mercenary, that he does not Act on base and ungenerous Principles, even when he is her Equal, because being absolute Master, she and all the Grants he makes her are in his Power, and there have been but too many instances of Husbands that by wheedling or threatning their Wives, by seeming Kindness or cruel Usage, have perswaded or forc'd them out of what has been settled on them. So that the Woman has in truth no security but the Man's Honour and Good-nature, a Security that in this present Age no wise Person would venture much upon. A Man enters into Articles very readily before Marriage, and so he may, for he performs no more of them afterwards than he thinks fit. A Wife must never dispute with her Husband, his Reasons are now no doubt on't better than hers, whatever they were before; he is sure to perswade her out of her Agreement, and bring her, it must be suppos'd, *Willingly*, to give up what she did vainly hope to obtain, and what she thought had been made sure to her. And if she shews any Refractoriness, there are ways enough to humble her; so that by right or wrong the Husband gains his Will. For Covenants betwixt Husband and Wife, like Laws in an Arbitrary Government, are of little Force, the Will of the Sovereign is all in all. Thus it is in Matter of Fact, I will not answer for the Right of it; for if the Woman's Reasons upon which those

Agreements are grounded are not Just and Good, why did he consent to them? Was it because there was no other way to obtain his Suit, and with an Intention to Annul them when it shall be in his Power? Where then is his Sincerity? But if her Reasons are good, where is his Justice in obliging her to quit them? He neither way acts like an equitable or honest Man.

But when a Woman Marrys unequally and beneath her self, there is almost Demonstration that the Man is Sordid and Unfair, that instead of Loving her he only Loves himself, trapans and ruines her to serve his own Ends. For if he had not a mighty Opinion of himself, (which temper is like to make an admirable Husband,) he cou'd never imagine that his Person and good Qualities should make compensation for all the advantages she quits on his account. If he had a real Esteem for her or valu'd her Reputation, he wou'd not expose it, nor have her Discretion call'd in Question for his sake; and if he truly Lov'd her he would not reduce her to Straits and a narrow Fortune, nor so much as lessen her way of Living to better his own. For since GOD has plac'd different Ranks in the World, put some in a higher and some in a lower Station, for Order and Beauty's sake, and for many good Reasons; tho' it is both our Wisdom and Duty not only to submit with Patience, but to be Thankful and well-satisfied when by his Providence we are brought low, yet there is no manner of Reason for us to Degrade our selves; on the contrary, much why we ought not. The better our Lot is in this World and the more we have of it, the greater is our leisure to prepare for the next; we have the more opportunity to exercise that God-like Quality, to tast that Divine Pleasure, Doing good to the Bodies and Souls of those beneath us. Is it not then ill Manners to Heaven, and an irreligious contempt of its Favours, for a Woman to slight that nobler Employment, to which it has assign'd her, and thrust her self down to a meaner Drudgery, to what is in the very literal Sense a caring for the things of the World, a caring not only to please, but to maintain a Husband?

And a Husband so chosen will not at all abate of his Authority and Right to Govern, whatever fair Promises he might make before. She has made him her Head, and he thinks himself as well qualify'd as the best to Act accordingly, nor has she given him any such Evidence of her Prudence as may dispose him to make an Act of Grace in her Favour. Besides, great Obligations are what Superiors cannot bear, they are more than can be return'd; to acknowledge, were only to reproach themselves with ingratitude, and therefore the readiest way is not to own but overlook them, or rather, as too many do, to repay them with Affronts and Injuries.

What then is to be done? How must a Man chuse, and what Qualities must encline a Woman to accept, that so our Marry'd couple may be as happy as that State can make them? This is no hard Question; let the Soul be principally consider'd, and regard had in the first Place to a good Understanding, a Vertuous Mind, and in all other respects let there be as much equality as may be. If they are good Christians and of suitable Tempers all will be well; but I should be shrewdly tempted to suspect their Christianity who Marry after any of those ways we have been speaking of, I dare venture to say, that they don't Act according to the Precepts of the Gospel, they neither shew the Wisdom of the Serpent, nor the Innocency of the Dove, they have neither so much Government of themselves, nor so much Charity for their Neighbours, they neither take such care not to Scandalize others, nor to avoid Temptations themselves, are neither so much above this World, nor so affected with the next, as they wou'd certainly be did the Christian Religion operate in their Hearts, did they rightly understand and sincerely Practise it, or Acted *indeed* according to the Spirit of the Gospel.

But it is not enough to enter wisely into this State, care must be taken of our Conduct afterwards. A Woman will not want being admonish'd of her Duty, the custom of the World, Economy, every thing almost reminds her of it. Governors do not often suffer their Subjects to forget Obedience through their want of demanding it, perhaps Husbands are but too forward on this occasion, and claim their Right oftner and more Imperiously than either Discretion or good Manners will justifie, and might have both a more chearful and constant Obedience paid them if they were not so rigorous in Exacting it. For there is a mutual Stipulation, and Love, Honour, and Worship, by which certain Civility and Respect at least are meant, are as much the Woman's due, as Love, Honour, and Obedience are the Man's, and being the Woman is said to be the weaker Vessel, the Man shou'd be more careful not to grieve or offend her. Since her Reason is suppos'd to be less, and her Passions stronger than his, he shou'd not give occasion to call that supposition in Question by his pettish Carriage and needless Provocations. Since he is the *Man*, by which very word Custom wou'd have us understand not only greatest strength of Body, but even greatest firmness and force

of Mind, he shou'd not play the *little Master* so much as to expect
to be cocker'd, nor run over to that side which the Women us'd
to be rank'd in; for according to the Wisdom of the *Italians, Will
you? Is spoken to sick Folks.*

Indeed Subjection, according to the Common Notion of it, is not
over easie, none of us whether Men or Women but have so good
an Opinion of our own Conduct as to believe we are fit, if not
to direct others, at least to govern our selves. Nothing but a sound
Understanding, and Grace the best improver of natural Reason, can
correct this Opinion, truly humble us, and heartily reconcile us to
Obedience. This bitter Cup therefore ought to be sweetned as much
as may be; for Authority may be preserv'd and Government kept
inviolable, without that nauseous Ostentation of Power which serves
to no end or purpose, but to blow up the Pride and Vanity of
those who have it, and to exasperate the Spirits of such as must
truckle under it.

Insolence 'tis true is never the effect of Power but in weak and
cowardly Spirits, who wanting true Merit and Judgment to support
themselves in that advantageous Ground on which they stand, are
ever appealing to their Authority, and making a shew of it to maintain
their Vanity and Pride. A truly great Mind and such as is fit to
Govern, tho' it may stand on its Right with its Equals, and modestly
expect what is due to it even from its Superiors, yet it never contends
with its Inferiors, nor makes use of its Superiority but to do them
Good. So that considering the just Dignity of Man, his great Wisdom
so conspicuous on all occasions! the goodness of his Temper and
Reasonableness of all his Commands, which make it a Woman's Interest
as well as Duty to be observant and Obedient in all things! that
his Prerogative is settled by an undoubted Right, and the Prescription
of many Ages; it cannot be suppos'd that he should make frequent
and insolent Claims of an Authority so well establish'd and us'd
with such moderation! nor give an impartial By-stander (cou'd such
an one be found) any occasion from thence to suspect that he is
inwardly conscious of the badness of his Title; Usurpers being always
most desirous of Recognitions and busie in imposing Oaths, whereas
a Lawful Prince contents himself with the usual Methods and Securities.

And since Power does naturally puff up, and he who finds himself
exalted, seldom fails to think he *ought* to be so, it is more suitable
to a Man's Wisdom and Generosity, to be mindful of his great
Obligations than to insist on his Rights and Prerogatives. Sweetness

of Temper and an Obliging Carriage are so justly due to a Wife, that a Husband who must not be thought to want either Understanding to know what is fit, nor Goodness to perform it, can't be suppos'd not to shew them. For setting aside the hazards of her Person to keep up his Name and Family, with all the Pains and Trouble that attend it, which may well be thought great enough to deserve all the respect and kindness that may be, setting this aside, tho' 'tis very considerable, a Woman has so much the disadvantage in *most*, I was about to say in *all* things, that she makes a Man the greatest Compliment in the World when she condescends to take him *for Better for Worse*. She puts her self intirely in his Power, leaves all that is dear to her, her Friends and Family, to espouse his Interests and follow his Fortune, and makes it her Business and Duty to please him! What acknowledgements, what returns can he make? What Gratitude can be sufficient for such Obligations? She shews her good Opinion of him by the great Trust she reposes in him, and what a Brute must he be who betrays that Trust, or acts any way unworthy of it? Ingratitude is one of the basest Vices, and if a Man's Soul is sunk so low as to be guilty of it towards her who has so generously oblig'd him, and who so intirely depends on him, if he can treat her Disrespectfully, who has so fully testify'd her Esteem of him, she must have a stock of Vertue which he shou'd blush to discern, if she can pay him that Obedience of which he is so unworthy.

Superiors indeed are too apt to forget the common Privileges of Mankind; that their Inferiors share with them the greatest Benefits, and are as capable as themselves of enjoying the supreme Good; that tho' the Order of the World requires an *Outward* Respect and Obedience from some to others, yet the Mind is free, nothing but Reason can oblige it, 'tis out of the reach of the most absolute Tyrant. Nor will it ever be well either with those who Rule or those in Subjection, even from the Throne to every Private Family, till those in Authority look on themselves as plac'd in that Station for the good and improvement of their Subjects, and not for their own sakes; not as the reward of their Merit, or that they may prosecute their own Desires and fulfil all their Pleasure, but as the Representatives of GOD whom they ought to imitate in the Justice and Equity of their Laws, in doing good and communicating Blessings to all beneath them: By which, and not by following the imperious Dictates of their own will, they become truly Great and Illustrious and Worthily fill their Place. And the Governed for their Part ceasing to envy the Pomp and Name of Authority, shou'd respect their Governours as plac'd in GOD's stead and contribute what they can to ease them of their real Cares, by a chearful, and ready compliance with their good endeavours, and by affording them the Pleasure of success in such noble and generous Designs.

For upon a due estimate things are pretty equally divided; those in Subjection as they have a less Glorious, so they have an easier task and a less account to give, whereas he who Commands has in a great measure the Faults of others to answer for as well as his own. 'Tis true he has the Pleasure of doing more good than a Private Person can, and shall receive the Reward of it when Time shall be no more, in compensation for the hazards he runs, the difficulties he at present encounters, and the large Account he is to make hereafter, which Pleasure and Reward are highly desirable and most worthy our pursuit; but they are Motives which such as usurp on their Governors, and make them uneasie in the due discharge of their Duty, never propose. And for those other little things that move their Envy and Ambition, they are of no Esteem with a just Considerer, nor will such as violently pursue, find their Account in them.

But how can a Man respect his Wife when he has a contemptible Opinion of her and her Sex? When from his own Elevation he looks down on them as void of Understanding, and full of Ignorance and Passion, so that Folly and a Woman are equivalent Terms with him? Can he think there is any Gratitude due to her whose utmost services he exacts as strict Duty? Because she was made to be a Slave to his Will, and has no higher end than to Serve and Obey him! Perhaps we arrogate too much to our selves when we say this Material World was made for our sakes; that its Glorious Maker has given us the use of it is certain, but when we suppose a thing to be made purely for our sakes, because we have Dominion over it, we draw a false Conclusion, as he who shou'd say the People were made for the Prince who is set over them, wou'd be thought to be out of his Senses as well as his Politicks. Yet even allowing that GOD who made everything in Number, Weight and Measure, who never acts but for some great and glorious End, an End agreeable to His Majesty, allowing that He Created such a Number of Rational Spirits merely to serve their fellow Creatures, yet how are these Lords and Masters helpt by the Contempt they shew of their poor humble Vassals? Is it not rather an hindrance to that Service they expect, as being an undeniable and constant Proof how unworthy they are to receive it?

None of GOD's Creatures absolutely consider'd are in their own Nature Contemptible; the meanest Fly, the poorest Insect has its Use and Vertue. Contempt is scarce a Human Passion, one may venture to say it was not in Innocent Man, for till Sin came into the World, there was nothing in it to be contemn'd. But Pride which makes every thing serve its purposes, wrested this Passion from its only use, so that instead of being an Antidote against Sin, it is become a grand promoter of it, nothing making us more worthy of that Contempt we shew, than when poor, weak, dependent Creatures as we are! we look down with Scorn and Disdain on others.

There is not a surer Sign of a noble Mind, a Mind very far advanc'd towards perfection, than the being able to bear Contempt and an unjust Treatment from ones Superiors evenly and patiently. For inward Worth and real Excellency are the true Ground of Superiority, and one Person is not in reality better than another, but as he is more Wise and Good. But this World being a place of Tryal and govern'd by general Laws, just Retributions being reserv'd for hereafter, Respect and Obedience many times become due for Order's sake to those who don't otherwise deserve them. Now tho' Humility keeps us from over-valuing our selves or viewing our Merit thro' a false and magnifying *Medium*, yet it does not put out our Eyes, it does not, it ought not to deprive us of that pleasing sentiment which attends our Acting as we ought to Act, which is as it were a foretast of Heaven, our present Reward for doing what is Just and Fit. And when a Superior does a Mean and unjust Thing, as all Contempt of one's Neighbour is, and yet this does not provoke his Inferiors to refuse that Observance which their Stations in the World require, they cannot but have an inward Sense of their own real Superiority, the other having no pretence to it, at the same time that they pay him an outward Respect and Deference, which is such a flagrant Testimony of the sincerest Love of Order as proves their Souls to be of the highest and noblest Rank.

A Man therefore for his own sake, and to give evidence that he has a Right to those Prerogatives he assumes, shou'd treat Women with a little more Humanity and Regard than is usually paid them. Your whissling Wits may scoff at them, and what then? It matters not, for they Rally everything tho' ever so Sacred, and rail at the Women commonly in very good Company. Religion, its Priests, and those its most constant and regular Professors, are the usual Subjects of their manly, mannerly and surprizing Jests. Surprizing indeed! not for the newness of the Thought, the brightness of the Fancy, or nobleness of Expression, but for the good Assurance with which such threadbare Jests are again and again repeated. But that your grave Dons, your Learned Men, and which is more, your Men of Sense as they wou'd be thought, should stoop so low as to make Invectives against the Women, forget themselves so much as to Jest with their Slaves, who have neither Liberty nor Ingenuity to make Reprizals! that they shou'd waste their Time, and debase their good Sense which fits them for the most weighty Affairs, such as are suitable to their profound Wisdoms and exalted Understandings! to render those poor Wretches more ridiculous and odious who are already in their Opinion sufficiently contemptible, and find no better exercise of their Wit and Satyr than such as are not worth their Pains, tho' it were possible to Reform them, this, this indeed may justly be wondred at!

I know not whether or no Women are allow'd to have Souls, if they have perhaps, it is not prudent to provoke them too much, lest silly as they are, they at last recriminate, and then what polite and well-bred Gentleman, tho' himself is concern'd, can forbear taking that lawful Pleasure which all who understand Raillery must tast, when they find his Jests who insolently began to peck at his Neighbour, return'd with Interest upon his own Head? And indeed Men are too Humane, too Wise to venture at it did they not hope for this effect, and expect the Pleasure of finding their Wit turn to such account; for if it be lawful to reveal a Secret, this is without doubt the whole design of those fine Discourses which have been made against the Women from our great Fore-fathers to this present Time! Generous Man has too much Bravery, he is too Just and too Good to assault a defenceless Enemy, and if he did inveigh against the Women it was only to do them Service! For since neither his Care of their Education, his hearty endeavours to improve their Minds, his wholsome Precepts, nor great Example cou'd do them good, as his last and kindest Essay, he resolv'd to try what Contempt wou'd do, and chose rather to expose himself by a seeming want of Justice, Equity, Ingenuity and Good-nature, than suffer Women to remain such vain and insignificant Creatures as they have hitherto been reckon'd! And truly Women are some degrees beneath what I have thus far thought them, if they do not make the best use of his kindness, improve themselves, and like Christians return it.

Let us see then what is their Part, what must they do to make the Matrimonial Yoke tolerable to themselves as well as pleasing to their Lords and Masters? That the World is an empty and deceitful Thing, that those Enjoyments which appear'd so desirable at a distance, which rais'd our Hopes and Expectations to such a mighty Pitch, which we so passionately coveted, and so eagerly pursued, vanish at our first approach, leaving nothing behind them but the Folly of Delusion, and the pain of disappointed Hopes, is a common Outcry; and yet as common as it is, tho' we complain of being deceiv'd this Instant, we do not fail of contributing to the Cheat the very next. Tho' in reality it is not the World that abuses us, 'tis we abuse ourselves, it is not the emptiness of that, but our own false Judgments, our unreasonable Desires and Expectations that Torment us; for he who exerts his whole strength to lift a Straw, ought not to complain of the Burden, but of his own disproportionate endeavour which gives him the pain he feels. The World affords us all the Pleasure a sound Judgment can expect from it, and answers all those Ends and Purposes for which it was design'd, let us expect no more than is reasonable, and then we shall not fail of our Expectation.

It is even so in the Case before us; a Woman who has been taught to think Marriage her only Preferment, the Sum-total of her Endeavours, the completion of all her hopes, that which must settle and make her Happy in this World, and very few, in their Youth especially, carry a Thought steadily to a greater distance; She who has seen a Lover dying at her Feet, and can't therefore imagine that he who professes to receive all his Happiness from her, can have any other Design or Desire than to please her; whose Eyes have been dazled with all the Glitter and Pomp of a Wedding, and who hears of nothing but Joy and Congratulations; who is transported with the Pleasure of being out of Pupillage and Mistress not only of her self but of a Family too: She who is either so simple or so vain, as to take her Lover at his Word either as to the Praises he gave her, or the Promises he made for himself; in sum, she whose Expectation has been rais'd by Court-ship, by all the fine things that her Lover, her Governess, and Domestic Flatterers say, will find a terrible disappointment when the hurry is over, and when she comes calmly to consider her Condition, and views it no more under a false Appearance, but as it truly is.

I doubt in such a View it will not appear over-desirable, if she regards only the present State of Things. Hereafter may make amends for what she must be prepar'd to suffer here, then will be her Reward, this is her time of Tryal, the Season of exercising and improving her Vertues. A Woman that is not Mistress of her Passions, that cannot patiently submit even when Reason suffers with her, who does not practise Passive Obedience to the utmost, will never be acceptable to such an absolute Sovereign as a Husband. Wisdom ought to Govern without Contradiction, but Strength however will be obey'd. There are but few of those wise Persons who can be content to be made yet wiser by Contradiction, the most will have their Will, and it is right because it is their's. Such is the vanity of Humane nature that nothing pleases like an intire Subjection; what Imperfections won't a Man over-look where this is not wanting! Tho' we live like Brutes, we wou'd have Incense offer'd us that is only due to Heaven it self, wou'd have an absolute and blind Obedience paid us by all over whom we pretend Authority. We were not made to Idolize one another, yet the whole strain of Courtship is little less than rank Idolatry: But does a Man intend to give, and not to receive his share in this Religious Worship? No such matter; Pride and Vanity and Self-love have their Designs, and if the Lover is so condescending as to set a Pattern in the time of his Addresses, he is so Just as to expect his Wife shou'd strictly Copy after it all the rest of her Life.

But how can a Woman scruple intire Subjection, how can she forbear to admire the worth and excellency of the Superior Sex, if she at all considers it? Have not all the great Actions that have been perform'd in the World been done by Men? Have not they founded Empires and overturn'd them? Do not they make Laws and continually repeal and amend them? Their vast Minds lay Kingdoms wast, no bounds or measures can be prescrib'd to their Desires. War and Peace depend on them, they form Cabals and have the Wisdom and Courage to get over all the Rubs which may lie in the way of their desired Grandeur. What is it they cannot do? They make Worlds and ruine them, form Systems of universal nature and dispute eternally about them; their Pen gives worth to the most trifling Controversie; nor can a fray be inconsiderable if they have drawn their Swords in't. All that the wise Man pronounces is an Oracle, and every Word the Witty speaks a Jest. It is a Woman's Happiness to hear, admire and praise them, especially if a little Ill-nature keeps them at any time from bestowing due Applauses on each other! And if she aspires no further, she is thought to be in her proper Sphere of Action, she is as wise and as good as can be expected from her!

She then who Marrys ought to lay it down for an indisputable Maxim, that her Husband must govern absolutely and intirely, and that she has nothing else to do but to Please and Obey. She must not attempt to divide his Authority, or so much as dispute it, to struggle with her Yoke will only make it gall the more, but must believe him Wise and Good and in all respects the best, at least he must be so to her. She who can't do this is no way fit to be a Wife, she may set up for that peculiar Coronet the ancient Fathers talk'd of, but is not qualify'd to receive that great reward, which attends the eminent exercise of Humility and Self-denial, Patience and Resignation, the Duties that a Wife is call'd to.

But some refractory Woman perhaps will say, how can this be? Is it possible for her to believe him Wise and Good who by a thousand Demonstrations convinces her and all the World of the contrary? Did the bare Name of Husband confer Sense on a Man, and the mere being in Authority infallibly qualifie him for Government, much might be done. But since a wise Man and a Husband are not Terms convertible, and how loth soever one is to own it, Matter of Fact won't allow us to deny, that the Head many times stands in need of the Inferior's Brains to manage it, she must beg leave to be excus'd from such high thoughts of her Sovereign, and if she submits to his Power, it is not so much Reason as Necessity that compels her.

Now of how little force soever this Objection may be in other respects, methinks it is strong enough to prove the necessity of a good Education, and that Men never mistake their true Interest more than when they endeavour to keep Women in Ignorance. Cou'd they indeed deprive them of their Natural good Sense at the same time they deny them the due improvement of it, they might compass their End; otherwise Natural Sense unassisted may run in to a false Track and serve only to punish him justly, who wou'd not allow it to be useful to himself or others. If Man's Authority be justly establish'd, the more Sense a Woman has, the more reason she will find to submit to it; if according to the Tradition of our Fathers, (who having had *Possession* of the Pen, thought they had also the best *Right* to it,) Women's Understanding is but small, and Men's

Partiality adds no Weight to the Observation, ought not the more care to be taken to improve them? How it agrees with the Justice of Men we enquire not, but certainly Heaven is abundantly more equitable than to enjoyn Women the hardest Task and give them the least Strength to perform it. And if Men Learned, Wise and Discreet as they are, who have as is said all the advantages of Nature, and without controversy have, or may have all the assistance of Art, are so far from acquitting themselves as they ought, from living according to that Reason and excellent Understanding they so much boast of, can it be expected that a Woman who is reckon'd silly enough in her self, at least comparatively, and whom Men take care to make yet more so, can it be expected that she shou'd constantly perform so difficult a Duty as intire Subjection, to which corrupt Nature is so averse?

If the Great and Wise *Cato*, a *Man*, a Man of no ordinary firmness and strength of Mind, a Man who was esteem'd as an Oracle, and by the Philosophers and great Men of his Nation equall'd even to the Gods themselves; If he with all his Stoical Principles was not able to bear the sight of a triumphant Conqueror, (who perhaps wou'd have Insulted and perhaps wou'd not,) but out of a Cowardly fear of an Insult, ran to Death to secure him from it; can it be thought that an ignorant weak Woman shou'd have patience to bear a continual Out-rage and Insolence all the days of her Life? Unless you will suppose her a very Ass, but then remember what the *Italians* say, to Quote them once more, since being *very* Husbands they may be presum'd to have Authority in this Case, *an Ass tho' slow if provok'd will kick.*

We never see or perhaps make sport with the ill Effects of a bad Education, till it come to touch us home in the ill conduct of a Sister, a Daughter, or Wife. Then the Women must be blam'd, their Folly is exclaim'd against, when all this while it was the wise Man's Fault, who did not set a better Guard on those who according to him stand in so much need of one. A young Gentleman, as a celebrated Author tells us, ought above all things to be acquainted with the State of the World, the Ways and Humours, the Follies, the Cheats, the Faults of the Age he is fallen into, he should by degrees be inform'd of the Vice in Fashion, and warn'd of the Application and Design of those who will make it their Business to corrupt him, shou'd be told the Arts they use and the Trains they lay, be prepar'd to be Shock'd by some and caress'd by others; warn'd who are like to oppose, who to mislead, who to undermine, and who to serve him. He shou'd be instructed how to know and distinguish them, where he shou'd let them see, and when dissemble the Knowledge of them and their Aims and Workings. Our Author is much in the right, and not to disparage any other Accomplishments which are useful in their kind, this will turn to more account than any Language or Philosophy, Art or Science, or any other piece of Good-breeding and fine Education that can be taught him, which are no otherwise excellent than as they contribute to this, as this does above all things to the making him a wise, a vertuous and useful Man.

And it is not less necessary that a young Lady shou'd receive the like Instructions, whether or no her Temptations be fewer, her Reputation and Honour however are to be more nicely preserv'd; they may be ruin'd by a little Ignorance or Indiscretion, and then tho' she has kept her Innocence, and so is secur'd as to the next World, yet she is in a great measure lost to this. A Woman cannot be too watchful, too apprehensive of her danger, nor keep at too great a distance from it, since Man whose Wisdom and Ingenuity is so much Superior to hers! condescends for his Interest sometimes, and sometimes by way of Diversion, to lay Snares for her. For tho' all Men are *Virtuosi*, Philosophers and Politicians, in comparison of the Ignorant and Illiterate Women, yet they don't all pretend to be Saints, and 'tis no great Matter to them if Women who were born to be their Slaves, be now and then ruin'd for their Entertainment.

But according to the rate that young Women are Educated, according to the way their Time is spent, they are destin'd to Folly and Impertinence, to say no worse, and which is yet more inhuman, they are blam'd for that ill Conduct they are not suffer'd to avoid, and reproach'd for those Faults they are in a manner forc'd into; so that if Heaven has bestowed any Sense on them, no other use is made of it, than to leave them without Excuse. So much and no more of the World is shewn them, as serves to weaken and corrupt their Minds, to give them wrong Notions, and busy them in mean Pursuits; to disturb, not to regulate their Passions; to make them timorous and dependant, and in a word, fit for nothing else but to act a Farce for the Diversion of their Governours.

Even Men themselves improve no otherwise than according to the Aim they take, and the End they propose; and he whose Designs are but little and mean, will be the same himself. Tho' Ambition, as 'tis usually understood, is a Foolish, not to say a Base and Pitiful

Vice, yet the Aspirings of the Soul after true Glory are so much its Nature, that it seems to have forgot it self and to degenerate, if it can forbear; and perhaps the great Secret of Education lies in affecting the Soul with a lively Sense of what is truly its Perfection, and exciting the most ardent Desires after it.

But, alas! what poor Woman is ever taught that she should have a higher Design than to get her a Husband? Heaven will fall in of course; and if she makes but an Obedient and Dutiful Wife, she cannot miss of it. A Husband indeed is thought by both Sexes so very valuable, that scarce a Man who can keep himself clean and make a Bow, but thinks he is good enough to pretend to any Woman, no matter for the Difference of Birth or Fortune, a Husband is such a Wonder-working Name as to make an Equality, or something more, whenever it is pronounc'd.

And indeed were there no other Proof of Masculine Wisdom, and what a much greater portion of Ingenuity falls to the Men than to the Women's Share, the Address, the Artifice, and Management of an humble Servant were a sufficient Demonstration. What good Conduct does he shew! what Patience exercise! what Subtilty leave untry'd! what Concealment of his Faults! what Parade of his Vertues! what Government of his Passions! How deep is his Policy in laying his Designs at so great a distance, and working them up by such little Accidents! How indefatigable is his Industry, and how constant his Watchfulness, not to slip any Opportunity that may in the least contribute to his Design! What a handsome Set of Disguises and Pretences is he always furnish'd with! How conceal'd does he lie! how little pretend, till he is sure that his Plot will take! And at the same time that he nourishes the Hope of being Lord and Master, appears with all the Modesty and Submission of an humble and unpretending Admirer.

Can a woman then be too much upon her Guard? Can her Prudence and Foresight, her early Caution, be reckon'd unnecessary Suspicion, or ill-bred Reserve, by any but those whose Designs they prevent, and whose Interest it is to declaim against them? it being a certain Maxim with the Men, tho' Policy or Good Breeding won't allow them to avow it always, that the Women were made for their Sakes and Services, and are in all respects their Inferiors, especially in Understanding; so that all the Compliments they make, all the Address and Complaisance they use, all the Kindness they profess, all the Service they pretend to pay, has no other Meaning, no other End, than to get the poor Woman into their Power, to govern her according to their Discretion. This is all pure Kindness indeed, and therefore no Woman has Reason to be offended with it; for considering how much she is expos'd in her own, and how safe in their Keeping, 'tis the wisest thing she can do to put her self under Protection! And then if they have a tolerable Opinion of her Sense, and not their Vanity but some better Principle disposes them to be something out of the way, and to appear more generous than the rest of their Sex, they'll condescend to dictate to her, and impart some of their Prerogative Books and Learning! 'Tis fit indeed that she should entirely depend on their Choice, and walk with the Crutches they are pleas'd to lend her; and if she is furnished out with some Notions to set her a prating, I should have said to make her entertaining and the Fiddle of the Company, her Tutor's Time was not ill bestowed: And it were a diverting Scene to see her stript like the Jay of her borrowed Feathers, but he, good Man, has not ill Nature enough to take Pleasure in it! You may accuse him perhaps for giving so much Encouragement to a Woman's Vanity, but your Accusation is groundless, Vanity being a Disease the Sex will always be guilty of; nor is it a Reproach to them, since Men of Learning and Sense are overrun with it.

But there are few Women whose Understandings are worth the Management, their Estates are much more capable of Improvement. No Woman, much less a Woman of Fortune, is ever fit to be her own Mistress, and he who has not the Vanity to think what much finer things he could perform had he the Management of her Fortune; or so much Partiality and Self-love, as to fancy it can't be better bestow'd than in making his; will yet be so honest and humble as to think that 'tis fit she should take his Assistance, as Steward at least. For the Good Man aspires no further, he would only take the Trouble of her Affairs off her Hand; and the Sense of her Condescention and his great Obligations, will for ever secure him against acting like a Lord and Master!

The Steps to Folly as well as Sin are gradual, and almost imperceptible, and when we are once on the Decline, we go down without taking notice on't; were it not for this, one cou'd not account for those strange unequal Matches we too often see. For there was a time no doubt, when a Woman could not have bore the very thought of what she has been afterwards betray'd into, it would have appear'd as shocking to her as it always does to other People; and had a Man been so impolitic as to discover the least intimation of such a Design, he had given her a sufficient Antidote against it. This your Wise Men are well satisfy'd of, and understand their own Interest too well to let their Design go bare-fac'd, for that would effectually put a barr to their Success. So innocent are they, that they had not the least Thought at first of what their Good Fortune afterwards leads them to! They would draw upon him, (if they wear a Sword) or fly in her Face who should let fall the least hint that they had such Intentions; and this very Eagerness to avoid the Suspicion, is a shrewd Sign that there is occasion for't.

But who shall dare to shew the Lady her Danger, when will it be seasonable to give her friendly Notice? If you do it e're she is resolv'd, tho' with all the Friendship and Tenderness imaginable, she will hardly forgive the Affront, or bear the Provocation; you offer her an Outrage, by entertaining such a Thought, and 'tis ten to one if you are not afterwards accus'd for putting in her Head what otherwise she could ne'er have dreamt of. And when no direct Proof can be offer'd, when matter of Prudence is the only thing in Question, every Body has so good an Opinion of their own Understanding as to think their own way the best. And when she has her Innocence and fair Intentions to oppose to your Fears and Surmises, and you cannot pretend to wish her better than she does her self, to be more disinteress'd and diligent in your Watchfulness, or to see farther in what so nearly concerns her, what can be done? Her ruin is commonly too far advanc'd to be prevented, e're you can in Good-breeding reach out a hand to help her. For if the Train has took, if she is entangled in the Snare, if Love, or rather a Blind unreasonable Fondness, which usurps the Name of that noble Passion, has gain'd on her, Reason and Perswasion may as properly be urg'd to the Folks in *Bethlem* [Bedlam] as to her. Tell her of this World, she is got above it, and has no regard to its impertinent Censures; tell her of the next, she laughs at you, and will never be convinc'd that Actions which are not expressly forbid can be Criminal, tho' they proceed from, and must necessarily be reduc'd to ill Principles, tho' they give Offence, are of ill Example, injure our Reputation, which next to our Innocence we are obliged as Christians to take the greatest care of, and in a word do more mischief than we can readily imagine. Tell her of her own Good, you appear yet more ridiculous, for who can judge of her Happiness but her self? And whilst our Hearts are violently set upon any thing, there is no convincing us that we shall ever be of another Mind. Our Passions want no Advocates, they are always furnish'd with plausible Pretences, and those very Prejudices, which gave rise to this unreasonable Passion, will for certain give her Obstinacy enough to justifie and continue in it. Besides, some are so ill advis'd as to think to support one Indiscretion with another, they wou'd not have it thought they have made a false Step, in once giving countenance to that which is not fit to be continued. Or perhaps the Lady might be willing enough to throw off the Intruder at first, but wanted Courage to get above the fear of his Calumnies, and the longer she suffers him to buz about her, she will find it the harder to get rid of his Importunities. By all which it appears that she who really intends to be secure, must keep at the greatest distance from Danger, she must not grant the *least* Indulgence, where such ill uses will be made of it.

And since the case is so, that Woman can never be in safety who allows a Man opportunity to betray her. Frequent Conversation does for certain produce either Aversion or Liking, and when 'tis once come to Liking, it depends on the Man's Generosity not to improve it farther, and where can one find an Instance that this is any security? There are very many indeed which shew it is none. How sensible soever a Woman may appear of another's Indiscretion, if she will tread in the same steps, tho' but for a little way, she gives us no assurance that she will not fall into the same Folly, she may perhaps intend very well, but she puts it past her Power to fulfil her good Intentions. Even those who have forfeited their Discretion, the most valuable thing next to their vertue, and without which vertue it self is but very weak and faint, 'tis like were once as well resolv'd as she, they had the very same Thoughts, they made the same Apologies, and their Resentment wou'd have been every whit as great against those who cou'd have imagin'd they shou'd so far forget themselves.

It were endless to reckon up the divers Stratagems Men use to catch their Prey, their different ways of insinuating which vary with Circumstances and the Ladies Temper. But how unfairly, how basely soever they proceed, when the Prey is once caught it passes for lawful Prize, and other Men having the same hopes and projects see nothing to find fault with, but that it was not their own Good Fortune. They may exclaim against it perhaps in a Lady's hearing, but it is only to keep themselves from being suspected, and to give the better Colour to their own Designs. Sometimes a Woman is cajol'd, and sometimes Hector'd, she is seduc'd to Love a Man, or aw'd into a Fear of him: He defends her Honour against another, or assumes the Power of blasting it himself; was willing to pass for one of no Consequence till he cou'd make himself considerable at her Cost. He might be admitted at first to be *her jest*, but he carries on the humour so far till he makes her his; he will either entertain or serve her as occasion offers, and some way or other gets himself intrusted with her Fortune, her Fame, or her Soul. Allow him but a frequent and free Conversation, and there's no manner of Question but that his Ingenuity and Application will at one time or other get the Ascendant over her.

And generally the more humble and undesigning a Man appears, the more improbable it looks that he should dare to pretend, the greater Caution shou'd be us'd against him. A bold Address and good Assurance may sometimes, but does not always, take. To a Woman of Sense an artificial Modesty and Humility is a thousand times more dangerous, for he only draws back to receive the more Encouragement, and she regards not what Advances she makes towards him, who seems to understand himself and the World so well, as to be incapable of making an ill use of them. Wou'd it not be unreasonable and a piece of Ill-breeding to be shy of him who has no Pretentions, or only such as are Just and Modest? What hurt in a Visit? or what if Visits grow a little more frequent? The Man has so much discernment, as to relish her Wit and Humour, and can she do less than be Partial to him who is so Just to her? He strives to please and to render himself agreeable, or necessary perhaps, and whoever will make it his Business may find ways enough to do it. For they know but little of Human Nature, they never consulted their own Hearts, who are not sensible what advances a well-manag'd Flattery makes, especially from a Person of whose Wit and Sense one has a good Opinion. His Wit at first recommends his Flatteries, and these in requital set off his Wit; and she who has been us'd to this high-season'd Diet, will scarce ever relish another Conversation.

Having got thus far to be sure he is not wanting to his good Fortune, but drives on to an Intimacy, or what they are pleas'd now a days, tho' very unjustly, to call a Friendship; all is safe under this sacred Character, which sets them above little Aims and mean Designs. A Character that must be conducted with the nicest Honour, allows the greatest Trusts, leads to the highest Improvements, is attended with the purest Pleasures and most rational Satisfaction.

And what if the malicious World, envious of his Happiness, shou'd take Offence at it, since he has taken all due Precautions, such unjust and ill-natur'd Censures are not to be regarded; for his part the distance that is between them checks all aspiring desires, but her Conversation is what he must not, cannot want, Life is insipid and not to be endur'd without it; and he is too much the Lady's Friend, has too just a Value for her to entertain a Thought to her disadvantage!

Now if once it is come to this, GOD help the poor Woman, for not much Service can be done her by any of her Friends on Earth. That Pretender to be sure will be the Darling, he will worm out every other Person, tho' ever so kind and disinterested. For tho' true Friends will endeavour to please in order to serve, their Complaisance never goes so far as to prove injurious; the beloved Fault is what they chiefly strike at, and this the Flatterer always sooths; so that at least he becomes the most acceptable Company, and they who are conscious of their own Integrity are not apt to bear such an unjust Distinction, nor is it by this time to any purpose to remonstrate the Danger of such an Intimacy. When a Man, and for certain much more when a Woman, is fallen into this Toyl, that is, when either have been so unwary and indiscreet as to let another find out by what Artifices he may manage their Self-love, and draw it over to his Party, 'tis too late for anyone who is really their Friend, to break the Snare and disabuse them.

Neither Sex cares to deny themselves that which pleases, especially when they think they may innocently indulge it; and nothing pleases more than the being admir'd and humour'd. We may be told of the Danger, and shown the Fall of others, but tho' their Misfortunes are ever so often or so lively represented to us, we are all so well assur'd of our own good Conduct, as to believe it will bring us safe off those Rocks on which others have been Shipwrackt. We suppose it in our Power to shorten the Line of our Liberty when ever we think fit, not considering that the farther we run, we shall be the more unwilling to Retreat and unable to judge when a Retreat is necessary. A Woman does not know that she is more than half lost when she admits of these Suggestions; that those Arguments she brings for continuing a Man's Conversation, prove only that she ought to have quitted it sooner; that Liking insensibly converts to Love, and that when she admits a Man to be her Friend, 'tis his Fault if he does not make himself her Husband.

And if Men even the Modestest and the best, are only in pursuit of their own Designs, when they pretend to do the Lady Service; if the Honour they wou'd seem to do her, tends only to lead her into an Imprudent and therefore a Dishonourable Action; and they have all that good Opinion of themselves as to take everything for Encouragement, so that she who goes beyond a bare Civility tho' she meant no more than Respect, will find it Interpreted a Favour and made ill Use of, (for Favours how Innocent soever, never turn to a Lady's advantage;) what shadow of a Pretence can a Woman have for admitting an intimacy with a Man whose Principles are known to be Loose and his Practices Licentious? can she expect to be safe with him who has ruin'd others, and by the very same Methods he takes with her? If an Intimacy with a Man of a fair Character gives Offence, with a Man of an ill One, 'tis doubly and trebly Scandalous. And suppose neither her Fortune nor Beauty can Tempt him, he has his ill-natur'd Pleasure in destroying that Vertue he will not Practise, or if that can't be done, in blasting the Reputation of it at least, and in making the World believe he has made a Conquest tho' he has found a Foil.

If the Man be the Woman's Inferior, besides all the Dangers formerly mention'd, and those just now taken notice of, she gives such a Countenance to his Vices as renders her in great measure partaker in them, and it can scarce be thought in such Circumstances, a Woman cou'd Like the Man if she were not reconcil'd to his Faults. Is he her Equal and no unsuitable Match, if his Designs are fair, why don't they Marry, since they are so well pleas'd with each other's Conversation, which in this State only can be frequently and safely allow'd? Is he her Better, and she hopes by catching him to make her Fortune, alas! the poor Woman is neither acquainted with the World nor her self, she neither knows her own Weakness nor his Treachery, and tho' he gives ever so much Encouragement to this vain Hope, 'tis only in order to accomplish her ruin. To be sure the more Freedom she allows, the more she lessens his Esteem, and that's not likely to encrease a real, tho' it may a pretended kindness; she ought to fly, if she wou'd have him pursue, the strictest Vertue and Reserve being the only way to secure him.

Religion and Reputation are so sure a Guard, such a security to poor defenceless Woman, that whenever a Man has ill Designs on her, he is sure to make a Breach in one or both of these, by endeavouring either to corrupt her Principles to make her less strict in Devotion, or to lessen her value of a fair Reputation, and wou'd perswade her that less than she imagines will secure her as to the next World, and that not much regard is to be given to the censures of this. Or if this be too bold at first, and will not pass with her, he has another way to make even her Love to Vertue contribute to its ruin, by perswading her it never Shines as it ought unless it be expos'd, and that she has no reason to Boast of her Vertue unless she has try'd it. An Opinion of the worst consequence that may be, and the most mischievous to a Woman, because it is calculated to feed her Vanity, and tends indeed to her utter Ruin. For can it be fit to rush into Temptations when we are taught every day to pray against them? If the Trials of our Vertue render it Illustrious, 'tis such Trials as Heaven is pleas'd to send us, not those of our own seeking. It holds true of both Sexes, that next to the Divine Grace, a Modest Distrust of themselves is their best Security, none being so often and so shamefully Foil'd, as those who depend most on their own Strength and Resolution.

As to the Opinion of the World, tho' one cannot say it is always just, yet generally it has a Foundation; great regard is to be paid to it, and very good use to be made of it. Others *may* be in fault for passing their Censures, but we certainly *are* so if we give them any the least just occasion. And since Reputation is not only one of the Rewards of Vertue, that which always ought, and generally does attend it, but also a Guard against Evil, an Inducement to Good, and a great Instrument in the Hand of the Wise to promote the common cause of Vertue, the being Prodigal of the one, looks as if we set no great value on the other, and she who abandons her good Name is not like to preserve her Innocence.

A Woman therefore can never have too nice a Sense of Honour, provided she does not prefer it before her Duty; she can never be too careful to secure her Character, not only from the suspicion of a Crime, but even from the shadow of an Indiscretion. 'Tis well worth her while to renounce the most Entertaining, and what some perhaps will call the most Improving Company, rather than give the World a just occasion of Suspicion or Censure. For besides the Injury that is done Religion, which enjoyns us to avoid the very Appearance of Evil, and to do nothing but what is of good Report, she puts her self too much in a Man's Power who will run such a risque for his Conversation, and expresses such a value for him, as cannot fail of being made use of to do her a mischief.

Preserve your distance then, keep out of the reach of Danger, fly if you wou'd be safe, be sure to be always on the Reserve, not such as is Morose and Affected, but Modest and Discreet, your Caution cannot be too great, nor your Foresight reach too far; there's nothing, or what is next to nothing, a little Amusement and entertaining Conversation lost by this, but all is hazarded by the other. A Man understands his own Merit too well to lose his time in a Woman's Company, were it not to divert himself at her cost, to turn her into a Jest or something worse. And wherever you see great Assiduities, when a Man insinuates into the Diversions and Humors of the Lady, Liking and Admiring whatever she does, tho' at the same time he seems to keep a due Distance, or rather exceeds in the profoundest Respect, Respect being all he dare at present pretend to; when a more than ordinary deference is paid; when something particular appears in the Look and Address, and such an Obsequiousness in every Action, as nothing cou'd engage a Man to, who never forgets the Superiority of his Sex, but a hope to be Observ'd in his turn: Then, whatever the Inequality be, and how sensible soever he seems to be of it, the Man has for certain his Engines at work, the Mine is ready to spring on the first opportunity, and 'tis well if it be not too late to prevent the poor Lady's Ruin.

To wind up this matter, if a Woman were duly Principled and Taught to know the World, especially the true Sentiments that Men have of her, and the Traps they lay for her under so many gilded Compliments, and such a seemingly great Respect, that disgrace wou'd be prevented which is brought upon too many Families, Women would Marry more discreetly, and demean themselves better in a Married State than some People say they do. The foundation indeed ought to be laid deep and strong, she shou'd be made a good Christian and understand why she is so, and then she will be everything else that is Good. Men need keep no Spies on a Woman's Conduct, need have no fear of her Vertue, or so much as of her Prudence and Caution, were but a due sense of true Honour and Vertue awaken'd in her, were her Reason excited and prepar'd to consider the Sophistry of those Temptations which wou'd perswade her from her Duty; and were she put in a way to know that it is both her Wisdom and Interest to observe it; She would then duly examine and weigh all the Circumstances, the Good and Evil of a Married State, and not be surpriz'd with unforeseen Inconveniences, and either never consent to be a Wife, or make a good one when she does. This would shew her what Human Nature is, as well as what it *ought* to be, and teach her not only what she may justly expect, but what she must be Content with; would enable her to cure some Faults, and patiently to suffer what she cannot cure.

Indeed nothing can assure Obedience, and render it what it ought to be, but the Conscience of Duty, the paying it for GOD's sake. Superiors don't rightly understand their own interest when they attempt to put out their Subjects Eyes to keep them Obedient. A Blind Obedience is what a Rational Creature shou'd never Pay, nor wou'd such an one receive it did he rightly understand its Nature. For Human Actions are no otherwise valuable than as they are conformable to Reason, but a blind Obedience is an Obeying *without Reason*, for ought we know *against* it. GOD himself does not require our Obedience at this rate, he lays before us the goodness and reasonableness of his Laws, and were there anything in them whose Equity we could not readily comprehend, yet we have this clear and sufficient Reason on which to found our Obedience, that nothing but what's Just and Fit, can be enjoyn'd by a Just, a Wise and Gracious GOD, but this is a Reason will never hold in respect of Men's Commands, unless they can prove themselves infallible, and consequently Impeccable too.

It is therefore very much a Man's Interest that Women should be good Christians, in this as in every other Instance, he who does his Duty, finds his own account in it. Duty and true Interest are one and the same thing, and he who thinks otherwise is to be pitied for being so much in the Wrong; but what can be more the Duty of the Head, than to Instruct and Improve those who are under Government? She will freely leave him the quiet Dominion of this World, whose Thoughts and Expectations are plac'd on the next. A Prospect of Heaven, and that only, will cure that Ambition which all Generous Minds are fill'd with; not by taking it away, but by placing it on a right Object. She will discern a time when her Sex shall be no bar to the best Employments, the highest Honour; a time when that distinction, now as much us'd to her Prejudice, shall be no more, but provided she is not wanting to her self, her Soul shall shine as bright as the greatest Heroe's. This is a true, and indeed the only consolation, this makes her a sufficient compensation for all the neglect and contempt the ill-grounded Customs of the World throw on her, for all the Injuries brutal Power may do her, and is a sufficient Cordial to support her Spirits, be her Lot in this World what it may.

But some sage Persons may perhaps object, that were Women allow'd to Improve themselves, and not amongst other discouragements driven back by those wise Jests and Scoffs that are put upon a Woman of Sense or Learning, a Philosophical Lady as she is call'd by way of Ridicule, they would be too Wise and too Good for the Men; I grant it, for vicious and foolish Men. Nor is it to be wonder'd, that he is afraid he shou'd not be able to Govern them were their Understandings improv'd, who is resolv'd not to take too much Pains with his own. But these 'tis to be hop'd are no very considerable Number, the foolish at least; and therefore this is so far from being an Argument against Women's Improvement, that it is a strong one for it, if we do but suppose the Men to be as capable of Improvement as the Women, but much more if according to Tradition we believe they have greater Capacities. This, if any thing, wou'd stir them up to be what they ought, and not permit them to wast their Time and abuse their Faculties, in the Service of their irregular Appetites and unreasonable Desires, and so let poor contemptible Women who have been their Slaves, excel them in all that is truly Excellent. This wou'd make them Blush at employing an immortal Mind no better than in making Provision for the Flesh to fulfil the Lusts thereof, since Women by a Wiser Conduct have brought themselves to such a reach of Thought, to such exactness of Judgement, such clearness and strength of Reasoning, such purity and elevation of Mind, such Command of their Passions, such regularity of Will and Affection, and in a word, to such a pitch of Perfection, as the Human Soul is capable of attaining in this Life by the Grace of GOD, such true Wisdom, such real Greatness, as tho' it does not qualifie them to make a Noise in this World, to found or overturn Empires, yet it qualifies them for what is infinitely better, a Kingdom that cannot be mov'd, an incorruptible Crown of Glory.

Besides, it were ridiculous to suppose that a Woman, were she ever so much improv'd, cou'd come near the topping Genius of the Men, and therefore why shou'd they envy or discourage her? Strength of Mind goes along with Strength of Body, and 'tis only for some odd Accidents which Philosophers have not yet thought worth while to enquire into, that the Sturdiest Porter is not the Wisest Man! As therefore the Men have the Power in their Hands, so there's no dispute of their having the Brains to manage it! Can we suppose there is such a thing as good Judgement and Sense upon Earth, if it is not to be found among them? Do not they generally speaking do all the great Actions and considerable Business of this World, and leave that of the next to the Women? Their Subtilty in forming Cabals and laying deep Designs, their Courage and Conduct in breaking through all Tyes Sacred and Civil to effect them, not only advances them to the Post of Honour, and keeps them securely in it for twenty or thirty Years, but gets them a Name, and conveys it down to Posterity for some Hundreds, and who wou'd look any further? Justice and Injustice are administred by their Hands, Courts and Schools are fill'd with these Sages; 'tis Men who dispute for Truth as well as Men who argue against it; Histories are writ by them, they recount each others great Exploits, and have always done so. All famous Arts have their Original from Men, even from the Invention of Guns to the Mystery of good Eating. And to shew that nothing is beneath their Care, any more than above their Reach, they have brought *Gaming* to an Art and Science, and a more Profitable and Honourable one too, than any of those that us'd to be call'd *Liberal!* Indeed what is it they can't perform, when they attempt it? The Strength of their Brains shall be every whit as Conspicuous at their Cups, as in a Senate-House, and when they please they can make it pass for as sure a Mark of Wisdom, to drink deep as to Reason profoundly; a greater proof of Courage and consequently of Understanding, to dare the Vengeance of Heaven it self, than to stand the Raillery of some of the worst of their fellow Creatures.

Again, it may be said, if a Wife's case be as it is here represented, it is not good for a Woman to Marry, and so there's an end of [the] Human Race. But this is no fair Consequence, for all that can justly be inferr'd from hence, is that a Woman has no mighty Obligations to the Man who makes Love to her, she has no reason to be fond of being a Wife, or to reckon it a piece of Preferment when she is taken to be a Man's Upper-Servant; it is no advantage to her in this World, if rightly manag'd it may prove one as to the next. For she who Marries purely to do Good, to Educate Souls for Heaven, who can be so truly mortify'd as to lay aside her own Will and Desires, to pay such as intire Submission for Life, to one whom she cannot be sure will always deserve it, does certainly perform a more Heroic Action than all the famous Masculine Heroes can boast of, she suffers a continual Martyrdom to bring Glory to GOD and Benefit to Mankind, which consideration indeed may carry her through all Difficulties, I know not what else can, and engage her to Love him who proves perhaps so much worse than a Brute, as to make this Condition yet more grievous than it needed to be. She has need of a strong Reason, of a truly Christian and well-temper'd Spirit, of all the Assistance the best Education can give her, and ought to have some good assurance of her own Firmness and Vertue, who ventures on such a Trial; and for this Reason 'tis less to be wonder'd at that Women Marry off in hast, for perhaps if they took time to consider and reflect upon it, they seldom wou'd Marry.

To conclude, perhaps I've said more than most Men will thank me for, I cannot help it, for how much soever I may be their Friend and humble Servant, I am more a Friend to Truth. Truth is strong, and sometime or other will prevail, nor is it for their Honour, and therefore one wou'd think not for their Interest, to be Partial to themselves and Unjust to others. They may fancy I have made some discoveries which like *Arcana Imperii*, ought to be kept secret, but in good earnest, I do them more Honour than to suppose their lawful Prerogatives need any mean Arts to support them. If they have Usurpt, I love Justice too much to wish Success and continuance to Usurpations, which tho' submitted to out of Prudence, and for Quietness sake, yet leave every Body free to regain their lawful Right whenever they have Power and Opportunity. I don't say that Tyranny *ought*, but we find in *Fact*, that it provokes the Oppress'd to throw off even a Lawful Yoke that sits too heavy: And if he who is freely Elected, after all his fair Promises and the fine Hopes he rais'd, proves a Tyrant, the consideration that he was one's own Choice, will not render more Submissive and Patient, but I fear more Refractory. For tho' it is very unreasonable, yet we see 'tis the course of the World, not only to return Injury for Injury, but Crime for Crime; both Parties indeed are Guilty, but the Aggressors have a double Guilt, they have not only their own, but their Neighbours ruin to answer for.

As to the Female Reader, I hope she will allow I've endeavour'd to do her Justice, nor betray'd her Cause as her Advocates usually do, under pretence of defending it. A Practice too mean for any to be Guilty of who have the least Sense of Honour, and who do any more than meerly pretend to it. I think I have held the Ballance even, and not being conscious of Partiality I ask no Pardon for it. To plead for the Oppress'd and to defend the Weak seem'd to me a generous undertaking; for tho' it may be secure, 'tis not always Honourable to run over to the strongest party. And if she infers from what has been said that Marriage is a very Happy State for Men, if they think fit to make it so; that they govern the World, they have Prescription on their side, Women are too weak to dispute it with them, therefore they, as all other Governours, are most, if not only accountable, for what's amiss, for whether other Governments in their Original, were or were not confer'd according to the Merit of the Person, yet certainly in this case, if Heaven has appointed the Man to Govern, it has qualify'd him for it: So far I agree with her. But if she goes on to infer, that therefore if a Man has not these Qualifications where is his Right? That if he misemploys, he abuses it? And if he abuses, according to modern Deduction, he forfeits it, I must leave her there. A peaceable Woman indeed will not carry it so far, she will neither question her Husband's Right nor his Fitness to Govern; but how? Not as an absolute Lord and Master, with an Arbitrary and Tyrannical sway, but as Reason Governs and Conducts a Man, by proposing what is Just and Fit. And the Man who acts according to that Wisdom he assumes, who wou'd have that Superiority he pretends to, acknowledg'd Just, will receive no Injury by any thing that has been offer'd here. A Woman will value him the more who is so Wise and Good, when she discerns how much he excels the rest of his noble Sex; the less he requires, the more will he Merit that Esteem and Deference, which those who are so forward to exact, seem conscious they don't deserve. So then the Man's Prerogative is not at all infring'd, whilst the Woman's Privileges are secur'd; and if any Woman think her self Injur'd, she has a Remedy in reserve which few Men will Envy or endeavour to Rob her of, the Exercise and Improvement of her Vertue here, and the Reward of it hereafter.

PART II
AN EDUCATION FOR
WOMEN

A Serious PROPOSAL TO THE LADIES FOR THE
Advancement of their True and Greatest INTEREST

PART 1

By a Lover of her SEX.

The Third Edition Corrected.

LONDON,
Printed by T.W. for R. Wilkin, at the King's Head in
St. Paul's Church-Yard,
1696

The Dedication
To her Royal Highness
the Princess Ann of Denmark

Madam,

What was at first address'd to the Ladies in General, as seeming not considerable enough to appear in your Royal Highnesses Presence, not being ill receiv'd by them, and having got the Addition of a Second Part, now presumes on a more Particular Application to Her who is the Principal of them, and whose Countenance and Example may reduce to Practice, what it can only Advise and Wish.

And when I consider you Madam as a Princess who is sensible that the Chief Prerogative of the Great is the Power they have of doing more good than those in an Inferior Station can, I see no cause to fear that your Royal Highness will deny Encouragement to that which has no other Design than the Bettering of the World, especially the most neglected part of it as to all Real Improvement, the Ladies. It is by the Exercise of this Power that Princes become truly Godlike, they are never so Illustrious as when they shine as Lights in the World by an Eminent and Heroic Vertue. A Vertue as much above Commendation as it is above Detraction, which sits equally Silent and Compos'd when Opprest with Praises or Pursu'd with Calumnys, is neither hurt by these nor better'd by the other; for the Service of GOD, and the Resembling Him, being its only Aim, His Approbation in a soft and inward Whisper, is more than the loud Huzza's and Plaudits of ten thousand Worlds.

I shall not therefore offend your Royal Ear with the nauseous strain of Dedications; for what can one say, when by how much the more any Person deserves Panegyric, by so much the less they endure it? That your Royal Highness may be All that is truly Great and Good, and have a Confluence of Temporal, Sanctify'd and Crown'd with Spiritual and Eternal Blessings, is the unfeigned and constant desire of

Madam,
Your Royal Highnesses
Most Humble and most Obedient Servant.

A Serious Proposal
to the Ladies, Part I

LADIES,

Since the Profitable Adventures that have gone abroad in the World have met with so great Encouragement, tho' the highest advantage they can propose, is an uncertain Lot for such matters as Opinion, not real worth, gives a value to; things which if obtain'd are as flitting and fickle as that Chance which is to dispose of them; I therefore persuade my self, you will not be less kind to a Proposition that comes attended with more certain and substantial Gain; whose only design is to improve your Charms and heighten your Value, by suffering you no longer to be cheap and contemptible. Its aim is to fix that Beauty, to make it lasting and permanent, which Nature with all the helps of Art cannot secure, and to place it out of the reach of Sickness and Old Age.... Wou'd have you all be wits, or what is better, Wise. Raise you above the Vulgar by something more truly illustrious, than a sounding Title or a great Estate. Wou'd excite in you a generous Emulation to excel in the best things, and not in such Trifles as every mean person who has but Money enough may purchase as well as you. Not suffer you to take up with the low thought of distinguishing your selves by any thing that is not truly valuable, and procure you such Ornaments as all the Treasures of the Indies are not able to purchase. Wou'd help you to surpass the Men as much in Vertue and Ingenuity, as you do in Beauty;

that you may not only be as lovely, but as wise as Angels. Exalt and Establish your Fame, more than the best wrought Poems and loudest Panegyricks, by ennobling your Minds with such Graces as really deserve it. And instead of the Fustian Complements and Fulsome Flatteries of your Admirers, obtain for you the Plaudit of Good Men and Angels, and the approbation of Him who cannot err. In a word, render you the Glory and Blessing of the present Age, and the Admiration and Pattern of the next.

And sure, I shall not need many words to persuade you to close with this *Proposal*.... Since you can't be so unkind to your selves, as to refuse your *real* Interest, I only entreat you to be so wise as to examine wherein it consists; for nothing is of worse consequence than to be deceiv'd in a matter of so great concern. 'Tis as little beneath your Grandeur as your Prudence, to examine curiously what is in this case offer'd you, and to take care that cheating Hucksters don't impose upon you with deceitful Ware. This is a Matter infinitely more worthy your Debates, than what Colours are most agreeable, or what's the Dress becomes you best. Your Glass will not do you half so much service as a serious reflection on your own Minds, which will discover Irregularities more worthy your Correction, and keep you from being either too much elated or depress'd by the representations of the other. 'Twill not be near so advantageous to consult with your Dancing-Master as with your own Thoughts, how you may with greatest exactness tread in the Paths of Vertue, which has certainly the most attractive *Air*, and Wisdom the most graceful and becoming *Mien*: Let these attend you and your Carriage will be always well compos'd, and ev'ry thing you do will carry its Charm with it. No solicitude in the adornation of your selves is discommended, provided you employ your care about that which is really your *self*; and do not neglect that particle of Divinity within you, which must survive, and may (if you please) be happy and perfect, when it's unsuitable and much inferiour Companion is mouldering into Dust. Neither will any pleasure be denied you, who are only desir'd not to catch at the Shadow and let the Substance go. You may be as ambitious as you please, so you aspire to the best things; and contend with your Neighbours as much as you can, that they may not out do you in any commendable Quality. Let it never be said, That they to whom pre-eminence is so very agreeable, can be tamely content that others shou'd surpass them in *this*, and precede them in a *better* World! Remember, I pray you, the famous

Women of former Ages, the *Orinda's*[1] of late, and the more Modern
Heroins, and blush to think how much is now, and will hereafter
be said of them, when you your selves (as great a Figure as you
make) must be buried in silence and forgetfulness! Shall your Emulation
fail *there only* where 'tis commendable? Why are you so preposterously
humble, as not to contend for one of the highest Mansions in the
Court of Heav'n? ... How can you be content to be in the World
like Tulips in a Garden, to make a fine *shew* and be good for nothing;
have all your Glories set in the Grave, or perhaps much sooner!
What your own sentiments are I know not, but I can't without
pity and resentment reflect, that those Glorious Temples on which
your kind Creator has bestow'd such exquisite workmanship, shou'd
enshrine no better than *Egyptian* Deities; be like a garnish'd Sepulchre,
which for all its glittering, has nothing within but emptiness or putrefaction! What a pity it is, that whilst your Beauty casts a lustre ✓
all around you, your Souls which are infinitely more bright and
radiant, ... shou'd be suffer'd to over-run with Weeds, lie fallow and
neglected, unadorn'd with any Grace! ... For shame let's abandon
that Old, and therefore one wou'd think, unfashionable employment
of pursuing Butter flies and Trifles! No longer drudge on in the
dull beaten road of Vanity and Folly, which so many have gone
before us, but dare to break the enchanted Circle that custom has
plac'd us in, and scorn the vulgar way of imitating all the Impertinencies
of our Neighbours. Let us learn to pride ourselves in something
more excellent than the invention of a Fashion; And not entertain
such a degrading thought of our own *worth*, as to imagine that
our Souls were given us only for the service of our Bodies, and
that the best improvement we can make of these, is to attract the
Eyes of Men. We value *them* too much, and our *selves* too little,
if we place any part of our desert in their Opinion; and don't think
our selves capable of Nobler Things than the pitiful Conquest of
some worthless heart. She who has opportunities of making an interest
in Heaven, of obtaining the love and admiration of GOD and Angels,
is too prodigal of her Time, and injurious to her Charms, to throw
them away on vain insignificant men. She need not make her self
so cheap, as to descend to court their Applauses; for at the greater
distance she keeps, and the more she is above them, the more effectually she secures their esteem and wonder. Be so generous then,

1   Katherine Philips, 'The Matchless Orinda'.

Ladies, as to do nothing unworthy of you; so true to your Interest, as not to lessen your Empire and depreciate your Charms. Let not your Thoughts be wholly busied in observing what respect is paid you, but a part of them at least, in studying to deserve it. And after all, remember that Goodness is the truest Greatness; to be wise for your selves the greatest Wit; and *that* Beauty the most desirable which will endure to Eternity.

Pardon me the seeming rudeness of this Proposal, which goes upon a supposition that there's something amiss in you, which it is intended to amend. My design is not to expose, but to rectifie your Failures. To be exempt from mistake, is a privilege few can pretend to, the greatest is to be past Conviction and too obstinate to reform. Even the *Men*, as exact as they wou'd seem, and as much as they divert themselves with our Miscarriages, are very often guilty of greater faults, and such, as considering the advantages they enjoy, are much more inexcusable. But I will not pretend to correct their Errors, who either are, or at least *think* themselves too wise to receive Instruction from a Womans Pen. My earnest desire is, That you Ladies, would be as perfect and happy as 'tis possible to be in this imperfect state; . . .. I would have you live up to the dignity of your Nature, and express your thankfulness to GOD for the benefits you enjoy by a due improvement of them: As I know very many of you do, who countenance that Piety which the men decry, and are the brightest Patterns of Religion that the Age affords; 'tis my grief that all the rest of our Sex do not imitate such Illustrious Examples, ... The Men perhaps will cry out that I teach you false ✓ Doctrine, for because by their seductions some amongst us are become very mean and contemptible, they would fain persuade the rest to be as despicable and forlorn as they. We're indeed oblig'd to them for their management, in endeavouring to make us so, who use all the artifice they can to spoil, and deny us the means of improvement. So that instead of inquiring why all Women are not wise and good, we have reason to wonder that there are any so. Were the Men as much neglected, and as little care taken to cultivate and improve them, perhaps they wou'd be so far from surpassing those whom they now dispise, that they themselves wou'd sink into the greatest stupidity and brutality. The preposterous returns that the most of them make, to all the care and pains that is bestow'd on them, renders this no uncharitable, nor improbable Conjecture. One wou'd ✓ therefore almost think, that the wise disposer of all things, foreseeing how unjustly Women are denied opportunities of improvement from *without* has therefore by way of compensation endow'd them with greater propensions to Vertue and a natural goodness of Temper within, which if duly manag'd, would raise them to the most eminent pitch of heroick Vertue. Hither, Ladies, I desire you wou'd aspire, 'tis a noble and becoming Ambition, and to remove such Obstacles as lie in your way is the design of this Paper. We will therefore enquire what it is that stops your flight, that keeps you groveling here below, like *Domitian* catching Flies when you should be busied in obtaining Empires.

Altho' it has been said by Men of more Wit than Wisdom, and ✓ perhaps of more malice than either, that Women are naturally incapable of acting Prudently, or that they are necessarily determined to folly, I must by no means grant it; that Hypothesis would render my endeavours impertinent, for then it would be in vain to advise the one, or endeavour the Reformation of the other. Besides, there are Examples in all Ages, which sufficiently confute the Ignorance and Malice of this Assertion.

The Incapacity, if there be any, is acquired not natural; and none of their Follies are so necessary, but that they might avoid them if they pleas'd themselves. Some disadvantages indeed they labour under, and what these are we shall see by and by and endeavour to surmount; but Women need not take up with mean things, since (if they are not wanting to themselves) they are capable of the best. Neither God nor Nature have excluded them from being Ornaments to their Families and useful in their Generation; there is therefore no reason they should be content to be Cyphers in the World, useless at the best, and in a little time a burden and nuisance to all about them. And 'tis very great pity that they who are so apt to over-rate themselves in smaller Matters, shou'd, where it most concerns them to know and stand upon their Value, be so insensible of their own worth. The Cause therefore of the defects we labour under is, if not wholly, yet at least in the first place, to be ascribed to the mistakes of our Education, which like an Error in the first Concoction, spreads its ill Influence through all our Lives.

. . . Women are from their very Infancy debar'd those Advantages, with the want of which they are afterwards reproached, and nursed up in those Vices which will hereafter be upbraided to them. So partial are Men as to expect Brick where they afford no Straw; and so abundantly civil as to take care we shou'd make good that obliging Epithet of *Ignorant*, which out of an excess of good Manners, they are pleas'd to bestow on us!

One would be apt to think indeed, that Parents shou'd take all possible care of their Childrens Education, not only for *their* sakes, but even for their *own*. And tho' the Son convey the Name to Posterity, yet certainly a great Part of the Honour of their Families depends on their Daughters. 'Tis the kindness of Education that binds our duty fastest on us: For the being instrumental to the bringing us into the World, is no matter of choice and therefore the less obliging; But to procure that we may live wisely and happily in it, and be capable of endless Joys hereafter, is a benefit we can never sufficiently acknowledge. To introduce poor Children into the World and neglect to fence them against the temptations of it, and so leave them expos'd to temporal and eternal Miseries, is a wickedness for which I want a Name; 'tis beneath Brutality; the Beasts are better natur'd for they take care of their offspring, till they are capable of caring for themselves. And if Mothers had a due regard to their Posterity, how *Great* soever they are, they wou'd not think themselves too *Good* to perform what Nature requires, nor through Pride and Delicacy remit the poor little one to the care of a Foster Parent. Or if necessity inforce them to depute another to perform *their* Duty, they wou'd be as choice at least, in the Manners and Inclinations, as they are in the complections of their Nurses, lest with their Milk they transfuse their Vices, and form in the Child such evil habits as will not easily be eradicated.

Nature as bad as it is and as much as it is complain'd of, is so far improveable by the grace of GOD, upon our honest and hearty endeavours, that if we are not wanting to our selves, we may all in *some*, tho' not in an *equal* measure, be instruments of his Glory, Blessings to this World, and capable of Eternal Blessedness in that to come. But if our Nature is spoil'd, instead of being improv'd at first; if from our Infancy we are nurs'd up in Ignorance and Vanity; are taught to be Proud and Petulant, Delicate and Fantastick, Humorous and Inconstant, 'tis not strange that the ill effects of this Conduct appear in all the future Actions of our Lives. And seeing it is Ignorance, either habitual or actual, which is the cause of all sin, how are they like to escape *this*, who are bred up in *that*? That therefore Women are unprofitable to most, and a plague and dishonour to some men is not much to be regretted on account of the *Men*, because 'tis the product of their own folly, in denying them the benefits of an ingenuous and liberal Education, the most effectual means to direct them into, and to secure their progress in the ways of Vertue.

For that Ignorance is the cause of most Feminine Vices, may be instanc'd in that Pride and Vanity which is usually imputed to us, and which I suppose if throughly sifted, will appear to be some way or other, the rise and Original of all the rest. These, tho' very bad Weeds, are the product of a good Soil, they are nothing else but Generosity degenerated and corrupted. A desire to advance and perfect its Being, is planted by GOD in all Rational Natures, to excite them hereby to every worthy and becoming Action; for certainly next to the Grace of GOD, nothing does so powerfully restrain people from Evil and stir them up to Good, as a generous Temper. And therefore to be ambitious of perfections is no fault, tho' to assume the Glory of our Excellencies to our selves, or to Glory in such as we really have not, are. And were Womens haughtiness express'd in disdaining to do a mean and evil thing, wou'd they pride themselves in somewhat truly perfective of a Rational nature, there were no hurt in it. But then they ought not to be denied the means of examining and judging what is so; . . .. She who rightly understands wherein the perfection of her Nature consists, will lay out her Thoughts and Industry in the acquisition of such Perfections: But she who is kept ignorant of the matter, will take up with such Objects as first offer themselves, and bear any plausible resemblance to what she desires; a shew of advantage being sufficient to render them agreeable baits to her who wants Judgment and Skill to discern between reality and pretence. From whence it easily follows, that she who has nothing else to value her self upon, will be proud of her Beauty, or Money and what that can purchase; and think her self mightily oblig'd to him, who tells her she has those Perfections which she naturally longs for. Her inbred self-esteem and desire of good, which are degenerated into Pride and mistaken Self-love, will easily open her Ears to whatever goes about to nourish and delight them; and when a cunning designing Enemy from without, has drawn over to his Party these Traytors within, he has the Poor unhappy Person, at his Mercy, who now very glibly swallows down his Poyson, because 'tis presented in a Golden Cup, and credulously hearkens to the most disadvantageous Proposals, because they come attended with a seeming esteem. She whose Vanity makes her swallow praises by the wholesale, without examining whether she deserves them, or from what hand they come, will reckon it but gratitude to think well of him who values her so much, and think she must needs be merciful to the poor despairing Lover whom her Charms have reduc'd to die at her feet. Love and Honour are what every one of us naturally esteem, they are excellent things in themselves and very worthy our regard, and by how much the readier we are to embrace what ever resembles them, by so much the more dangerous it is that these venerable Names should be wretchedly abus'd and affixt to their direct contraries, yet this is the Custom of the World: And how can she possibly detect the fallacy, who has no better Notion of either than what she derives from Plays and Romances? How can she be furnished with any solid Principles whose very Instructors are Froth and emptiness? Whereas Women were they rightly Educated, had they obtain'd a well inform'd and discerning Mind, they would be proof against all those Batteries, see through and scorn those little silly Artifices which are us'd to ensnare and deceive them. Such an one would value her self only on her Vertue, and consequently be most chary of what she esteems so much. She would know, that not what others *say*, but what she her self *does*, is the true Commendation and the only thing that exalts her; . . ..

Whence is it but from ignorance, from a want of Understanding to compare and judge of things, to chuse a right End, to proportion the Means to the End, and to rate ev'ry thing according to its proper value, that we quit the Substance for the Shadow, Reality for Appearance, and embrace those very things which if we understood we shou'd hate and fly, but now are reconcil'd to, merely because they usurp the Name, tho' they have nothing of the Nature of those venerable Objects we desire and seek? Were it not for this delusion, is it probable a Lady who passionately desires to be admir'd, shou'd ever consent to such Actions as render her base and contemptible? Wou'd she be so absurd as to think either to get love, or to keep it, by those methods which occasion loathing and consequently end in hatred? Wou'd she reckon it a piece of her Grandeur, or hope to gain esteem by such excesses as really lessen her in the eyes of all considerate and judicious persons? Wou'd she be so silly as to look big and think her self the better person, because she has more Money to bestow profusely, or the good luck to have a more ingenious Taylor or Milliner than her Neighbour? Wou'd she, who by the regard she pays to Wit, seems to make some pretences to it, undervalue her Judgment so much as to admit the Scurrility and profane noisy Nonsense of men, whose Fore-heads are better than their Brains, to pass under that Character? Wou'd she be so weak as to imagine that a few airy Fancies joyn'd with a great deal of Impudence and ill-nature (the right definition of modern Wit) can bespeak him a Man of sense, who runs counter to all the sense and reason that ever appear'd in the World? than which nothing can be an Argument of greater shallowness, unless it be to regard and esteem him for it. Wou'd a Woman, if she truly understood her self, be affected either with the praises or calumnies of those worthless persons, whose Lives are a direct contradiction to Reason, a very sink of corruption, by whom one wou'd blush to be commended, lest they shou'd be mistaken for Partners in or Connivers at their Crimes? Will she who has a jot of discernment think to satisfy her greedy desire of Pleasure, with those promising nothings that have again and again deluded her? Or will she to obtain such Bubbles, run the risque of forfeiting Joys infinitely satisfying and eternal? In sum, did not ignorance impose on us, we would never lavish out the greatest part of our Time and Care, on the decoration of a Tenement, in which our Lease is so very short, and which for all our industry, may lose it's Beauty e'er that Lease be out, and in the mean while neglect a more glorious and durable Mansion! We wou'd never be so curious of the House and so careless of the Inhabitant, whose beauty is capable of great improvement and will endure for ever without diminution or decay!

Thus Ignorance and a narrow Education lay the Foundation of Vice, and Imitation and Custom rear it up. Custom, that merciless torrent that carries all before it, and which indeed can be stem'd by none but such as have a great deal of Prudence and a rooted Vertue. For 'tis but Decorous that she who is not capable of giving better Rules, shou'd follow those she sees before her, least she only change the instance and retain the absurdity. 'Twou'd puzzle a considerate Person to account for all that Sin and Folly that is in the World (which certainly has nothing in it self to recommend it) did not Custom help to solve the difficulty.... 'Tis Custom therefore, that Tyrant Custom, which is the grand motive to all those irrational choices which we daily see made in the World, so very contrary to our *present* interest and pleasure, as well as to our Future. We think it an unpardonable mistake not to do as our neighbours do, and part with our Peace and Pleasure as well as our Innocence and Vertue, meerly in complyance with an unreasonable Fashion. And having inur'd our selves to Folly, we know not how to quit it;

we go on in Vice, not because we find satisfaction in it, but because we are unacquainted with the Joys of Vertue.

Add to this the hurry and noise of the World, which does generally so busy and pre-ingage us, that we have little time and less inclination to stand still and reflect on our own Minds. Those impertinent Amusements which have seiz'd us, keep their hold so well and so constantly buz about our Ears, that we cannot attend to the Dictates of our Reason . . .. By an habitual inadvertency we render our selves incapable of any serious and improveing thought, till our minds themselves become as light and frothy as those things they are conversant about . . ..

When a poor Young Lady is taught to value her self on nothing but her Cloaths, and to think she's very fine when well accoutred; When she hears say that 'tis Wisdom enough for her to know how to dress her self, that she may become amiable in his eyes, to whom it appertains to be knowing and learned; who can blame her if she lay out her Industry and Money on such Accomplishments, and sometimes extends it farther than her misinformer desires she should? When she sees the vain and the gay, making Parade in the World and attended with the Courtship and admiration of the gazing herd, no wonder that her tender Eyes are dazled with the Pageantry, and wanting Judgement to pass a due Estimate on them and their Admirers, longs to be such a fine and celebrated thing as they? What tho' she be sometimes told of another World, she has however a more lively perception of this, and may well think, that if her Instructors were in earnest when they tell her of *hereafter*, they would not be so busied and concerned about what happens *here*. She is it may be, taught the Principles and Duties of Religion, but not Acquainted with the Reasons and Grounds of them; being told 'tis enough for her to believe, to examine why, and wherefore, belongs not to her. And therefore, though her Piety may be tall and spreading, yet because it wants foundation and Root, the first rude Temptation overthrows and blasts it, or perhaps the short liv'd Gourd decays and withers of its own accord. But why should she be blamed for setting no great value on her Soul, whose noblest Faculty her Understanding is render'd useless to her? Or censur'd for relinquishing a course of Life, whose Prerogatives she was never acquainted with, and tho' highly reasonable in it self, was put upon the embracing it with as little reason as she now forsakes it? For if her Religion it self be taken up as the Mode of the Country, 'tis no strange thing that she lays it down again in conformity to the Fashion. Whereas she whose Reason is suffer'd to display it self ..... who is a Christian out of Choice, not in conformity to those among whom she lives; .... she who is not only eminently and unmoveably good, but able to give a Reason *why* she is so, is too firm and stable to be mov'd by the pitiful Allurements of sin, too wise and too well bottom'd to be undermined and supplanted by the strongest Efforts of Temptation. Doubtless a truly Christian Life requires a clear Understanding as well as regular Affections, that both together may move the Will to a direct choice of Good and a stedfast adherence to it. For tho' the heart may be honest, it is but by chance that the Will is right if the Understanding be ignorant and Cloudy. And what's the reason that we sometimes see persons unhappily falling off from their Piety, but because 'twas their Affections, not their Judgement, that inclin'd them to be Religious? Reason and Truth are firm and immutable, she who bottoms on them is on sure ground, Humour and Inclination are sandy Foundations, and she who is sway'd by her Affections more than by her Judgement, owes the happiness of her Soul in a great measure to the temper of her Body; her Piety may perhaps blaze high but will not last long. .... Their Devotion becomes ricketed, starv'd and contracted in some of it's vital parts, and disproportioned and over-grown in less material instances; whilst one Duty is *over-done* to commute for the neglect of another, and the mistaken person thinks the being often on her knees, attones for all the miscarriages of her Conversation: .....

And now having discovered the Disease and its cause, 'tis proper to apply a Remedy; single Medicines are too weak to cure such complicated Distempers, they require a full Dispensatory; and what wou'd a good Woman refuse to do, could she hope by that to advantage the greatest part of the World, and improve her Sex in knowledge and true Religion? I doubt not, Ladies, but that the Age, as bad as it is, affords very many of you who will readily embrace whatever has a true tendency to the Glory of GOD and your mutual Edification, to revive the ancient Spirit of Piety in the World and to transmit it to succeeding Generations. I know there are many of you who so ardently love God, as to think no time too much to spend in his service, nor any thing too difficult to do for his sake; and bear such a hearty goodwill to your Neighbours, as to grudge no Prayers or Pains to reclaim and improve them. I have therefore no more to do but to make the Proposal, to prove that it will answer these great and good Ends, and then 'twill be easy to obviate the Objections that Persons of more Wit than Vertue may happen to raise against it.

Now as to the Proposal, it is to erect a *Monastery*, or if you will (to avoid giving offence to the scrupulous and injudicious, by names which tho' innocent in themselves, have been abus'd by superstitious Practices,) we will call it a *Religious Retirement*, and such as shall have a double aspect, being not only a Retreat from the World for those who desire that advantage, but likewise, an Institution and previous discipline, to fit us to do the greatest good in it; such an Institution as this (if I do not mightily deceive my self) would be the most probable method to amend the present and improve the future Age. For here those who are convinc'd of the emptiness of earthly Enjoyments, who are sick of the vanity of the world and its impertinencies, may find more substantial and satisfying enter-
✓ tainments, and need not be confin'd to what they justly loath. Those who are desirous to know and fortify their weak side, first do good to themselves, that hereafter they may be capable of doing more good to others; or for their greater security are willing to avoid *temptation*, may get out of that danger which a continual stay in view of the Enemy, and the familiarity and unwearied application of the Temptation may expose them to; and gain an opportunity to look into themselves to be acquainted at home and no longer the greatest strangers to their own hearts. Such as are willing in a more peculiar and undisturb'd manner, to attend the great business they came into the world about, the service of GOD and improvement of their own Minds, may find a convenient and blissful recess from the noise and hurry of the World . . ..

You are therefore Ladies, invited into a place, where you shall suffer no other confinement, but to be kept out of the road of sin: You shall not be depriv'd of your grandeur, but only exchange the vain Pomps and Pageantry of the world, empty Titles and Forms of State, for the true and solid Greatness of being able to despise them. You will only quit the Chat of insignificant people for an ingenious Conversation; the froth of flashy Wit for real Wisdom; idle tales for instructive discourses. The deceitful Flatteries of those who under pretence of loving and admiring you, really served their *own* base ends for the seasonable Reproofs and wholsom Counsels of your hearty wellwishers and affectionate Friends, which will procure you those perfections your feigned lovers pretended you had, and kept you from obtaining . . .. Happy Retreat! which will be the introducing you into such a *Paradise* as your Mother *Eve* forfeited, where you shall feast on Pleasures, that do not like those of the World, disappoint your expectations, pall your Appetites, and by the disgust they give you put you on the fruitless search after new Delights, which when obtain'd are as empty as the former; but such as will make you *truly* happy *now*, and prepare you to be *perfectly* so hereafter. Here are no Serpents to deceive you, whilst you entertain your selves in these delicious Gardens. No Provocations will be given in this Amicable Society, but to Love and to good Works, which will afford such an entertaining employment, that you'll have as little inclination as leisure to pursue those Follies, which in the time of your ignorance pass'd with you under the name of love, altho' there is not in nature two more different things, than *true Love* and that *brutish Passion* which pretends to ape it. Here will be no Rivalling but for the of Love of GOD, no Ambition but to procure his Favour, to which nothing will more effectually recommend you, than a great and dear affection to each other. Envy that Canker, will not here disturb your Breasts; for how can she repine at anothers well-fare, who reckons it the greatest part of her own? No Covetousness will gain admittance in this blest abode, but to amass huge Treasures of good Works, and to procure one of the brightest Crowns of Glory. You will not be solicitous to encrease your Fortunes, but to enlarge your Minds, esteeming no Grandeur like being conformable to the meek and humble JESUS. So that you only withdraw from the noise and trouble, the folly and temptation of the world, that you may more peaceably enjoy your selves, and all the innocent Pleasures it is able to afford you, and particularly that which is worth all the rest, a Noble Vertuous and Disinteress'd Friendship. . . . In fine, the place to which you are invited is a Type and Antepast of Heav'n, where your Employment will be as there, to magnify GOD, to love one another, and to communicate that useful *knowledge*, which by the due improvement of your time in Study and Contemplation you will obtain, and which when obtain'd, will afford you a much sweeter and more durable delight, than all those pitiful diversions, those revellings and amusements, which now thro your ignorance of better, appear the only grateful and relishing Entertainments.

But because we were not made for our selves, nor can by any means so effectually glorify GOD and do good to our own Souls, as by doing Offices of Charity and Beneficence to others: . . .. your

Retreat shall be so manag'd as not to exclude the good Works of an *Active*, from the pleasure and serenity of a *Contemplative* Life, but by a due mixture of both retain all the advantages and avoid the inconveniences that attend either. It shall not so cut you off from the world as to hinder you from bettering and improving it, but rather qualify you to do it the greatest Good, and be a Seminary to stock the Kingdom with pious and prudent Ladies, whose good Example it is to be hop'd, will so influence the rest of their Sex, that Women may no longer pass for those little useless and impertinent Animals, which the ill conduct of too many has caus'd 'em to be mistaken for.

We have hitherto consider'd our Retirement only in relation to Religion, which is indeed its *main*, I may say its *only* design; nor can this be thought too contracting a word, since Religion is the adequate business of our lives, and largely consider'd, takes in all we have to do, nothing being a fit employment for a rational Creature, which has not either a *direct* or *remote* tendency to this great and *only* end. But because, as we have all along observ'd. Religion never appears in it's true Beauty, but when it is accompanied with Wisdom and Discretion; and that without a good Understanding, we can scarce be *truly*, but never *eminently* Good; being liable to a thousand seductions and mistakes (for even the men themselves, if they have not a competent degree of Knowledge, are carried about with every wind of Doctrine) Therefore, one great end of this Institution shall be, to expel that cloud of Ignorance which Custom has involv'd us in, to furnish our minds with a stock of solid and useful Knowledge, that the Souls of Women may no longer be the only unadorn'd and neglected things. It is not intended that our *Religious* shou'd waste their time, and trouble their heads about such unconcerning matters, as the vogue of the world has turn'd up for Learning, the impertinency of which has been excellently expos'd by an ingenious pen,[1] but busy themselves in a serious enquiry after *necessary* and *perfective* truths, something which it *concerns* them to know, and which tends to their real interest and perfection, and what that is the excellent Author just now mention'd will sufficiently inform them. Such a course of Study will neither be too troublesome nor out of the reach of a Female Virtuoso; for it is not intended she shou'd spend her hours in learning *words* but *things*, and therefore no more Languages than

1   John Norris, *Reflections upon the Conduct of Human Life*, 1690.

are necessary to acquaint her with useful Authors. Nor need she trouble her self in turning over a great number of Books, but take care to understand and digest a few well-chosen and good ones. Let her but obtain right Ideas, and be truly acquainted with the nature of those Objects that present themselves to her mind, and then no matter whether or no she be able to tell what fanciful people have said about them: And throughly to understand Christianity as profess'd by the *Church* of *England*, will be sufficient to confirm her in the truth, tho' she have not a Catalogue of those particular errors which oppose it. Indeed a Learned Education of the Women will appear so unfashionable, that I began to startle at the singularity of the proposition, but was extremely pleas'd when I found a late ingenious Author (whose Book I met with since the writing of this) agree with me in my Opinion. For speaking of the Repute that Learning was in about 150 years ago, "*It was so very modish* (says he) *that the fair Sex seem'd to believe that Greek and Latin added to their Charms; and Plato and Aristotle untranslated, were frequent Ornaments of their Closets. One wou'd think by the effects, that it was a proper way of Educating them, since there are no accounts in History of so many great Women in any one Age, as are to be found between the years 15 and 1600.*" (Mr Wotton's Reflect. on Ant. and Mod. Learn. p.349, 350.)[1]

For since GOD has given Women as well as Men intelligent Souls, why should they be forbidden to improve them? Since he has not denied us the faculty of Thinking, why shou'd we not (at least in gratitude to him) employ our Thoughts on himself their noblest Object, and not unworthily bestow them on Trifles and Gaities and secular Affairs? Being the Soul was created for the contemplation of Truth as well as for the fruition of Good, is it not as cruel and unjust to preclude Women from the knowledge of the one as from the enjoyment of the other? Especially since the Will is blind, and cannot chuse but by the direction of the Understanding; or to speak more properly, since the Soul always *Wills* according as she *Understands*, so that if she Understands amiss, she Wills amiss. And as Exercise enlarges & exalts any Faculty, so thro' want of using it becomes crampt & lessened; if therefore we make little or no use of our Understandings, we shall shortly have none to use; and the more contracted and unemploy'd the deliberating and directive Power

1   William Wotton (1666–1726), *Reflections upon Ancient and Modern Learning*, 1694.

is, the more liable is the elective to unworthy and mischievous options. What is it but the want of an ingenious Education, that renders the generality of Feminine Conversations so insipid and foolish and their solitude so insupportable? Learning is therefore necessary to render them more agreeable and useful in company, and to furnish them with becoming entertainments when alone, that so they may not be driven to those miserable shifts, which too many make use of to put off their Time, that precious Talent that never lies on the hands of a judicious Person. And since our Happiness in the next World, depends so far on those dispositions which we carry along with us out of this, that without a right habitude and temper of mind we are not capable of Felicity; and seeing our Beatitude consists in the contemplation of the divine Truth and Beauty, as well as in the fruition of his Goodness, can Ignorance be a fit preparative for Heaven? Is't likely that she whose Understanding has been busied about nothing but froth and trifles, shou'd be capable of delighting her self in noble and sublime Truths? Let such therefore as deny us the improvement of our Intellectuals, either take up *his* Paradox, who said *that Women have no Souls*, which at this time a day, when they are allow'd to Brutes, wou'd be as unphilosophical as it is unmannerly, or else let them permit us to cultivate and improve them. There is a sort of Learning indeed which is worse than the greatest Ignorance: A Woman may study Plays and Romances all her days, and be a great deal more knowing but never a jot the wiser. Such a knowledge as this serves only to instruct and put her forward in the practice of the greatest Follies, yet how can they justly blame her who forbid, or at least won't afford opportunity of better? A rational mind *will* be employ'd, it will never be satisfy'd in doing nothing, and if you neglect to furnish it with good materials, 'tis like to take up with such as come to hand.

We pretend not that Women shou'd teach in the Church, or usurp Authority where it is not allow'd them; permit us only to understand our *own* duty, and not be forc'd to take it upon trust from others; to be at least so far learned, as to be able to form in our minds a true Idea of Christianity, it being so very necessary to fence us against the danger of these *last* and *perilous days*, in which Deceivers a part of whose Character is to *lead captive silly Women*, need not *creep into Houses* since they have Authority to proclaim their Errors on the *House top*. And let us also acquire a true Practical Knowledge such as will convince us of the absolute necessity of *Holy Living* as well as of *Right Believing*, and that no Heresy is more dangerous than that of an ungodly and wicked Life. And since the *French Tongue* is understood by most Ladies, methinks they may much better improve it by the study of Philosophy (as I hear the *French Ladies* do) *Des Cartes*, *Malebranche* and others, than by reading idle *Novels* and *Romances*. 'Tis strange we shou'd be so forward to imitate their Fashions and Fopperies, and have no regard to what really deserves our Imitation! And why shall it not be thought as genteel to understand *French Philosophy*, as to be accoutred in a *French Mode*? Let therefore the famous Madam *D'acier*, *Scudéry*;[1] Etc. and our own incomparable *Orinda*, excite the Emulation of the English Ladies.

The Ladies, I'm sure, have no reason to dislike this Proposal, but✓ I know not how the Men will resent it to have their enclosure broke down, and Women invited to tast of that Tree of Knowledge they have so long unjustly *Monopoliz'd*. But they must excuse me, if I be as partial to my own Sex as they are to theirs, and think Women as capable of Learning as Men are, and that it becomes them as well. For I cannot imagine wherein the hurt lies, if instead of doing mischief to one another, by an uncharitable and vain Conversation, Women be enabled to inform and instruct those of their own Sex at least; the Holy Ghost having left it on record, that *Priscilla* as well as her Husband, catechiz'd the eloquent *Apollos* and the great Apostle found no fault with her. It will therefore be very proper for our Ladies to spend part of their time in this Retirement, in adorning their minds with useful Knowledge.

To enter into the detail of the particulars concerning the Government of the *Religious*, their Offices of Devotion, Employments, Work,

---

1   René Descartes (1596–1650), French philosopher whose main works were *Discours de la Méthode* (1637) and *Principes de la Philosophie* (1644). Among the many profoundly influenced by his ideas were the Cambridge Platonists in the mid-seventeenth century. Père Nicolas Malebranche (1638–1715), French philosopher of the Cartesian school and mathematician; he published *De la Recherche de la Vérité* (1674), *Conversations Chrétiennes* (1677) and *Traité de la Nature et de la Grâce* (1680) – all of which were translated into English in the mid-90s. He was much admired by John Norris, 'the last of the Cambridge Platonists'. Anne Lefebvre Dacier (1654?–1720), French classical scholar who edited and translated several classical authors. Madeleine de Scudéry (1607–1701), novelist who established her own salon (la societé du Samedi) under the pseudonym of Sappho. Her novels were immensely popular and were translated into English. Among the best known were *Artamène ou le Grand Cyrus* (1648–53), part of which was devoted to a discussion of female education, and *Clélie* (1654–61).

etc. is not now necessary. Suffice it at present to signify, that they will be more than ordinarily careful to redeem their Time, spending no more of it on the Body than the necessities of Nature require, but by a judicious choice of their Employment and a constant industry about it, so improve this invaluable Treasure, that it may neither be buried in Idleness, nor lavish'd out in unprofitable concerns. For a stated portion of it being daily paid to GOD in Prayers and Praises, the rest shall be employ'd in innocent, charitable, and useful Business; either in study in learning themselves or instructing others, for it is design'd that part of their Employment be the Education of those of their own Sex; or else in spiritual and corporal Works of Mercy, relieving the Poor, healing the Sick, mingling Charity to the Soul with that they express to the Body, instructing the Ignorant, counselling the Doubtful, comforting the Afflicted, and correcting those that err and do amiss.

And as it will be the business of their lives, their meat and drink to *know* and *do* the Will of their Heavenly Father, so will they pay a strict conformity to all the Precepts of their holy Mother the *Church*, whose sacred Injunctions are too much neglected, even by those who pretend the greatest zeal for her. For besides the daily performance of the Publick Offices after the Cathedral manner, in the most affecting and elevating way, the celebration of the Holy Eucharist every Lords Day and Holyday, and a course of solid instructive Preaching and Catechizing; our *Religious*, considering that the holy JESUS punctually observ'd the innocent usages of the *Jewish* Church, and tho' in many instances the *reason* of the Command ceas'd as to him, yet he wou'd obey the *letter* to avoid giving offence and to set us an admirable pattern of Obedience; therefore, tho' it may be thought such pious Souls have little occasion for the severities of fasting and mortification, yet they will consider it as a special part of their Duty to observe all the Fasts of the Church, *viz. Lent, Ember,* and *Rogation-days, Fridays* and *Vigils*; times so little heeded by the most, that one wou'd scarce believe them set apart for Religious Purposes, did we not find them in the antiquated Rubricks. And as their Devotion will be regular, so shall it likewise be solid and substantial. They will not rest in the mere out-side of Duty, nor fansie the performance of their Fasts and Offices will procure them license to indulge a darling Vice: But having long since laid the Ax to the root of sin, and destroy'd the whole body of it, they will look upon these holy times of recollection and extraordinary Devotion (without which Fasting signifies little) as excellent means to keep it down, and to pluck up every the least Fibre that may happen to remain in them. But we intend not by this to impose any intolerable burden on tender Constitutions, knowing that our Lord has taught us, that Mercy is to be prefer'd before Sacrifice: and that Bodily Exercise profiteth but a little, the chief business being to obtain a divine and God-like temper of Mind.

And as this institution will strictly enjoyn all pious and profitable Employments, so does it not only permit but recommend harmless and ingenious Diversions, Musick particularly and such as may refresh the Body without enervating the Mind. They do a disservice to Religion who make it an enemy to innocent Nature, and injure the Almighty when they represent him as imposing burdens that are not to be born. Neither GOD nor Wise men will like us the better for an affected severity and waspish sourness. . . .

As to *Lodging, Habit* and *Diet,* they may be quickly resolv'd on by the Ladies who shall subscribe; who I doubt not will make choice of what is most plain and decent, what Nature not Luxury requires. And since neither Meat nor Cloaths commend us unto GOD, they'll content themselves with such things as are fit and convenient, without occasioning scruple to themselves or giving any trouble or offence to others. She who considers to how much better account that Money will turn which is bestow'd on the Poor, than that which is laid out in unnecessary Expences on her self, needs no Admonitions against superfluities. . . .

In a word, this happy Society will be but one Body, whose Soul is love, animating and informing it, and perpetually breathing forth it self in flames of holy desires after GOD and acts of Benevolence to each other. Envy and Uncharitableness are the Vices only of little and narrow hearts, and therefore 'tis suppos'd, they will not enter here amongst persons whose Dispositions as well as their Births are to be Generous. Censure will refine into Friendly Admonition, all Scoffing and offensive Railleries will be abominated and banish'd hence, where not only the Words and Actions; but even the very Thoughts and Desires of the *Religious* tend to promote the most endearing Love and universal Good-will. Thus these innocent and holy Souls shou'd run their Race, measuring their hours by their Devotions, and their days by the charitable Works they do. . . .

And to the end that these great designs may be the better pursu'd and effectually obtain'd, care shall be taken that our Religious be under the tuition of persons of irreproachable Lives, of a consummate Prudence, sincere Piety and unaffected Gravity. No Novices in Religion, but such as have spent the greatest part of their lives in the study and practice of Christianity; who have lived *much*, whatever the time of their abode in the world has been. Whose Understandings are clear and comprehensive, as well as their Passions at command and Affections regular, and their Knowledge able to govern their Zeal. Whose scrutiny into their own hearts has been so exact, they fully understand the weaknesses of humane Nature, are able to bear with its defects, and by the most prudent methods procure its Amendment.... Who have the perfect government of themselves, and therefore rule according to Reason not Humour, consulting the good of the Society, not their own arbitrary sway. Yet know how to assert their Authority when there is just occasion for it, and will not prejudice their Charge by an indiscreet remissness and loosning the Reins of discipline. ... And that every one who comes under this holy Roof may be such an amiable, such a charming Creature, what faults they bring with them shall be corrected by sweetness not severity; by friendly Admonitions, not magisterial Reproofs; Piety shall not be roughly impos'd, but wisely insinuated, by a perpetual Display of the Beauties of Religion in an exemplary Conversation, the continual and most powerful Sermon of an holy Life. And since Inclination can't be forc'd, and nothing makes people more uneasy than the fettering themselves with unnecessary Bonds, there shall be no Vows or irrevocable Obligations, not so much as the fear of Reproach to keep our Ladies here any longer than they desire. No: Ev'ry act of our *Religious* Votary shall be voluntary and free, and no other tye but the Pleasure, the Glory and Advantage of this blessed Retirement to confine her to it.

And now I suppose, you'll save me the labour of proving, that this Institution will very much serve the ends of Piety and Charity; it is methinks self-evident, and the very Proposal sufficient proof. But if it will not promote these great ends, I shall think my self mightily oblig'd to him who will shew me what will; for provided the good of my Neighbour be advanc'd, 'tis very indifferent to me whether it be by my method or by anothers. Here will be no impertinent Visits, no foolish Amours, no idle Amusements to distract our Thoughts and waste our precious time; a very little of which is spent in Dressing, that grand devourer and its concomitants, and no more than necessity requires in sleep and eating; so that here's a vast Treasure gain'd, which for ought I know may purchase an happy Eternity. But we need not rest in generals, a cursory view of some particulars will sufficiently demonstrate the great usefulness of such a Retirement; which will appear by observing first a few of those inconveniencies to which Ladies are expos'd by living in the World, and in the next place the positive advantages of a Retreat.

And first, as to the inconviencies of living in the World; no very small one is that strong *Idea* and warm perception it gives us of its Vanities; since these are ever at hand, constantly thronging about us, they must necessarily push aside all other Objects, and the Mind being prepossess'd and gratefully entertain'd with those pleasing Perceptions which external Objects occasion, takes up with them as its only Good, is not at leisure to last those delights which arise from a Reflection on it self, nor to receive the *Ideas* which such a Reflection conveys, and consequently forms all its Notions by such *Ideas* only as it derives from sensation, being unacquainted with those more excellent ones which arise from its own operations and a serious reflection on them, and which are necessary to correct the mistakes and supply the defects of the other. From whence arises a very partial knowledge of things, nay, almost a perfect ignorance in things of the greatest moment. For tho' we are acquainted with the Sound of some certain words, *viz, God, Religion, Pleasure* and *Pain, Honour* and *Dishonour*, and the like; yet having no other *Ideas* but what are convey'd to us by those Trifles we converse with, we frame to our selves strange and awkard notions of them, conformable only to those *Ideas* sensation has furnish'd us with, which sometimes grow so strong and fixt, that 'tis scarce possible to introduce a new Scheme of Thoughts and so to disabuse us, especially whilst these Objects are thick in our way.

Thus she who sees her self and others respected in proportion to that Pomp and Bustle they make in the world, will form her Idea of Honour accordingly. She who has relish'd no Pleasures but such as arise at the presence of outward Objects, will seek no higher than her Senses for her Gratification. And thus we may account for that strange insensibility, that appears in some people when you speak to them of any serious Religious matter.... I have sometimes smil'd betwixt scorn and pity, to hear Women talk as gravely and concernedly about some trifling disappointment from their Milliner or Taylor, as if it had related to the weightiest concerns of their Souls, nay, perhaps more seriously than others who wou'd pass for

Good, do about their eternal Interest; but turn the talk that way, and they grow as heavy and cold as they were warm and sensible before. And whence is this, but because their heads are full of the one, and quite destitute of such Ideas as might give them a competent notion of the other, and therefore to discourse of such matters, is as little to the purpose as to make Mathematical Demonstrations to one who knows not what an Angle or Triangle means. Hence by the way, will appear the great usefulness of judicious Catechizing, which is necessary to form clear Ideas in the mind, without which it can receive but little benefit from the Discourses of the Pulpit, and perhaps the neglect of the former, is the reason that the great plenty of the latter has no better effect. By all which it appears, that if we wou'd not be impos'd on by false Representations and Impostures, if we wou'd obtain a due knowledge of the most important things, we must remove the little Toys and Vanities of the world from us, or our selves from them; enlarge our Ideas, seek out new Fields of knowledge, whereby to rectify our first mistakes.

From the same Original, *viz.* the constant flattery of external Objects, arises that querulousness and delicacy observable in most Persons of fortune, and which betrays them to many inconveniences. For besides that it renders them altogether unfit to bear a change, which considering the great uncertainty and swift vicissitudes of worldly things, the Greatest and most established ought not to be unprepar'd for; it likewise makes them perpetually uneasy, abates the delight of their enjoyments, for such persons will very rarely find all things to their mind, and then some little disorder which others wou'd take no notice of, like an aching Tooth or Toe, spoils the relish of their Joys. And tho' many great Ladies affect this temper, mistaking it for a piece of Grandeur, 'tis so far from that, that it gives evidence of a poor weak Mind, a very childish Humour, that must be cocker'd and fed with Toys and Baubles to still its forwardness, and is like the crazy stomach of a sick Person, which no body has reason to be fond of or desire.

This also disposes them to Inconstancy, for she who is continually supply'd with variety knows not where to fix; a Vice which some Women seem to be proud of, and yet nothing in the world so reproachful and degrading, because nothing is a stronger indication of a weak and injudicious mind. For it supposes us either so ignorant as to make a wrong Choice at first, or else so silly as not to know and stick to it, when we have made a right one. . . .

A constant Scene of Temptations and the infection of ill company, is another great danger which conversing in the world exposes to. 'Tis a dangerous thing to have all the opportunities of sinning in our power, and the danger is increas'd by the ill Precedents we daily see of those who take them. *Liberty* (as somebody says) *will corrupt an Angel*, and tho' it is indeed more glorious to conquer than to fly, yet since our Vertue is so visibly weakned in other instances, we have no reason to presume on't in this. 'Tis become no easy matter to secure our Innocence in our necessary Civilities and daily Conversations, in which if we have the good luck to avoid such as bring a necessity on us, either of seeming rude to them, or of being really so to GOD Almighty, whilst we tamely hear him, our best Friend and Benefactor affronted and swallow it, at the same time, that we wou'd reckon't a very pitiful Spirit to hear an Acquaintance traduc'd and hold our Tongue; yet if we avoid this Trial, our Charity is however in continual danger, Censoriousness being grown so modish, that we can scarce avoid being active or passive in it; so that she who has not her pert jest ready to pass upon others, shall as soon as her back is turn'd become a Jest her self for want of Wit.

In consequence of all this, we are insensibly betray'd to a great loss of time, a Treasure whose value we are too often quite ignorant of till it be lost past redemption. And yet considering the shortness and uncertainty of Life, the great work we have to do, and what advantages accrew to us by a due management of our time, we cannot reconcile it with prudence to suffer the least minute to escape us. . . .

In the last place, by reason of this loss of time and the continual hurry we are in, we can find no opportunities for thoughtfulness and recollection; we are so busied with what passes abroad, that we have no leisure to look at home, nor to rectifie the disorders there. And such an unthinking mechanical way of living, when like Machines we are condemn'd every day to repeat the impertinencies of the day before, shortens our Views, contracts our Minds, exposes to a thousand practical Errors, and renders Improvement impossible, because it will not permit us to consider and recollect, which is the only means to attain it. So much for the inconveniences of living in the World; if we enquire concerning Retirement, we shall find ✓ it does not only remove all these, but brings considerable advantages of its own.

161

For first, it helps us to mate Custom and delivers us from its Tyranny, which is the most considerable thing we have to do, it being nothing else but the habituating our selves to Folly that can reconcile us to it. But how hard is it to quit an old road? What courage as well as prudence does it require? How clear a Judgment to overlook the Prejudices of Education and Example and to discern what is best, and how strong a Resolution notwithstanding all the Scofs and Noises of the world to adhere to it? For Custom has usurpt such an unaccountable Authority, that she who would endeavour to put a stop to its Arbitrary Sway and reduce it to Reason, is in a fair way to render her self the Butt for all the Fops in Town to shoot their impertinent Censures at. And tho' a wise Woman will not value their Censure, yet she cares not to be the subject of their Discourse. The only way then is to retire from the World, as the *Israelites* did out of *Ægypt*, lest the Sacrifice we must make of its Follies shou'd provoke its Spleen.

This also puts us out of the road of Temptation, and very much redeems our Time, cutting off those extravagancies on which so much of it was squandred away before, and furnishing us constantly with good employment, secures us from being seduc'd into bad. . . .

And by that Learning which will be here afforded, and that leisure we have to enquire after it, and to know and reflect on our own minds, we shall rescue our selves out of that woful incogitancy we have slipt into, awaken our sleeping Powers and make use of that reason which GOD has given us. We shall then begin to wonder at our Folly, that amongst all the pleasures we formerly pursued, we never attended to that most noble and delicious one which is to be found in the chase of truth; and bless our selves at last, that our eyes are open'd to discern, how much more pleasantly we may be entertain'd by our own Thoughts, than by all the Diversions which the world affords us. . . . 'Tis a very unseemly thing to jump from our Diversions to our Prayers; as if when we have been entertaining our selves and others with Vanity, we were instantly prepar'd to appear in the sacred presence of GOD. But a Religious Retirement and holy Conversation, will procure us a more serious Temper, a graver Spirit, and so both make us habitually fit to approach, and likewise stir us up to be more careful in our actual preparations when we do. For besides all other improvements of Knowledge, we shall hereby obtain truer Notions of GOD than we were capable of before, which is of very great consequence, since the want of right apprehensions concerning him, is the general cause of Mistakes in Religion, of Errors in Speculation, and Indecorums in Practice; for as GOD is the noblest Object of our Understanding, so nothing is more necessary or of such consequence to us as to busie our thoughts about him. And did we rightly consider his Nature, we shou'd neither dare to forget him, nor draw near to him with unclean hands and unholy hearts.

[A paragraph is omitted here.]

Farther yet, besides that holy emulation which a continual view of the brightest and most exemplary Lives will excite in us, we shall have opportunity of contracting the purest and noblest Friendship; a Blessing, the purchase of which were richly worth all the World besides! For she who possesses a worthy Person, has certainly obtain'd the richest Treasure. . . . Probably one considerable cause of the degeneracy of the present Age, is the little true Friendship that is to be found in it; or perhaps you will rather say that this is the effect of our corruption. The cause and the effect are indeed reciprocal; for were the World better there wou'd be more Friendship, and were there more Friendship we shou'd have a better World. But because *Iniquity abounds*, therefore the *love of many* is not only *waxen cold*, but quite benumb'd and perish'd. But if we have such narrow hearts, be so full of mistaken Self-love, so unreasonably fond of our selves, that we cannot spare a hearty Goodwill to one or two choice Persons, how can it ever be thought, that we shou'd well acquit our selves of that Charity which is due to all Mankind? For Friendship is nothing else but Charity contracted; it is (in the words of an admired Author) a kind of revenging our selves on the narrowness of our Faculties, by exemplifying that extraordinary Charity on one or two, which we are willing, but not able to exercise towards all. And therefore 'tis without doubt the best Instructor to teach us our duty to our Neighbour, and a most excellent Monitor to excite us to make payment as far as our power will reach. . . . That institution therefore must needs be highly beneficial, which both disposes us to be Friends our selves and helps to find them. But by Friendship I do not mean any thing like those intimacies that are abroad in the World, which are often combinations in evil and at best but insignificant dearnesses, as little resembling true Friendship, as modern Practice does Primitive Christianity. But I intend by it the greatest usefulness, the most refin'd and disinteress'd Benevolence, a love that thinks nothing within the bounds of Power and Duty, too much to do or suffer for its Beloved; And makes no distinction betwixt its Friend and its self, except that in Temporals it prefers her interest. But tho' it be very desirable to obtain such a Treasure, such a Medicine of Life as the wise man speaks, yet the danger is great least being deceiv'd in our choice, we suck in Poyson where we expected Health. And considering how apt we are to disguise our selves, how hard it is to know our own hearts much less anothers, it is not advisable to be too hasty in contracting so important a Relation; before that be done, it were well if we could look into the very Soul of the beloved Person, to discover what resemblance it bears to our own, and in this Society we shall have the best opportunities of doing so. There are no Interests here to serve, no contrivances for another to be a stale to; the Souls of all the *Religious* will be open and free, and those particular Friendships must be no prejudice to the general Amity....

But to hasten; such an Institution will much confirm us in Vertue and help us to persevere to the end, and by that substantial Piety and solid knowledge we shall here acquire, fit us to propagate Religion when we return into the World. An habitual Practice of Piety for some years will so root and establish us in it, that Religion will become a second Nature, and we must do strange violences to our selves, if after that we dare venture to oppose it.... And then what a blessed World shou'd we have, shining with so many stars of *Vertue*, who not content to be happy themselves alone, for that's a narrowness of mind too much beneath their God-like temper, would like the glorious Lights of Heaven, or rather like him who made them, diffuse their benign Influences where-ever they come. Having gain'd an entrance into Paradise themselves, they wou'd both shew the way, and invite others to partake of their felicity. In stead of that Froth and Impertinence, that Censure and Pragmaticalness, with which Feminine Conversations so much abound, we should hear their tongues employ'd in making Proselytes to heaven, in running down Vice, in establishing Vertue and proclaiming their Makers Glory. 'Twou'd be more genteel to give and take instructions about the ornaments of the Mind, than to enquire after the Mode; and a Lecture on the Fashions wou'd become as disagreeable as at present any serious discourse is. Not the Follies of the Town, but the Beauties and the Love of JESUS wou'd be the most polite and delicious Entertainments. 'Twould be thought as rude and barbarous to send our Visitors away uninstructed, as our foolishness at present reckons it to introduce a pertinent and useful Conversation. Ladies of Quality ✓ wou'd be able to distinguish themselves from their Inferiors, by the blessings they communicated and the good they did. For this is their grand Prerogative, their *distinguishing Character*, that they are plac'd in a condition which makes that which is every ones *Chief* business, to be their *Only* employ. They have nothing to do but to glorifie GOD, and to benefit their Neighbours, and she who does not thus improve her Talent, is more vile and despicable than the meanest Creature that attends her.

And if after so many Spiritual Advantages, it be convenient to mention Temporals, here Heiresses and Persons of Fortune may be kept secure from the rude attempts of designing Men; And she who has more Money than Discretion, need not curse her Stars for being expos'd a prey to bold importunate and rapacious Vultures. She will not here be inveigled and impos'd on, will neither be bought nor sold, nor be forc'd to marry for her own quiet, when she has no inclination to it, but what the being tir'd out with a restless importunity occasions. Or if she be dispos'd to marry, here she may remain in safety till a convenient Match be offer'd by her Friends, and be freed from the danger of a dishonourable one. Modesty requiring that a Woman should not love before Marriage, but only make choice of one whom she can love hereafter; She who has none but innocent affections, being easily able to fix them where Duty requires.

And though at first I propos'd to my self to speak nothing in particular of the employment of the Religious, yet to give a Specimen how useful they will be to the World, I am now inclin'd to declare, that it is design'd a part of their business shall be to give the best Education to the Children of Persons of Quality, who shall be attended ✓ and instructed in lesser Matters by meaner Persons deputed to that Office, but the forming of their minds shall be the particular care of those of their own Rank, who cannot have a more pleasant and useful employment than to exercise and encrease their own knowledge, by instilling it into these young ones, who are most like to profit under such Tutors. For how can their little Pupils forbear to credit them, since they do not decry the World (as others may be thought to do) because they cou'd not enjoy it, but when they had it in their power, were courted and caress'd by it, for very good Reasons and on mature deliberation, thought fit to relinquish and despise its offers for a better choice? Nor are mercenary people on other accounts capable of doing so much good to young Persons; because having often but short views of things themselves, sordid and low Spirits, they are not like to form a generous temper in the minds of the Educated. Doubtless 'twas well consider'd of him, who wou'd not trust the breeding of his Son to a Slave, because nothing great or excellent could be expected from a person of that condition.

And when by the increase of their Revenue, the *Religious* are enabled to do such a work of Charity, the Education they design to bestow on the Daughters of Gentlemen who are fallen into decay will be no inconsiderable advantage to the Nation. For hereby many Souls will be preserv'd from great Dishonours and put in a comfortable way of subsisting, being either receiv'd into the House if they incline to it, or otherwise dispos'd of. It being suppos'd that prudent Men will reckon the endowments they here acquire a sufficient *Dowry*, and that a discreet and vertuous Gentlewoman will make a better Wife than she whose mind is empty tho' her Purse be full.

But some will say, May not People be good without this confinement? may they not live at large in the World, and yet serve GOD as acceptably as here? 'Tis allow'd they may; truly wise and vertuous Souls will do it by the assistance of GOD's Grace in despite of all temptations; and I heartily wish that all Women were of this temper. But it is to be consider'd, that there are *tender* Vertues who need to be screened from the ill Airs of the World: many persons who had *begun* well might have gone to the Grave in peace and innocence, had it not been their misfortune to be violently tempted. For those who have honest Hearts have not always the strongest Heads; and sometimes the enticements of the World and the subtil insinuations of such as lie in wait to deceive, may make their Heads giddy, stagger their Resolutions, and overthrow all the fine hopes of a promising beginning. 'Tis fit therefore, such tender *Cyons* shou'd be transplanted, that they may be supported by the prop of Vertuous Friendship, and confirm'd in Goodness by holy Examples, which alas! they will not often meet with in the World. And, such is the weakness of humane Nature, bad People are not so apt to be better'd by the Society of the Good, as the Good are to be corrupted by theirs. Since therefore we daily pray against temptation, it cannot be amiss if we take all prudent care to avoid it, and not out of a vain presumption face the danger which GOD may justly permit to overcome us for a due correction of our Pride. . . . Besides, she has need of an establish'd Vertue and consummated Prudence, who so well understands the great end for which she came into the World, and so faithfully pursues it, that not content to be wise and good her self alone, she endeavours to propagate Wisdom and Piety to all within her Sphere; But neither this Prudence nor heroic Goodness are easily attainable amidst the noise and hurry of the world, we must therefore retire a while from its clamour and importunity, if we generously design to do it good, and having calmly and sedately observ'd and rectify'd what is amiss in our selves, we shall be fitter to promote a Reformation in others. A devout Retirement will not only strengthen and confirm our Souls, that they be not infected by the worlds Corruptions, but likewise so purify and refine them, that they will become Antidotes to expel the Poyson in others, and spread a salutary Air on ev'ry Side.

If any object against a Learned Education, that it will make Women vain and assuming, and instead of correcting encrease their Pride: I grant that a smattering in Learning may, for it has this effect on the Men, none so Dogmatical and so forward to shew their Parts as your little *Pretenders* to Science. But I wou'd not have the Ladies content themselves with the *shew*, my desire is, that they shou'd not rest tell they obtain the *Substance*. And then, she who is most knowing will be forward to own with the wise *Socrates* that she knows nothing: nothing that is matter of Pride and Ostentation; nothing but what is attended with so much ignorance and imperfection, that it cannot reasonably elate and puff her up. The more she knows, she will be the less subject to talkativeness and its sister Vices, because she discerns, that the most difficult piece of Learning is to know when to use and when to hold ones Tongue, and never to speak but to the purpose.

But the men if they rightly understand their own interest, have no reason to oppose the ingenious Education of the Women, since 'twou'd go a great way towards reclaiming the men, great is the influence we have over them in their Childhood, in which time if a Mother be discreet and knowing as well as devout, she has many opportunities of giving such a *Form* and *Season* to the tender Mind of the Child, as will shew its good effects thro' all the stages of his Life. But tho' you should not allow her capable of doing *good*, 'tis certain she may do *hurt*: If she do not *make* the Child, she has power to *marr* him, by suffering her fondness to get the better of discreet affection. But besides this, a good and prudent Wife wou'd wonderfully work on an ill man; he must be a Brute indeed, who cou'd hold out against all those innocent Arts, those gentle persuasives and obliging methods she wou'd use to reclaim him. Piety is often offensive when it is accompanied with indiscretion; but she who is as Wise as Good, possesses such Charms as can hardly fail of prevailing. Doubtless her Husband is a much happier Man and more likely to abandon all his ill Courses, than he who has none to come home to, but an ignorant, forward and fantastick Creature. An ingenious Conversation will make his life comfortable, and he who can be so well entertain'd at home, needs not run into Temptations in search of Diversions abroad. The only danger is that the Wife be more knowing than the Husband; but if she be 'tis his own fault, since he wants no opportunities of improvement; unless he be a natural *Block-head*, and then such an one will need a wise Woman to govern him, whose prudence will conceal it from publick Observation, and at once both cover and supply his defects. Give me leave therefore to hope, that no Gentleman who has honourable designs, will hence-forward decry Knowledge and Ingenuity in her he would pretend to Honour; If he does, it may serve for a Test to distinguish the feigned and unworthy from the real Lover.

Now who that has a spark of Piety will go about to oppose so Religious a design? What generous Spirit that has a due regard to the good of Mankind, will not be forward to advance and perfect it? Who will think 500 pounds too much to lay out for the purchase of so much Wisdom and Happiness? Certainly we shou'd not think them too dearly paid for by a much greater Sum, did not our pitiful and sordid Spirits set a much higher value on Money than it deserves. But granting so much of that dear Idol were given away, a person thus bred, will easily make it up by her Frugality & other Vertues; if she bring less, she will not waste so much as others do in superflous and vain Expences. Nor can I think of any expedient so useful as this to Persons of Quality who are over-stock'd with Children, for thus they may honourably dispose of them without impairing their Estates. Five or six hundred pounds may be easily spar'd with a Daughter, when so many thousands would go deep; and yet as the world goes be a very inconsiderable Fortune for Ladies of their Birth, neither maintain them in that *Port* which Custom makes almost necessary, nor procure them an equal Match, those of their own Rank (contrary to the generous custom of the *Germans*) chusing rather to fill their Coffers than to preserve the purity of their Blood, and therefore think a weighty Bag the best Gentility, preferring a wealthy Upstart before the best Descended and best Qualified Lady; their own Extravagancies perhaps having made it necessary, that they may keep up an empty shadow of Greatness, which is all that remains to shew what their Ancestors have been.

Does any think their Money lost to their Families when 'tis put in here? I will only ask what course they can take to save it, and at once to preserve their Money, their Honour and their Daughters too? Were they sure the Ladies wou'd die unmarried, I shou'd commend their Thrift, but Experience has too often shewn us the vanity of this expectation. For the poor Lady having past the prime of her Years in Gaity and Company, in running the Circle of all the Vanities of the Town, having spread all her Nets and us'd all her Arts for Conquest, and finding that the Bait fails where she wou'd have it take; and having all this while been so over-careful of her Body, that she had no time to improve her Mind, which therefore affords her no safe retreat, now she meets with Disappointments abroad, and growing every day more and more sensible, that the respect which us'd to be paid her decays as fast as her Beauty; quite terrified with the dreadful Name of *Old Maid*, which yet none but Fools will reproach her with, nor any wise Woman be afraid of; to avoid this terrible *Mormo*,[1] and the scoffs that are thrown on superanuated Virgins, she flies to some dishonourable Match as her last, tho' much mistaken Refuge, to the disgrace of her Family and her own irreparable Ruin. And now let any Person of Honour tell me, if it were not richly worth some thousand Pounds, to prevent all this mischief, and the having an idle Fellow, and perhaps a race of beggarly Children to hang on him and to provide for?

Cou'd I think of any other Objection I wou'd consider it; there's nothing indeed which witty Persons may not argue *for* and *against*, but they who duly weigh the Arguments on both sides, unless they be extreamly prejudiced, will easily discern the great usefulness of this Institution. The *Beaux* perhaps, and topping Sparks of the Town will ridicule and laugh at it. For Vertue her self as bright as she is, can't escape the lash of scurrilous Tongues; the comfort is, whilst they impotently endeavour to throw dirt on her, they are unable to soil her Beauty, and only defile and render themselves the more contemptible. They may therefore if they please, hug themselves in their own dear folly, and enjoy the diversion of their own insipid Jests. She has but little Wisdom and less Vertue, who is to be frighted from what she judges reasonable, by the scoffs and insignificant noises

---

1   From the Greek *mormŏ* (Xenophon) meaning bugbear.

of ludicrous Wits and pert Buffoons. And no wonder that such as they who have nothing to shew for their pretences to Wit, but some scraps of Plays and blustring Non-sense; who fansie a well adjusted Peruke is able to supply their want of Brains, and that to talk *much* is a sign of Ingenuity, tho't be never so little to the purpose, no wonder that they object against our *Proposal*: 'Twou'd indeed spoil the Trade of the gay fluttering Fops, who wou'd be at a loss, had they no body as impertinent as themselves to talk with. The Criticism of their Dress wou'd be useless, and the labour of their *Valet de Chambre* lost, unless they cou'd peaceably lay aside their Rivalling, and one Ass be content to complement and admire another. For the Ladies wou'd have more discernment than to esteem a Man for such Follies as shou'd rather incline them to scorn and despise him. They wou'd never be so sottish as to imagine, that he who regards nothing but his own brutish Appetite, shou'd have any real affection for them, nor ever expect Fidelity from one who is unfaithful to GOD and his own Soul. They wou'd not be so absurd as to suppose, that Man can esteem them who neglects his Maker; for what are all those fine Idolatries, by which he wou'd recommend himself to his pretended Goddess, but mockery and delusion from him who forgets and affronts the true Deity? They wou'd not value themselves on account of the Admiration of such incompetent Judges, nor consequently make use of those little trifling Arts that are necessary to recommend them to such Admirers; Neither wou'd they give them opportunity to profess themselves their Slaves so long till at last they become their Masters.

What now remains, but to reduce to Practice that which tends so very much to our advantage. Is Charity so dead in the world that none will contribute to the saving their own and their neighbours Souls? Shall we freely expend our Money to purchase Vanity, and often find none for such an eminent good Work, which will make the Ages to come arise and call us Blessed? I wou'd fain persuade my self better things, and that I shall one day see this *Religious Retirement* happily setled, and its great designs wisely and vigorously pursu'd; and methinks I have already a Vision of that lustre and glory our Ladies cast far and near; Let me therefore intreat the rest of our Sex, who tho' at liberty in the world, are the miserable Slaves of their own vile affections, let me intreat them to lay aside their Prejudices and whatever borders on Envy and Malice, and with impartial eyes to behold the Beauties of our *Religious*. The native innocency and unaffectedness of whose Charms, and the unblameable Integrity of their Lives, are abundantly more taking than all the curious Artifices and studied Arts the other can invent to recommend them, even bad men themselves being Judges, who often betray a secret Veneration for that vertue they wou'd seem to despise and endeavour to corrupt. . . .

There is a sort of Bravery and Greatness of Soul, which does more truly ennoble us than the highest Title, and it consists in living up to the dignity of our Natures, being so sensible of our own worth as to think our selves too great to do a degenerate and unbecoming thing; in passing indifferently thro' Good and Evil Fortune, without being corrupted by the one or deprest by the other. For she that can do so, gives evidence that her Happiness depends not on so mutable a thing as this World; but, in a due subserviency to the Almighty, is bottom'd only on her own great Mind. This is the richest Ornament, and renders a Woman glorious in the lowest Fortune. So shining is real worth, that like a Diamond it loses not its lustre tho' cast on a Dunghill. Whereas, she who is advanc'd to some eminent Station and wants this natural and solid Greatness, is no better than Fortunes *May-game*, rendered more conspicuous that she may appear the more contemptible. Let those therefore who value themselves only on external accomplishments, consider how liable they are to decay, and how soon they may be depriv'd of them, and that supposing they shou'd continue, they are but sandy Foundations to build Esteem upon. What a disappointment will it be to a Ladies Admirer as well as to her self, that her Conversation shou'd lose or endanger the Victory her eyes had gain'd! For when the Passion of a Lover is Exchang'd for the Indifference of a Husband, and a frequent review has lessen'd the wonder which her Charms at first had rais'd, she'll retain no more than such a formal respect as decency and good breeding will require, and perhaps hardly that, but unless he be a very good man (and indeed the world is not over full of 'em) her worthlessness has made a forfeit of his Affections, which are seldom fixt by any other thing than Veneration and Esteem. Whereas a wise and good Woman is useful and valuable in all Ages and Conditions: she who chiefly attends the *one thing needful*, the *good part which shall not be taken from her*, lives a cheerful and pleasant Life, innocent and sedate, calm and tranquil, and makes a glorious Exit; being translated from the most happy life on Earth, to unspeakable happiness in Heaven; a fresh and fragrant Name embalming her Dust, and extending its Perfume to succeeding Ages. Whilst the Fools, and the worst sort of them the wicked, live as well as die in Misery, go out in a snuff, leaving nothing but stench and putrefaction behind them.

To close all, if this *Proposal* which is but a rough draught and rude Essay, and which might be made much more beautiful by a better Pen, give occasion to wiser heads to improve and perfect it, I have my end. For imperfect as it is, it seems so desirable, that she who drew the Scheme is full of hopes, it will not want kind hands to perform and compleat it. But if it miss of that, it is but a few hours thrown away, and a little labour in vain, which yet will not be lost, if what is here offer'd may serve to express her hearty Good-will, and how much she desires your Improvement, who is Ladies, *Your very humble Servant.*

Excerpts from, *A Serious Proposal to the Ladies, Part II: Wherein a Method is offer'd for the Improvement of their Minds*, 1697

[Part I of *A Serious Proposal*, 1694, had got a favourable reception, but this was not enough to satisfy Mary Astell. She would rather have had her proposal condemned, she said, 'than to find it receiv'd with some Approbation, and yet no body endeavouring to put it in Practice'.]

From '*The Introduction*, Containing a farther Perswasive to the Ladies to endeavour the Improvement of their Minds.'

pp.4–7 Why won't you begin to think, and no longer dream away your Time in a wretched incogitancy? Why does not a generous Emulation fire your Hearts and inspire you with Noble and Becoming Resentments? The Men of Equity are so just as to confess the errors which the Proud and Inconsiderate had imbib'd to your prejudice, and that if you allow them the preference in Ingenuity, it is not because you *must*, but because you *will*. Can you be in Love with servitude and folly? Can you dote on a mean, ignorant and ignoble Life? An Ingenious Woman is no Prodigy to be star'd on, for you have it in your power to inform the World, that you can every one of you be so, if you please yourselves. It is not enough to wish and to would it, or t'afford a faint Encomium upon what you

173

pretend is beyond your Power; Imitation is the heartiest Praise you can give, and is a Debt which Justice requires to be paid to every worthy Action. ...If you *approve*, why don't you *follow*? And if you *Wish*, why shou'd you not *Endeavour*?...

...Are you afraid of being out of the ordinary way and therefore admir'd and gaz'd at? Admiration does not use to be uneasy to our Sex, a great many Vanities might be spar'd if we consulted only our own conveniency and not other peoples Eyes and Sentiments:... Why should not we assert our Liberty, and not suffer every Trifler to impose a Yoke of Impertinent Customs on us?... she shall never do any thing Praiseworthy and excellent who is not got above unjust Censures, and too steady and well resolv'd to be sham'd from her Duty by the empty Laughter of such as have nothing but airy Noise and Confidence to recommend them....

Is it the difficulty of attaining the Bravery of the Mind, the Labour and Cost that keeps you from making a purchase of it? Certainly they who spare neither Money nor Pains t'obtain a gay outside and make a splendid appearance, who can get over so many difficulties, rack their brains, lay out their time and thoughts in contriving, stretch their Relations Purses in procuring, nay and rob the very Poor, to whom the Overplus of a full Estate, after the owners Necessaries and decent Conveniencies according to her Quality are supplied, is certainly due, they who can surmount so many difficulties, cannot have the face to pretend any here. Labour is sweet when there's hope of success....

pp.9–10   I'me unwilling to believe there are any among you who are obstinately bent against what is praiseworthy in themselves, and Envy or Detract from it in others; who won't allow any of their Sex a capacity to write Sense, because they want it, or exert their Spleen where they ought to show their Kindness or Generous Emulation; who sicken at their Neighbours Virtues, or think anothers Praises a lessening of their Character; or meanly satisfie ill-nature by a dull Malicious Jest at what deserves to be approv'd and imitated....

pp.15–18   They think they've been bred up in Idleness and Impertinence, and study will be irksome to them, who have never employ'd their mind to any good purpose, and now when they wou'd they want the method of doing it; They have been barbarously us'd, their Education and greatest Concerns neglected, whilst their imprudent Parents and Guardians were busied in managing their Fortunes and regulating their Mien; who so their Purse was full and their outside plausible, matter'd not much the poverty and narrowness of their minds, have taught them perhaps to repeat their Catechism and a few good Sentences, to read a Chapter and *say* their Prayers, tho' perhaps with as little Understanding as a Parrot, and fancied this was Charm enough to secure them against the temptations of the present world and to waft them to a better; and so through want of use and by misapplying their Thoughts to trifles and impertinencies, they've perhaps, almost lost those excellent Capacities which probably were afforded them by nature for the highest things ... But let me intreat them to consider that there's no Ignorance so shameful, no Folly so absurd as that which refuses Instruction, be it upon what account it may. All good Persons will pity not upbraid their former unhappiness, as not being their own but other Peoples fault; whereas they themselves are responsible if they continue it, since that's an Evidence that they are silly and despicable, not because they *cou'd* not, but because they *wou'd* not be better Informed. But where is the shame of being taught? for who is there that does not need it? Alas, Human Knowledge is at best defective, and always progressive, so that she who knows the most has only this advantage, that she has made a little more speed than her Neighbours....

pp.20–1   And having (in the former essay) assign'd the reasons why they are so little improv'd, ... which reasons are chiefly Ill-nurture, Custom, loss of Time, the want of Retirement, or of knowing how to use it, so that by the disuse of our Faculties we seem to have lost them if we ever had any; ... we then proceeded to propose a Remedy for those Evils ... it was in general propos'd to acquaint them with Judicious Authors, give them opportunity of Retirement and Recollection and put them in a way of Ingenious Conversation, whereby they might enlarge their prospect, rectify their false Ideas, form in their Minds adequate conceptions of the End and Dignity of their Natures, not only have the Name and common Principles of Religion floating in their Heads and sometimes running out at their Mouths, but understand the design and meaning of it, and have a just apprehension, a lively sentiment of its Beauties and Excellencies; ....

From '*The Second Part of the Proposal to the Ladies*'

pp.35–7   The first thing I shall advise against is Sloth, and what may be joyn'd with it a stupid Indifference to any thing that is excellent; shall I call it Contentedness with our Condition how low and imperfect soever it be? I will not abuse the Word so much, 'tis rather an ungenerous inglorious Laziness, we doze on in a Circle with our Neighbours, and so we get but Company and Idleness enough, we consider not for what we were made, and what the Condition of our present State requires. And we think our selves good humble Creatures for this, who busy not our Heads with what's out of our Sphere and was never design'd for us, but acquiesce honestly and contentedly in such Employments as the generality of Women have in all Ages been engaged in: for why shou'd we think so well of our selves as to fancy we can be wiser and better than those who have gone before? . . .

p.64   Truths merely Speculative and which have no influence upon Practice, which neither contribute to the good of Soul or Body, are but idle Amusements, an impertinent and criminal wast of Time. To be able to speak many Languages, to give an Historical Account of all Ages Opinions and Authors, to make a florid Harangue, or defend right or wrong the Argument I've undertaken, may give me higher thoughts of my Self but not of God. . . .

pp.123–4   GOD does nothing in vain, he gives no Power or Faculty which he has not allotted to some proportionate use, if therefore he has given to Mankind a Rational Mind, every individual Understanding ought to be employ'd in somewhat worthy of it. The Meanest Person shou'd think as *Justly*, tho' not as *Capaciously*, as the greatest Philosopher. And if the Understanding be made for the Contemplation of Truth, and I know not what else it can be made for, either there are many Understandings who are never able to attain what they were design'd and fitted for, which is contrary to the Supposition that God made nothing in Vain, or else the very meanest must be put in a way of attaining it: Now how can this be if all that which goes to the composition of a Knowing Man in th'account of the World, be necessary to make one so? All have not leisure to Learn Languages and pore on Books, nor Opportunity to Converse with the Learned; but all may *Think*, may use their own Faculties rightly, and consult the Master who is within them.

pp.202–3   I am therefore far from designing to put Women on a vain pursuit after unnecessary and useless Learning, nor wou'd by any means persuade them to endeavour after Knowledge cou'd I be convinced that it is improper for 'em. Because I know very well that tho' a thing be never so excellent in it self, it has but an ill grace if it be not suitable to the Person and Condition it is apply'd to. Fine Cloaths and Equipage do not become a Beggar, and a Mechanic who must work for daily bread for his Family, wou'd be wickedly Employ'd shou'd he suffer 'em to starve whilest he's solving Mathematical Problems. If therefore Women have another Duty incumbent on 'em, and such as is inconsistent with what we here advise, we do ill to take them from it: But to affirm this is to beg the Question, and it is what I will never grant till it be better prov'd than as yet it appears to be. For if the Grand Business that Women as well as Men have to do in this World be to prepare for the next, ought not all their Care and Industry to Centre here? And since the matter is of Infinite Consequence is it equitable to deny 'em the use of any help? If therefore Knowledge were but any ways Instrumental, tho' at the remotest distance, to the Salvation of our Souls, it were fit to apply ourselves to it;

p.205 ...So it cannot be thought sufficient that Women shou'd but just know whats Commanded and what Forbid, without being inform'd of the Reasons why, since this is not like to secure them in their Duty. For we find a Natural Liberty within us which checks at an Injunction that has nothing but Authority to back it;

pp.209–12   As unnecessary as it is thought for Women to have Knowledge she who is truly good finds very great use of it not only in the Conduct of her own Soul but in the management of her Family, in the Conversation of her Neighbours and in all Concerns of Life. Education of Children is a most necessary Employment, perhaps the chief of those who have any; But it is as Difficult as it is Excellent when well perform'd; and I question not but that the mistakes which are made in it, are a principal Cause of that Folly and Vice, which is so much complain'd of and so little mended. Now this, at least the foundation of it, on which in a great measure the success of all depends, shou'd be laid by the Mother, for Fathers find other Business, they will not be confin'd to such a laborious work, they have not such opportunities of observing a Child's Temper, nor are the greatest part of 'em like to do much good, since Precepts contradicted by Example, seldom prove effectual. Neither are Strangers so proper for it, because hardly any thing besides Paternal Affection can sufficiently quicken the Care of performing, and sweeten the labour of such a task. But Tenderness alone will never discharge it well, she who wou'd do it to purpose must thoroughly understand Human nature, know how to manage different Tempers Prudently, be Mistress of her own, and able to bear with all the little humours and follies of Youth, neither Severity nor Lenity are to be always us'd, it wou'd ruin some to be treated in that manner which is fit for others. As Mildness makes some ungovernable, and as there is a stupor in many from which nothing but Terrors can rouse them, so sharp Reproofs and Solemn Lectures serve to no purpose but to harden others, in faults from which they might be won by an agreeable Address and tender application.

Nor will Knowledge lie dead upon their hands who have no Children to Instruct; the whole World is a single Lady's Family, her opportunities of doing good are not lessen'd but encreas'd by her being unconfin'd. Particular Obligations do not contract her Mind, but her Beneficence moves in the largest Sphere. And perhaps the Glory of Reforming this Prophane and Profligate Age is reserv'd for you Ladies, and that the natural and unprejudic'd Sentiments of your Minds being handsomely express'd, may carry a more strong conviction than the Elaborate Arguments of the Learned.

p.279 No discouragements shou'd shock us, no ungrateful returns shou'd sower our Temper, but we must expect and be prepar'd to bear many repulses and wild disorders, and patiently sustain that greatest uneasiness to a Christian Mind, the bitter appearance that our Hopes are lost, and that all the Labour of our Love is ineffectual! We must abound both in Good Nature and Discretion, and not seldom make use of quite contrary Means to bring about the End we aim at.

pp.284–6 It is not my intention that you shou'd seclude yourselves from the World. I know it is necessary that a great number of you shou'd live in it; but it is Unreasonable and Barbarous to drive you into't, e're you are capable of doing Good in it, or at least of keeping Evil from yourselves. Nor am I so fond of my Proposal, as not to lay it aside very willingly did I think you cou'd be sufficiently serv'd without it. But since such Seminaries are thought proper for the men, since they enjoy the fruits of those Noble Ladies Bounty who were the foundresses of several of their Colleges, why should we not think that such ways of Education wou'd be as advantageous to the Ladies or why shou'd we despair of finding some among them who will be as kind to their own Sex as their Ancestors have been to the other? ...They must either be very Ignorant or very Malicious who pretend that we wou'd imitate Foreign Monastries, or object against us the Inconveniencies that they are subject to;

a little attention to what they read might have convinc'd them that our Institution is rather *Academical* than *Monastic* . . . So that it is altogether beside the purpose to say 'tis too Recluse, or prejudicial to an Active Life; 'tis as far from that as a Lady's Practising at home is from being a hindrance to her dancing at Court. For an Active Life consists not barely in *Being in the World*, but in *doing much Good in it*. And therefore it is fit we Retire a little, to furnish our Understandings with useful Principles, to set our Inclinations right, and to manage our Passions, and when this is well done, but not till then, we may safely venture out.

pp.287–8   She who makes the most Grimace at a Woman of Sense, who employs all her little skill in endeavouring to render Learning and Ingenuity ridiculous, is yet very desirous to be thought Knowing in a Dress, in the Management of an Intreague, in Coquetry or good Houswifry. . . .

pp.290–1   The Men therefore may still enjoy their Prerogatives for us, we mean not to intrench on any of their Lawful Privileges . . . They may busy their Heads with Affairs of State, and spend their Time and Strength in recommending themselves to an uncertain Master, or a more giddy Multitude, our only endeavour shall be to be absolute Monarchs in our own Bosoms. They shall still if they please dispute about Religion, let 'em give us leave to Understand and Practise it. And whilst they have unrival'd the Glory of speaking as *many* Languages as *Babel* afforded, we only desire to express ourselves Pertinently and Judiciously in *One*. We will not vie with them in thumbing over Authors, nor pretend to be walking Libraries, provided they'll but allow us a competent Knowledge of the Books of God, Nature I mean and the Holy Scriptures: And whilst they accomplish themselves with the Knowledge of the World, and experiment all the Pleasures and Follies of it, we'll aspire no further than to be intimately acquainted with our own Hearts. And sure the Complaisant and Good natur'd Sex will not deny us this; nor can they who are so well assur'd of their own Merit entertain the least Suspicion that we shall overtop them. It is upon some other account therefore that they object against our Proposal. . . .

PART III
LOVE AND FRIENDSHIP,
FAITH AND REASON

Excerpts from *A Collection of Poems humbly presented and Dedicated to the most Reverend Father in God William by Divine Providence Lord Archbishop of Canterbury etc.*, 1689[1]

May it please your Grace

Next to the committing of a Crime, the doing of that which stands in need of an Apology, has ever been most disagreeable to me. But since we cannot command our own circumstances, and are therefore sometimes inforced to do, not as we would but as we can; this, tho it will not excuse us in the commission of an evil may be allowed to Apologise for a less proper and less becoming Action. Of which sort your Grace may justly reckon, this my repeated boldness and importunity, as I must needs confess it in a person of my sex, and meanness, to intrude into so venerable a presence, with nothing else to recommend me but a few trifles, which even themselves stand in need of an excuse. It is not without pain and reluctancy, that I break from my beloved obscurity, (which is so agreeable to my temper and proper for my sex,) to expose to so

---

1   This *Collection of Poems* sent to Archbishop Sancroft comes from Rawlinson MSS. poet. 154:50 in the Bodleian Library. Their authenticity is clear from a comparison of the handwriting with that of Mary Astell's signed letter to Dr. Dodwell of March 11th, 1705/6 (See MS.Eng.Letters. C28) They have not been published before but see Ruth Perry, *A 17th Century Feminist Poet*, in the T.L.S., 20.8.82 where Stanza IV of the first poem appears. This collection was apparently one of two sent to Sancroft. The second, however is undated, so it may have preceded that of 1689.

judicious a Censure, those mean productions which a little reading, a small experience, and smaller fancy, has made shift to bring forth; and yet I may say as David did in another case is there not a Cause? Not to mention what your Grace does not love to hear, but what I must always remember with Honour and Veneration, that real worth (and not only external Greatness) which is the true motive to veneration and esteem: Permit me to say, that the Condiscention and Candor, with which your Grace was pleased to receive a poor unknown, who hath no place to fly unto, and none that careth for her Soul, when even my Kinsfolk had failed, and my familiar Friends had forgotten me; this my Lord, hath emboldened me to make an humble tender of another offering which tho but of Goats hair and Badger Skins, is the best I have to give, and therefore I hope may not be altogether unacceptable.

May your Grace be pleased to receive it with your wonted Charity and Goodness, and pass a favourable censure upon the failure of a Woman's pen, who would very thankfully be informed of her errours and amend them; and permit me with all Humility to profess myself

My Lord,
    Your Graces
    Most humble, thankfull,
    and obedient Servant,
        M.A.

In Emulation of Mr. Cowley's Poem call'd the Motto Jan 7, 1687/8

I

What shall I do? not to be Rich or Great,
  Not to be courted and admir'd,
  With Beauty blest, or Wit inspir'd,
Alas! these merit not my care and sweat,
  These cannot my Ambition please,
My high born Soul shall never stoop to these,
But something I would be that's truly great
In 'ts self, and not by vulgar estimate.

II

If this low World were always to remain,
  If th'old Philosphers were in the right
  Who wou'd not then, with all their might
Study and strive to get themselves a name?
  Who wou'd in soft repose lie down,
Or value ease like being ever known?
But since Fames trumpet has so short a breath,
Shall we be fond of that which must submit to Death?

III

Nature permits not me the common way,
  By serving Court, or State, to gain
  That so much valu'd trifle, Fame;
Nor do I covet in Wit's Realm to sway:
  But O ye bright illustrious few,
What shall I do to be like some of you?
Whom this misjudging World dos underprize,
Yet are most dear in Heav'ns all-righteous eyes!

IV

How shall I be a Peter or a Paul?
  That to the Turk and Infidel,
  I might the joyfull tydings tell,
And spare no labour to convert them all:
  But ah my sex denies me this,

185

And Mary's Priviledge I cannot wish;
Yet hard I hear my dearest Saviour say,
They are more blessed who his Word obey.

V

Up then my sluggard Soul, Labour and Pray,
   For if with Love enflam'd thou be,
   Thy Jesus will be born in thee,
And by thy ardent Prayers thou can'st make way,
   For their Conversion whom thou may'st not teach,
Yet by a good Example always Preach:
And tho' I want a Persecuting Fire,
I'll be at lest a Martyr in desire.

Solitude   Ap.8.1684

I
Now I with gen'rous Cowley* see,
This trifling World and I shall ne're agree.
Nature in business me no share affords,
And I no business find in empty words:
   I dare not all the morning spend
   To dress my body, and not lend
A minuit to my Soul, nor can think fit,
To sell the Jewel for the Cabinet.

II
My unpolish'd converse Ladies fly,
'Twill make you dull, I have no railery,
I cannot learn the fashionable art,
To laugh at Sin, and censure true desert.
   Alas I no experience have,
   With my weak eyes to make a slave,
Nor am I practis'd in that am'rous flame,
Which has so long usurpt Loves sacred name.

III
No satisfaction can I find
In balls and revelling, my thinking mind,
Can't reconcile 'em with a mournfull Spirit,
Nor with the solid comfort they'l inherit
   Who here love sorrows; Complement
   I am as guiltless of as paint,
No fucus[1] for my mind or face I use,
Nor am acquainted with the modern Muse.

IV
O happy Solitude, may I
My time with thee, and some good books employ!
No idle visits rob me of an hour,
No impertinents those precious drops devour.
   Thus blest, I shall while here below
   Antedate Heav'n; did Monarchs know
What 'tis with God, and Cherubims to dwell,
With Charles[2] they'd leave their Empires for a Cell.

*See Cowley's The Wish.
1   Fucus = cosmetic.   2   Charles V. abdicated 1555.

[Untitled Poem]

I

Awake my Lute, daughters of Musick come,
To Allelujahs tune my tongue,
My heart already hath the Canticle begun:
And leaps for Joy, because its business is
In a better world than this.
Blessed be God and evermore extoll'd,
Who wou'd not let me fetter'd be with Gold:
Nor to a dang'rous World expose weak me,
By giving opportunitie
For ev'ry sin, which wanton appetite
Too easily can entertain,
Nor needs temptations to invite;
Did we but know the secret bane,
The perdue poyson, hidden aconite,
Which Riches do infold,
Not all its charms, nor all its shining would
Persuade us to the Love of Gold.
Happy am I who out of danger sit,
Can see and pitty them who wade thro it;
Need take no thought my treasure to dispose,
What I ne'er had I cannot fear to lose:
Nor am concern'd what I must wear or buy,
To shew my plenty and my vanity.

II

From my secure and humble seat,
I view the ruins of the Great.
And dare look back on my expired days,
To my low state there needs no shameful ways.
O how uneasy shou'd I be,
If tied to Custom and formalitie,
Those necessary evils of the Great,
Which bind their hands, and manacle their feet.
Nor Beauty, Parts, nor Portion are expose
My most beloved Liberty to lose.
And thanks to Heav'n my time is all my own;
I when I please can be alone;

Nor Company, nor Courtship steal away
That treasure they can ne're repay.
No Flatterers, no Sycophants,
My dwelling haunts,
Nor am I troubl'd with impertinents.
Nor busy days, nor sleepless nights infest
My Quiet mind, nor interrupt my rest.
My Honour stands not 'on such a ticklish term
That ev'ry puff of air can do it harm.
But these are blessings I had never known,
Had I been great, or seated near a Throne.
My God, forever blessed be thy name!
That I'me no darling in the list of Fame.
While the large spreading Cedars of the Wood,
Are by their eminence expos'd to storms,
I who beneath their observation stood,
Am undisturb'd with such alarms.
None will at me their sharp detractions throw,
Or strive to make me less who am already low.

III

I thank thee Lord that I am Friendless too,
Tho that alas be hard to do!
Tho I have wearied Heav'n with Prayers,
And fill'd its bottles with my tears.
Tho I always propos'd the noblest end,
Thy glory in a Friend
And never any earthly thing requir'd,
But this thats better part divine,
And for that reason was so much desir'd;
Yet humbly I submit,
To that most perfect will of thine,
And thank thee cause thou hast denied me it.
Thrice blessed be thy Jealousie,
Which wou'd not part
With one small corner of my heart,
But hast engross'd it all to Thee!
Thou would'st not let me ease my burthens here,
Which none on Earth cou'd bear,
Nor in anothers troubles share;

O sweet exchange thy Joys are mine,
And thou hast made my sorrows thine.
Now absence will not break my heart,
Jesus and I can never part,
By night, or day, by Land, or sea,
His right hand shades, his left hands under me,
Nor shall I need to shed a tear,
Because my Friend is dead or I must leave her here.

IV

If I can thank for this, what cannot I
Receive with chearful mind, and perfect joy?
No want so sharply doth affect the heart,
No loss nor sickness causeth such a smart,
No racks nor tortures so severely rend,
As the unkindness of a darling Friend.
Yet ev'n this bitter pil has done me good,
Without it I had hardly understood,
The baseness which attends
On ev'ry sin, because it is
Ingratitude and black perfidiousness,
To thee my God the best of Friends.
Thus by th'assistance of thy grace,
Joyn'd with a lively Faith, and honest mind,
In most untastfull things I pleasure find,
And beauty in the darkest sorrows face.
The eater brings forth meat, the strong affords
Like Samson's Lion, sweetness to thy Servants boards.
Who has the true Elixir, may impart
Pleasure to all he touches, and convert
The most unlikely grief to Happiness.
Vertue this true Elixir is,
'Tis only Vertue this can do,
And with this choicest Priviledge invest,
Can make us truly happy now,
And afterwards for ever blest.

Excerpts from *Letters concerning the Love of God,* between the Author of *The Proposal to the Ladies* and Mr. John Norris[1]

From '*To the Reader*'

The Letters here laid open to thy View are a late Correspondence between myself and a Gentlewoman, and to add to thy Wonder, a young Gentlewoman. Her Name I have not the Liberty to publish. For her Person, as her Modesty will not suffer me to say much of her, so the present Productions of her Pen make it utterly needless to say anything, unless it be by way of Prevention to obviate a Diffidence in some who from the surprising Excellency of these Writings may be tempted to question whether my Correspondent be really a Woman or no. To whom my Answer is, that indeed I did not see her write these Letters, but that I have all the moral and reasonable Assurance that she did write them, and is the true Author of them, that can be had in a thing of this Nature, and I hope my Credit may be good enough with those that know me to be believed upon my serious Word where there is no other Satisfaction to be given.

From '*The Preface*'

[Mary Astell's Letter replying to Norris's appeal to her to agree

---

1   Published by J. Norris, Rector of Bemerton nr. Sarum, 1695

191

to publish the Letters. Having suggested Norris publish his own letters which would stand by themselves, she goes on:]

I cannot imagine to what Purpose mine will serve, unless it be to decoy those to a Perusal of them, who wanting Piety to read a Book for its Usefulness, may probably have the Curiosity to inquire what can be the Product of a Woman's Pen, and to excite a generous Emulation in my Sex, persuade them to leave their insignificant Pursuits for Employments worthy of them. For if one to whom Nature has not been over liberal, and who has found but little Assistance to surmount its Defects, by employing her Faculties the right way, and by a moderate Industry in it, is inabled to write tolerable Sense, what may not they perform who enjoy all that Quickness of Parts and other Advantages which she wants? And I heartily wish they would make the Experiment, so far am I from coveting the Fame of being singular, that 'tis my very great Trouble it should be any bodies Wonder to meet with an Ingenious Woman.

If therefore you over-rule me, and resolve to have these Papers go abroad, it shall be on these Conditions; first, that you make no mention of my Name, no not so much as the initial Letters; and next, that you dedicate them to a Lady whom I shall name to you,[1] or else give me leave to do it. For though none can be less fond of Dedications, or has so little Ambition to be known to those who are called great, yet out of the Regard I owe to the Glorious Author of all Perfection I cannot but pay a very great Respect to one who so nearly resembles him ... One whom now we have duly stathe [?stated] the Measures, I may venture to say, I love with the greatest Tenderness, for all must love her who have any Esteem for Unfeigned Goodness, who value an early Piety and eminent Virtue.... A Lady, whom for the good of our Sex I would endeavour to describe, were I capable to write the Character of a compleat and finished Person; but it requires a Soul as bright, as lovely, as refined as her Ladyships, to give an exact Description of such Perfections! A Lady who dedicates that Part of her Life intirely to her Maker's Service, which the generality think too short to serve themselves. Who in the Bloom of her Years, despising the Temptations of Birth and Beauty, and whatever may withdraw her from *Mary's* noble Choice, has made such Advances in Religion, that if she hold on at this rate, she'll quickly outstrip our Theory, and oblige the World with what was never more wanted

1   Lady Catherine Jones. See Introduction pp.9–10.

than now, an exact and living Transcript of Primitive Christianity. So good she is that even Envy itself has never a *But* to interfere with her Praises, and though women are not forward to commend one another, yet I never met with any that had seen or heard of her, who did not willingly pay their Eulogies to this admirable Person, and if Praise be due to any Mortal, doubtless she may lay the greatest Claim to it. But not to relie wholly on Report, I my self have observed in her so much Sweetness and Modesty, so free from the least Tincture of Vanity, so insensible of that Worth which all the World admires; such a constant and regular Attendance on the publick Worship of GOD, Prayers and Sacraments; such a serious, reverent and unaffected Devotion, so fervent and so prudent, so equally composed of Heat and Light, so removed from all Formality, and the Extremes of Coldness and Enthusiasme, as gave me a lively Idea of Apostolical Piety, and made me every Time I prayed by her, fancy my self in the Neighbourhood of Seraphick Flames! But ... my Expressions are too flat, my Colours too dead to draw such a lovely Piece! Would to GOD we would all transcribe, not this imperfect Copy, but that incomparable Original she daily gives us; that Ladies may be at last convinced that the Beauty of the Mind is the most charming Amiableness, because most lasting and most divine, and that no Ornaments are so becoming to a Lady as the Robe of Righteousness and the Jewels of Piety.

From Letter I

To Mr. Norris,
Sir,
Though some morose Gentlemen wou'd perhaps remit me to the Distaff or Kitchin, or at least to the Glass and the Needle, the proper Employments as they fancy of a Woman's Life; yet expecting better things from the more Equitable and Ingenious Mr. *Norris*, who is not so narrow-Soul'd as to confine Learning to his own Sex, or to envy it in ours, I presume to beg his Attention a little to the Impertinencies of a Woman's Pen. And indeed Sir, there is some reason why I, though a Stranger, should Address to you for the Resolution of my Doubts and Information of my Judgement, since you have increased my Natural Thirst for Truth, and set me up for a *Virtuoso*. For though I can't pretend to a Multitude of Books,

Variety of Languages, the Advantages of Academical Education, or any Helps but what my own Curiosity afford; yet, *Thinking* is a Stock that no Rational Creature can want, if they know how to use it; . . ..

Reading the other day the Third Volume of your Excellent Discourses[1] . . . . a difficulty arose which without your assistance I know not how to solve.

Methinks there is all the reason in the World to conclude, *That God is the only efficient Cause of all our Sensations*; and you have made it as clear as the Day; and it is equally clear from the Letter of the Commandment, *That God is not only the Principal, but the sole Object of our Love*: But the reason you assign for it, namely, *Because he is the only efficient Cause of our Pleasure*, seems not equally clear. For if we must Love nothing but what is Lovely, and nothing is Lovely but what is our Good, and nothing is our Good but what does us Good, and nothing does us Good but what causes Pleasure in us; may we not by the same way of arguing say, That which causes Pain in us does not do us Good, (for nothing you say does us Good but what Causes Pleasure) and therefore can't be our Good, and if not our Good then not Lovely and consequently not the proper, much less the only Object of our Love? Again, if the Author of our Pleasure, be upon that account the only Object of our Love, then by the same reason the Author of our Pain can't be the Object of our Love; and if both these Sensations be produced by the same Cause, then that Cause is at once the Object of our Love, and of our Aversion; for it is as natural to avoid and fly from Pain, as it is to follow and pursue Pleasure?

So that if these Principles, viz., *That God is the Efficient Cause of our Sensations* (Pain as well as Pleasure) *and that he is the only Object of our Love*, be firm and true, as I believe they are; it will then follow, either that the being the Cause of our Pleasure is not the true and proper Reason why that Cause should be the Object of our Love, (for the Author of our Pain has as good a Title to our Love as the Author of our Pleasure;) Or else, if nothing be the Object of our Love but what does us Good, then something else does us Good besides what causes Pleasure? Or to speak more properly, the Causes of all our Sensations, Pain as well as Pleasure being the only Object of our Love, and nothing being Lovely but

---

1   John Norris, *Practical Discourses on several Divine Subjects*, Vol.3, 1693.

what does us Good, consequently, that which Causes Pain does us Good as well as that which Causes Pleasure; and therefore it can't be true, That nothing does us Good but what causes Pleasure.'....

From Letter III

Permit me to add a Word or two more which is a greater Concernment to me because of practical Consideration; you have fully convinc'd me that God is the only proper Object of my Love, and I am sensible 'tis the highest Injustice to him and Unkindness to my self to defraud him of the least Part of my Heart; but I find it more easie to recognise his Right than to secure the Possession. Though I often say in your Pathetick and Divine Words, *No, my fair Delight, I will never be drawn off from the Love of Thee by the Charms of any of thy Creatures*, yet alas, *sensible* Beauty does too often press upon my Heart, whilst *intelligible* is disregarded. For having by Nature a strong Propensity to friendly Love, which I have all along encouraged as a good Disposition to Vertue, and do still think it so if it may be kept within the due Bounds of Benevolence. But having likewise thought till you taught me better, that I need not cut off all Desire from the Creature, provided it were in Subordination to, and for the sake of the Creator: I have contracted such a Weakness, I will not say by Nature (for I believe Nature is often very unjustly blam'd for what is owing to *Will* and *Custom*) but by voluntary Habit, that it is a very difficult thing for me to love at all, without something of Desire. Now I am loath to abandon all Thoughts of Friendship, both because it is one of the brightest Virtues, and because I have the noblest Designs in it. Fain wou'd I rescue my Sex, or at least as many of them as come within my little Sphere, from that meanness of Spirit into which the Generality of 'em are sunk, perswade them to pretend some higher Excellency than a well-chosen Pettycoat, or a fashionable Commode; and not wholly lay out their Time and Care in the Adoration of their Bodies, but bestow a Part of it at least on the Embellishment of their Minds, since inward Beauty will last when outward is decayed. But though I can say without boasting that none ever loved more generously than I have done, yet perhaps never any met with more ungrateful Returns which I can attribute to nothing so much as the kindness of my best Friend, who saw how apt my Desires were to stray from him, and therefore

195

by these frequent Disappointments would have me learn more Wisdom than to let loose my Heart to that which cannot satisfie. And though I have in some measure rectified this Fault, yet still I find an agreeable Movement in my Soul towards her I love, and a strong Indication of somewhat more than pure Benevolence; for there's no Reason that we should be uneasie because others won't let us do them all the good we would. And though your Distinction be very ingenious, "That we may seek Creatures *for* our good, but not love them *as* our good", yet methinks 'tis too nice for common Practice; and through the Deception of our Senses, and Hurry of our Passions, we shall be too apt to reckon that our good whose Absence we find uneasie to us. Be pleased therefore to oblige me with a Remedy for this Disorder, since what you have already writ has made a considerable Progress towards a Cure, but not quite perfected it. Thus you see Sir, what a Trouble you have brought upon your self by your obliging Condescensions to
Worthy sir,
Your most humble and thankful Servant

From Letter V

Hitherto I have courted Truth with a kind of Romantick Passion, in spite of all Difficulties and Discouragements: for Knowledge is thought so unnecessary an Accomplishment for a Woman, that few will give themselves the Trouble to assist them in the Attainment of it.

Excerpts from *The Christian Religion as Profess'd by a Daughter of the Church of England* In a Letter to the Right Honourable T.L., C.I., 1705

pp.5–7   If we wou'd Judge to purpose, we must free ourselves from Prejudice and Passion, must examine and prove all things, and not give our assent till forc'd to do so by the evidence of Truth. And when we are sure we have found the Truth, we ought to stick to it with an heroick Constancy and immoveable Resolution; which is a valour that does not misbecome a Woman, let it be nick-nam'd Pride or Obstinacy, or what Folks please. For without it we can never be good Christians, we are hardly Rational Creatures, but shall be *blown about with every wind of Doctrine, by the cunning craftiness of those who lie in wait to Deceive.*

If God had not intended that Women shou'd use their Reason, He wou'd not have given them any, for He does nothing in vain. If they are to use their Reason, certainly it ought to be employ'd about the noblest Objects, and in business of the greatest Consequence, therefore in Religion . . .

I am a Christian then, and a member of the Church of *England*, not because I was Born in *England*, and Educated by Conforming Parents, but because I have, according to the very best of my Understanding, and with some application and industry, examin'd the Doctrine and Precepts of Christianity, the Reasons and Authority on which it is built.

p.36   Most of, if not all, the Follies and Vices that Women are subject to, (for I meddle not with the Men) are owing to our paying too great a deference to other People's judgments, and too little to our own, in suffering others to judge for us, when GOD has not only allow'd, but requir'd us to judge for ourselves.

pp.103–4 A Woman may *put on the whole Armour of God* without degenerating into a Masculine Temper; she may *take the Shield of Faith, the Sword of the Spirit, the Helmet of Salvation, and the Breast-plate of Righteousness* without any offence to the Men, and they become her as well as they do the greatest Hero. I cou'd never understand why we are bred Cowards; sure it can never be because our Masters are afraid we shou'd Rebel, for Courage wou'd enable us to endure their Injuries, to forgive and to despise them! It is indeed so necessary a Virtue that we can't be good Christians without it; for till we are got above the fear of Death, 'Tis in any bodies power to make us renounce our hopes of Heaven. And it can't be suppos'd that Men envy us our Portion there; since however desirous they are to engross *this* World, they do not seem so covetous of *the other*.

pp.141–3 (Mary Astell replies to Damaris Masham's *Discourse concerning the Love of God* (1696) in which John Norris's idea that God was the sole object of our love is opposed on the grounds that 'it unfits men for society'.)

Among which [the objections made in the Discourse], that which they seem most afraid of, is dispeopling the World and driving Folks into *Monasteries*, tho' I see none among us for them to run into were they ever so much inclin'd; but have heard it generally complain'd of by very good *Protestants*, that Monasteries were Abolish'd instead of being Reform'd: And tho' none that I know of plead for Monasteries, strictly so call'd, in *England*, or for any thing else but a reasonable provision for the Education of one half of Mankind, and for a safe retreat so long and no longer than our Circumstances make it requisite...

pp.142–3 But may we not hope from the magnificence of a truly Glorious Prince, every Year of whose Reign may be reckon'd not by the addition of new Extortions and Oppressions to drain Her Subjects and enrich Foreigners, but by an encrease of new Bounties and Acts of Goodness to Her own people, as well as a Generous exertion of Her Power to Establish the Tranquillity of *Europe*; That since Her Subjects in general have had so Liberal a Portion of Her Royal Beneficence, and the Clergy more particularly, an Act that will embalm Her Majesties Name to future Generations and sound Her Praise louder than all the Ravages and Victories of Usurping and Ambitious Men, nay even than Her own Glorious Victories, truly Glorious in that they do not dispossess a Rightful Owner, but secure his Empire, *Whilst the Name of the Wicked* who dispossess Lawful Sovereigns, who destroy God's Heritage, and root up the Order and Government of His Church, *shall Rot*: May we not hope that She will not do less for Her own Sex than She has already done for the other; but that the next Year of Her Majesties Annals will bear date, from Her Maternal and Royal Care of the most helpless part of Her Subjects. If She over-looks us we have no further prospect; for where-ever other People may carry their views, we of the *Church of England* have no hope beyond our *Present Sovereign*.

...For what but the Love of GOD can justly restrain Sovereign Princes from being Injurious, or excite them to be Just and Gracious to their People? Those who think the Awe of God's Sovereignty but a poor Restraint, and are therefore for Subjecting them to the Coercion of the People, against the Laws of this Nation as well as against the Doctrine of the Church, against Scripture, and Common Sense, shew too little regard to any Religion, whatever they may talk about it, to be look'd upon by any but a heedless Mob as its Defenders; and are *in truth,* what *St. Paul* and his Fellow Christians were *falsely* accus'd of being, *The Men that have turn'd the World upside down.*

pp.178–9 ...A little Practice of the World will convince us, That Ladies are as grand Politicians, and every whit as Intriguing as any Patriot of the Good-old-cause. Perhaps because the gentleness of their Temper makes them fitter to insinuate and gain Proselytes; or that being less suspected they may be apter to get and to convey Intelligence, and are therefore made the Tools of Crafty and Designing Demagogues... How busie looks and grand concern about that Bill and t'other promotion, how whispers and cabals, eternal disputes and restless solicitations, with all the equipage of Modern Politicians, become the Ladies, I have not skill to determine. But if there be anything Ridiculous in it, I had rather leave the Observation to the Men, as being both more proper for their Wit, and more agreeable to their Inclinations.[1]

1 Mary Astell was not exceptional in her failure even to envisage women using politics to further their own cause. Even the Levellers' demand for an extension of the franchise was carefully restricted to adult males. Here Mary Astell reveals how she equated politics with intrigue and with exactly that faction-fighting of which she so heartily disapproved. As she had Nokes suggest in the Prefatory Discourse to *Moderation Truly Stated* (1704) 'Intriguing and Politick Ladies are on the Factious Side'.

pp.219–20 . . . No body can say, that generally speaking, it is unlawful for any Woman to Converse with any Man, there may perhaps be some advantage in it, he may assist her in her Worldly Affairs, may Improve her Understanding, or be the Guide of her Soul. But yet, if either the Privacy, or Frequency, or any other Circumstances attending this Conversation, is of Ill Report, or gives occasion of Scandal; either by affording those who will make an ill use of such an Intimacy, a pretence to encourage themselves in it by her Example; or by bringing a Suspicion or blemish on her Reputation, or any other way; She is oblig'd in Conscience to remove the Stumbling-block, either by changing those circumstances which gave the Scandal; or else by that which is much the best, because the only sure proof of *Innocence*, by breaking off the Conversation.[1]

pp.275–6 One may remember a time perhaps, when they have thought they cou'd not be happy unless another was so; but this was venturing too much on an uncertain bottom, it was besides the Command, and therefore so far from being Excellent, that it was not Prudent. For we are commanded only to Love our Neighbours *as* our Selves, and to wish them all the Good we wish to our own Souls, but we are not to make our selves uneasie because they *Will* be Unhappy.[2]

pp.292–3 I wou'd never advise a Woman to study to improve her Mind, if I did not think her capable; and few things mortify me more than the not being able to persuade her to make a Trial. For cou'd we but once excite in each other's Breast a noble thirst after Perfection, placing our Perfection in that wherein it truly consists, the greatest difficulty were past, we might go on with Pleasure, and prosper in our Attempt.

But to what study shall we apply ourselves? some Men say Heraldry is a pretty Study for a Woman, for this reason, I suppose, that she may know how to Blazon her Lord and Master's great Achieve-

---

1 This passage serves to emphasise just what difficulties lay in the way of women's friendships with men however much women might value that friendship. It's revealing of the censoriousness of society where women's behaviour was concerned. The only friendships that were safe for women were with their own sex. It helps to explain why Mary Astell thought that women, in order to pursue their education, must withdraw from society.

2 Is Mary Astell recalling here her early and unhappy friendship with Lady Catherine Jones? (see Introduction p.9) The passage closely resembles her Letter III to John Norris (see above pp.195–6).

ments! They allow us Poetry, Plays, and Romances, to Divert us and themselves; and when they would express a particular Esteem for a Woman's Sense, they recommend History; tho' with Submission, History can only serve us for Amusement and a Subject of Discourse. For tho' it may be of Use to the Men who govern Affairs, to know how their Fore-fathers Acted, yet what is this to us, who have nothing to do with such Business? Some good Examples indeed are to be found in History, tho' generally the bad are ten for one; but how will this help our Conduct, or excite in us a generous Emulation? since the Men being the Historians, they seldom condescend to record the great and good Actions of Women; and when they take notice of them, 'tis with this wise Remark, That such Women *acted above their Sex.* By which one must suppose they wou'd have their Readers understand, That they were not Women who did those Great Actions, but that they were Men in Petticoats!

pp.296–7   Except in the Duties of our Christian calling, and the little Economy of a House, Women's Lives are not Active, conse-quently they ought to be Contemplative; ... And since it is allow'd on all hands, that the Mens Business is without Doors and that theirs is an Active Life; Women who ought to be Retir'd are for this reason design'd by Providence for Speculation: ... And I make no question but Improvements might be made in the Sciences, were not Women enviously excluded from this their proper Business. Quick-ness and Penetration our Masters vouchsafe to allow us, whilst they deny us Judgment, and I own it is too true, That too many of us have given them just reason, Gratitude apart. For it is no great sign of Prudence to chuse a Service when we are Free; or if a Service must be taken, not to stay till we are offer'd one thats creditable. But this case excepted, I am at a loss to find those instances in which Men in general judge better than Women, even without abate-ment for the advantages of their Education, which yet in reason ought to be allow'd.

p.298   The more intirely we depend on God, we are so much the Wiser and Happier, but the less we depend on Men so much the better. If a Woman takes them for the only Oracles of Wisdom, I give her up for lost, it being certain that she will find them so Crafty ... as to serve their own Ends whatever becomes of her.

pp.323–4   The Sphere allotted to us Women who are Subjects, allows us no room to Serve our Country either with our Counsel or our Lives. We have no Authority to Preach Vertue, or to Punish Vice.

As we have not the Guilt of Establishing Iniquity by Law, so neither can we Execute Judgement and Justice. And since we are not allow'd a share in the Honourable Offices in the Commonwealth, we ought to be asham'd and scorn to drudge, in the mean Trade of Faction and Sedition.

pp.353–4 The course of the World does not often lodge *Power and Authority* in Women's hands, tho' by the use is made of them, when Providence has plac'd them there, one may reasonably conclude, That as it does not show the Justice, so neither is it for the Interest of Men to withold them. For besides that Glorious Example we have all in view, which is the delight of *English* Hearts, and on which the Eyes of all *Europe* are fixt with Admiration, we have many Ancient Precedents to show how Power and Greatness *ought* to be and how they *have* been us'd by Ladies.

pp.359–60 And therefore when Mankind are generally corrupt, so that Charity it self can hardly Think or Speak well of them, St. Peter's advice is certainly to take place, *Save your selves from this untoward Generation, Beware of men* as our Lord directed, keep as much out of their way as innocently as you can, not only by reason of the Injury one may suffer in their Temporal Affairs but chiefly because of the damage that may happen to the Mind.

pp.402–3 (An answer to Locke's, *The Reasonableness of Christianity*, 1695) And tho' my Religion is not so *short* as what he prescribes to the Ladies, yet I hope it is *Plain* and *Practicable*. There are *no Sublime Notions or Mysterious Reasonings in it*; none *of the Notions and Language that the Books and Disputes of Religion are fill'd with*; Nor any thing but such *plain Propositions and short Reasonings about things familiar* to our *Minds*, as need not *amaze any part of Mankind, no not the Day Labourers and Tradesmen, the Spinsters and Dairy Maids*, who may very easily *comprehend* what a Woman cou'd write. A Woman who has not the least Reason to imagine that her Understanding is any better than the rest of her Sex's. All the difference, if there be any, arising only from her Application, her Disinterested and Unprejudic'd Love to Truth, and unwearied pursuit of it, notwithstanding all Discouragements, which is in every Woman's power as well as in hers... she consulted no Divine, nor any other Man, scarce any Book except the Bible, on the Subject of this Letter, being willing to follow the thread of her own Thoughts.

PART IV
POLEMIC: RELIGIOUS
AND POLITICAL

A FAIR WAY WITH THE DISSENTERS AND THEIR PATRONS.

Not Writ by Mr. L.....y, or any other Furious
Jacobite, whether Clergyman or Layman;
but by a very Moderate Person and Dutiful
Subject to the QUEEN.

LONDON:

Printed by E.P. for R. Wilkin, at the King's Head in
St. Paul's Church-yard, 1704.

A Fair Way with
the Dissenters[1]

WELL! If in Disputes in Print and Disputes at *Billingsgate*, which, as they are manag'd, are equally scolding, he were to carry the day who rails loudest and longest; Wo be to the poor Church and its Friends, they could never shew their Faces or hold up their Heads against the everlasting Clamour of their Adversaries. For what Thunder may we expect from those *too violent Spirits*, which these meek and good Christians *do not deny* they have *among them*, when even your *Moderate Men*, your *Men of Temper*, those hearty Advocates for *Peace and Union*, who even *challenge* us to it, as much as to say, that we may have *Peace and Union* with them if we dare; when these good Souls, not at all given to *Revenge themselves, against the Christian Principle*, being only *forced to expose others for their own just Vindication, and who had much rather live in peace, and bury the Iniquities*,

---

1   Mr. L.....y, referred to on the title page is almost certainly Charles Leslie (1650–1722), Non-juror and Jacobite who was violently anti-dissent. He wrote *The Wolf Stript of his Shepherd's Cloathing etc.*, 1704, in answer to James Owen's *Moderation a Virtue*, 1703, and in support of the bill against Occasional Conformity.

   I have followed Mary Astell's use of italics which unless otherwise stated cover quotations from Daniel Defoe's *More Short-Ways with the Dissenters*, London, 1704, to which this pamphlet is an answer.

   To the original text Mary Astell added a Postscript on *Moderation still a Virtue*, 1704, the second contribution of the Rev. James Owen to the debate on Occasional Conformity. This is omitted here.

the Rebellion, King-killing, Persecution Principles, etc. of theirs and our Forefathers, than come to an Account; for which no doubt they have their Reasons. When even these meek Lambs, who never Insult their Brethren, are forced to make use of Rudeness, Ill-manners, Opprobrious Language, Bitter Scurrilous Invectives, Rallying and Bullying, Barbarous Designs, Fools Coat, Knaves Coat and Traitors Coat, (tho when a Coat fits a Man, according to Cyrus his Justice, he ought to wear it) Lampooning, Insolent Behaviour, Gallows and Galleys, Essence of Persecution, Gall not a little and Prejudice to Extremity, Positive Untruths, and, but that the word sticks a little in their Throats, they'd almost said Lies, but Falshood and Prevarication, Positive Falsities, are what they make no scruple at all of uttering, Envy, Pride, ungoverned Passion, Black Notions, full of Malice and empty of Charity, Genuine Forgery. Are forced to call a Minister of Christ, a Fury made up of a Complication of Malice, intolerable Pride, Bigotted Zeal, and Bloody, Hellish, Unchristian Principles; accuse him of Debauching the Pulpit, and Scandalising the Ministerial Function, and with an Heart full of Malice, through a Mouth full of Cursing and Bitterness, to lay the Trifles of Drunkeness and Lewdness to the charge of two Famous Universities, besides those more substantial Crimes of Unjust and Unfair Terms and Imposed Oaths, that is, Oaths to be true to the Government in Church and State, which if they were laid aside, the honest conscientious Dissenters, to get in two thousand of their Children, would venture the poor Babies Morals, in relation to the former Trifles of Lewdness and Drunkenness, nay even the Danger of being infected with Farce in their Sermons and Buffoonery in their Preaching, which, for ought any one knows, may be suck'd in by them in a more natural Air. And to say all in a word, to accuse the whole Church of Want of Justice, of Treachery, Barbarities, Injustices, (according to the English of these Correctors of our Stile and Manners) and Ingratitude to Dissenters.

A heavy Charge! and what can be said to't? for were I ever so much disposed to bluster and make a noise, to treat these Folks with all that Contempt that is due to little Scriblers and Busiebodies, who, either for Bread, and to deserve their Wages of the Party, or out of an innate Love to Mischief, alarm the Mob, and impose upon the Ignorant and Careless Reader, by venting bold Slanders and notorious Untruths, in a plausible Stile and with some shews of Probability, with an Insolence peculiar to themselves, and a matchless Effrontery; yet alas for me! I go to Church every day, and of course hear the Scripture read in the Liturgy, and this has so dampt my Courage, that I dare not bring a *Railing tho a true Accusation* no not against the *Devil* himself, but can only say with Michael, the *Prince* of the Church, *The Lord rebuke thee.*

But Anger and Ill Language apart, and to deliver them from the fear of that which their Charity and good Nature would be so loth to find, that our *Discourses are Banter,* and our *Preaching Buffoonry;* I shall frankly own with an Ingenuity they would do well to practise, that the *Total Destruction of Dissenters as a Party* (the Barbarous Usage that *More Short Ways* is so afraid of) is indeed our Design. 'Tis the Design of all honest Men and good Christians, even of the Dissenters themselves, if they may be believed, and if they are not notorious Hypocrites. And supposing the Bill against *Occasional Conformity* aim'd at this, which is the very worst that Wit or Malice can charge it with; no violence was done in the least to the *Toleration Act,* no *Ruin,* no Injury wou'd have followed to Dissenters; nothing indeed could have been more for their Interest and Real Good. For if I do not make it out before I have done, that to strike at *the Root of the Dissenting Interest, to extirpate and destroy* Dissention, and hinder its *Succession in the Nation,* neither hurts the Consciences, the Persons, nor the Estates of the Dissenters, *then I do nothing;* and promise to pull in my Horns and tamely be condemn'd, to hear only their Sermons and read all their Pamphlets, and in fine, to be *Daniel Burgess*[1] and *Defoe's* Convert.

To the Business then; How often have we been told of the *fatal Consequences of our Divisions,* that *Disunion first weakens, and then destroys the Body Politick;* and that if we *are acted by the Spirit of Disunion, 'tis a sign the things of our Peace are hid from us, and that we are judicially devoted to Destruction;* and are therefore call'd upon *to heal the Breaches,* by the great Advocates for what they term *Moderation,* being assur'd by them of the Dissenters willingness to come to *Terms of Accommodation,* that henceforth there may be no more Divisions amongst us, but that the Protestant Interest may be strengthened, and we may *all be Brethren?* Where then is the harm of putting an end to the *Dissenting Party,* and removing all Marks of Distinction? Is not this what we really, and what they at least seemingly desire? Both sides agree in the end, tho' they cannot agree about the means of doing it.

---

1   Daniel Burgess (1645–1713), Presbyterian minister famous for his preaching. The Sacheverell mob was to gut his London meeting house in 1710.

Now suppose St. *Peter* and St. *Paul*, or Men who act by their Authority, are influenc'd by their Spirit, and preach nothing but their Doctrine, shou'd prevail upon our Dissenters to *mark such as cause Divisions and to avoid* them, and to maintain *the Unity of the Spirit in the Bond of Peace*; would not this be the *ruin of Dissenters as a Party*, and totally *destroy the Succession of them in this Nation*. On the other hand, to make a supposition that may please them better; suppose Dissenters were agreed among themselves, and that they were able to tell us what will satisfie them; suppose *the Men of Moderation, who gave Peace to the Dissenters*, shou'd open their Arms, and the Doors of their Church as wide as Heart could wish, not leaving a Ceremony, or so much as the Creed and Lords Prayer, to offend a Conscientious Dissenting Brother; wou'd you be Coy? wou'd you still draw back, for fear of *Destroying the Succession of Dissenters*? no I warrant ye, Dissenters know their Interest a little better. So then I hope I have made good my Point, that Dissenters may be destroy'd as a Party, without any the least Damage, either to the Consciences or Interests of Dissenters. If I am in the wrong, pray tell me what your Writers mean by Moderate Episcopacy, by Comprehension and Union? are these only pretty words to draw us on to make our Court, that you may have the Honour of rejecting us; and may shew the World what great Offers you refuse, only for the dear sake of the Dissenting Party and Interest? And that Division is so sweet a thing, so many Markets are to be made by't, that you wou'd not, scarce for Heaven it self for it's a place of Union, have Dissention extirpated; but had much rather part with Apostolical Succession, than with a Succession of Dissenters?

So then, Brother *Short-ways* has a little over-shot him self, in being so violently concern'd for the Destruction of Dissenters as a Party. The poor Man was to blame to discover the Mystery, it should have been kept among Friends, whilst the World has been amus'd with tender Consciences and grievous Persecutions; that is, in plain *English*, the keeping a Man out of a Place, who can't come into't but by violating his Conscience. For *some* there are who *have Charity* little enough to suggest, that this is *the very Essence of Persecution*: and truly one can't but think that *Short ways* is of this mind, when he affirms it to be a *Positive Untruth*, that Episcopacy is Persecuted in *Scotland*: No says he, the *Church has fair Quarter* there; and how does he make it out? Why they *may enjoy the Advantages of Places and Preferments*, as often as the Queen thinks fit to give them, *a*

thing we are denied here, says he: We have Liberty of Conscience
'tis true, Indulged us by Law, whilst they are not allow'd to Worship
GOD after their own Way, so much as in Private, so far as Presbyterians can hinder it, notwithstanding the Queens desire and Letter
on their behalf; and therefore from these Premises it undeniably
follows, that they have *fair Quarter*, and we are Persecuted for Conscience sake. Admirable Logick; only to be learn'd in Mr *Morton's*
Academy,[1] for *Oxford* and *Cambridge* are never like to *match* it. Let
this then pass for the Second Mistake, I would not for the World
say *Positive Untruth*, much less that broad Ill-manner'd word *Lies*,
which our Friend *Short-ways* has happen'd to fall into.

A third may be his talking for Peace and Union in one Page,
and in a little while being very angry at any thing that looks like
preventing Posterity, from keeping up a *Succession of* Dissenters *in this
Nation*. This is, says he, a *striking at the Root of the Dissenters Interest*;
their Interest then, say I, is the main of their Religion; and Division
is the Principal Article of their Faith. The Dissenters either believe
our Communion Sinful and Damnable, or they do not believe it
so; if the first, then they do that which so much provokes *Short-ways*,
when he supposes it done by Mr. S.[2] towards Dissenters, they exclude
us from hopes of Salvation; nay, they themselves do wilfully commit
a Sin for *filthy Lucres sake*, as often as they become *Occasional Conformists* for Preferment. But if our Communion is not absolutely Sinful,
but only would be so to them, because they doubt of it, and because
their Consciences are tender, which is the only justifiable Reason
for granting Liberty of Conscience; what necessity of Nursing up
their Children in the same Doubts and Scruples? which, make the
best of them, are but Weaknesses; must the Off-springs Consciences
needs be of the same Cut and Fashion with their Fore-father? And
were it not better both for their own Posterity, and for the Nation
in general (to which certainly these great Pretenders to Publick
Spiritedness ought to have some regard) to lay the Seeds of Dissention
as much out of their Childrens way as possible, and not beat into
their Heads such Fancies and Prejudices as would ne'er come there,

1 Charles Morton (1627–1698), Puritan divine. From the 1670s he ran a Dissenting
Academy at Stoke Newington – the chief of the dissenting schools in which
he attempted to provide an education in no way inferior to that of the universities.
Defoe was a pupil at the Academy and spoke highly of the education he had
received there.

2 Dr. Henry Sacheverell – see footnote p.212.

were they not drove in by an awkward Education, or afterwards taken up upon Worldly and Unchristian Views, and for Temporal Advantage? *Short-ways* may call it *Nonsense* as long as he please, but surely could a Method be found out to prevent Posterity from falling into the Separation, it would be one of the greatest Benefits could be done this Kingdom, and no manner of Prejudice to the Toleration. Suppressing of their Schools would be a very good and necessary Work, were it like to destroy a Faction; which sure could do no manner of hurt to a truly Conscientious Dissenter. As for such as would keep up the Party and Separation to perpetuity, unless we're resolv'd to wink very hard and to take no warning of the Precipice, they plainly shew us, that the Ruin of the Church is the thing they are resolv'd on, and that their fear of being prevented in this Design is the only matter that Alarms them, how loudly soever they may Clamour, with their pretended Fears of their own Destruction.

Fourthly, It is not true that Mr. *Sacheverel*[1] is the *Real Author of the Shortest-way*, or else your Friend *Defoe* is a *Plagiary*; that *Original* of Honesty, Truth and Ingenuity, being Printed among his *Handicrafts*, with his own *shining* Face in the front of them. As for Mr *Sacheverel*, and those other Gentlemen whom *Short-ways* is so free with, they are of Age let them answer for themselves. Tho' if the *Revd. B.....op*, the *Esq; M....*, the *Dr. H....*,[2] be any where but *in nubibus*, they ought to *be expos'd, or the Slander silenc'd*. *Short-ways* wants no assurance that I can find, to speak out in Words at length, or if the modest Man's diffidence restrain him, there's a Mr. *Defoe*, who spares ne'er a Sovereign Prince in *Christendom*, will do it for him. And since

---

1 Dr. Henry Sacheverell (1674?–1724), political preacher. Replaced Francis Atterbury as chief propagandist of the High Church movement in the early years of the eighteenth century. His first major sermon preached in June 1702, *The Political Union: A Discourse showing the Dependence of Government on Religion*, was violently anti-dissent and was among those publications which provoked Defoe's *The Shortest Way with the Dissenters*, 1702. See too all subsequent references to Sacheverell or Mr. S.

2 The passage referred to in Defoe reads: 'What tho' a Reverend B....op had frequently said we shou'd never be well in England till all the Dissenters were serv'd as the *Huguenots* in France? What tho' Esq: M..... has given it under his Hand, that he heartily prays God would give her Majesty the Grace to put all that was wrote there in the Book call'd *The Shortest Way* in Execution? What tho' Dr. H..... frequently has Preach'd and Printed too, that the Dissenters were a Brood of Traytors, and the Spawn of the Rebels, and not fit to live?'

this exalted Person, and many of his rigid Dissenting Brethren, damn *Occasional Conformity*, and have writ against it, even in Contradiction to Patriarch *How*;[1] what harm I pray for a poor Church-man to *Banter* it a little, and to take a *loose* after the Mode of the Times, now Madness is so much in Fashion? And it is not improbable, that *Short-ways* has discovered the true cause of the Politick Dissenters rigour against Brother *Occasional*; they would have the Government know, what they tell you a Bishop has prov'd, was Queen *Elizabeth's* Practise, that *Persons of Different Religions*, ought to be admitted, without Scruple or Caution, *into Places of Trust*; the Laws notwithstanding, which can never be injur'd by being dispens'd with in Favour of Dissenters, and then *the Test would cease*, and *Occasional Conformity would die of course*; and so no need of a Bill, the Business is done without it.

Fifthly, *Short-ways* manner of Proof, that his Tutor *Morton's*[2] Politicks *were not Antimonarchial*, nor *Destructive* to our *Constitution*, I know not whether to call a Falshood or a Flam. For tho' the antient *Manuscripts now above 25 Years old, are left at the Publishers for any one to peruse*; yet who this Publisher is, the Man in the Moon can tell; for my part I read no Direction to find him, either in Book or Title Page. But one needs not thumb over and wear these choice Papers, *Short-ways* lets us know how well he profited under such Instructions, both in the Art of Reasoning and in Politicks. For "Justice, says he, *"which is the end*, is superiour to the King that Executes, *"who is the means*; therefore, Evil Administring Princes may be Depos'd!" Who but a Dissenter could ever have had Brains enough to pick this out of Mr. *Sacheverel's* Sermon! Tho' it follows most undeniably by a Chain of Mr *Hobbes's* Consequences: As thus, "The Regular Administration of Justice, is the Grand End and Design, both of Government and Law;" (says *Mr Sacheverel*.)

Now the End is always superiour to the Means,

Therefore Justice is superiour to the King, (says *Shortways*.)

Therefore the People are so; for you know the People and Justice are Terms Synonymous.

Therefore they may Execute Justice when the King neglects it,

---

1   John Howe (1630–1705), Presbyterian who was ejected in 1662 under the Uniformity Act. In 1700 he entered into controversy with Defoe over Occasional Conformity. Howe favoured this practice and so was strongly against the Bill to prevent it.

2   Charles Morton, see footnote p.211.

for they always do it Impartially, they never *over-turn and destroy the end of Government*, nor Judge amiss in their own Cause!

Therefore *Deposing Tyrannick Evil-Administrating Princes cannot be criminal!* and as to the *Learning* and *Honesty* of this *Performance*, let any *Oxonian match* it, and *out-do it if he can*. Especially taking in the *Design they own*, as *Short-ways* tells p.14 "of maintaining their Just Rights and Privileges as *English* men, and by all lawful Means to oppose and suppress all sorts of Tyranny and Oppression, as well Ecclesiastical as Civil." *Other Designs* they have not, nor do we, or need we charge them with other, for this is sufficient to do the Business, if either their Writings or their Practices may be allowed to explain it. And because I do not love to make endless Repetitions, I shall refer my Reader for this Explanation to *Dissenters Sayings,*[1] or if this is out of Print, let him consult *Moderation truly Stated,*[2] where he may find *such unanswerable Proofs, from such Just Authorities and Plain Matters of Fact,* (which, tho' *Short-ways* boasts of, yet is only produced by his Opposers, and which Dissenters have but little to say to,) as make it out beyond a Contradiction, that Dissenters are by Principle and Practice irreconcileable Enemies to our Government in Church and State, declar'd Opposers of Liberty of Conscience, when they themselves have the Power in their Hands, and the bitterest Persecutors. So justly might Mr *Sacheverel* appeal to the Histories of our Kingdom, whether ever they gave the Church the least Favour or Quarter, when they had her under their Power.

In short, all Government in the Church, except their own Discipline is Tyranny. Let the worthy Mr *Baxter* be my witness, who tells us, "That *English* Prelacy is the Product of Proud Ambition and Arrogancy, and contrary to the express Command of Christ; that it is a Government that gratifieth the Devil and Wicked Men, and that Bishops are Thorns and Thistles and the Military Instruments of the Devil".[3] And "What is this Prelacy? (says Dr. *Owen*)[4] a mere

1 Roger L'Estrange, *The Dissenters' Sayings published in their own words*, 1681.

2 Mary Astell, *Moderation Truly Stated etc.*, 1704 (Clearly produced earlier in the same year as *A Fair Way with the Dissenters and their Patrons*, 1704.)

3 Richard Baxter, *Five Disputations of Church-Government, and Worship etc.*, 1659, pp.45,36.There is also a margin reference to 'Concord' and an indecipherable page reference. If this was meant to be Baxter's *Christian Concord*, 1653, I was unable to find her reference.

4 Dr. John Owen (1616–83), Independent divine. Mary Astell's reference is to the Thanksgiving Sermon he preached on 14 October 1651, for the victory at Worcester over the invading Scottish army led by Charles.

Antichristian Encroachment upon the Inheritance of Christ." And as for the State, every Government, and all even the mildest Administration is, in their Gibberish, Tyranny, if it does not pass through their hands, and is not managed according to their Humours. And their *Lawful Means* of *Suppressing Tyranny*[1] are just of the same piece with their Definitions of Tyranny. For if Seditious Pamphlets and Practices, Slanders and false Representations, speaking Evil of Dignities, Cabals and Conjurations, hounding on the Mob on the Crowns best Subjects, and the like, be lawful Means, these they practise under Queen ANNE. If *Rye-house* Conspiracies, *Bothwell-Bridge* and *West Country* Rebellions be so, these and more they have practised against Princes who frankly forgave them their Father's Murder, and their own twelve years Banishment. If usurping all Royal Authority, and maintaining a Bloody Civil War against their Sovereign, and at last, with an unheard of Impudence, arraigning him at their Bar, and beheading him at his own Palace-Gate; if these be *Lawful Means* we are sure they have made use of them. But then I pray what Means can be unlawful? These are the Dissenters gradual Steps in suppressing what they call Tyranny, and when we catch them upon the first Round of the Ladder, we may, without Breach of Charity, conclude, that they mean, as soon as they are able, to mount to the top of it.

Sixthly, *Short-Ways* will have it that my Lord *Clarendon's* History[2] tells us that K. *Charles I brought all the Calamities of Civil War upon his own head.* Bless me! what hideous Spectacles Prejudice and Prepossession are upon a Reader's nose! But when our Brother *Short Ways* has laid these aside, has wip'd his Eyes, and is willing to see clearly, I would then advise him to another Perusal of that excellent and useful History, which he will find to be point blank against his Assertion, and particularly I recommend to him p. 52, 71, 166, 206, of Vol I by which it appears, that the King had remov'd every Shadow of a Grievance, and that the like *Peace and Plenty and Universal Tranquillity was never enjoy'd by any Nation*, till miserably interrupted by these Enemies of Peace with their Unjust and Unreasonable Clamours.

Seventhly, *Short-Ways* is under a great mistake when he tell us, in his Admirable English, That "The Barbarisms and Bloody Doings us'd with the Episcopal Party in *Scotland* amounted to few". It seems

---

1   It has proved impossible to identify this pamphlet.
2   *The History of the Rebellion and Civil Wars in England*, in 3 vols., 1702–4.

then there were *some* Barbarous and Bloudy Doings, and if there were *any*, her Majesty has too much Wisdom and Goodness to think them *Trivial*. But whether they were few or many, the Accounts of their Sufferings, and several Books that were publish'd not long after the Revolution, besides many Living Witnesses, will inform the Reader. And convince him, that many Clergy-men were outed and ill-us'd, not for refusing the Oaths to the Government, for they took them as soon as they came into *England*, but merely because in their Consciences they approv'd of, and adher'd to Episcopacy. And as for Presbyterian Justice and Moderation, I refer him to Mr. *Kirkwood's* Case,[1] and to those Authorities and plain matters of Fact he so largely treats of.

Eighthly, Poor *Short-ways* was but little oblig'd to his Neighbours, when they suffer'd him to fall into so gross an Error, as to tell us that Dr. *Tennison*[2] was that *Incumbent at St. Giles's*, whom the Bishop of London refused to suspend for Preaching against Popery. Why, every body can tell him that Dr. *Sharpe*,[3] the present most Reverend Archbishop of *York*, was the Man. But alas! this truly Pious and Learned Archbishop has *honestly appeared* for the *Bill against Occasional Conformity*.

Ninthly, What does *Short-ways* mean by making those Bishops who were sent to the Tower, the only *Refuge, Deliverers and Restorers* of the *Church*, together with the Bishop of *London*? Does not the good Man know that five of those seven were *Non-jurors*, and that the sixth, the now Bishop of *Exeter*, as also the Bishop of *London*, are none of his *Men of Moderation*, who appear'd against the *Occasional Bill*? It is very true that the Church has great Obligations to those worthy Prelates and their Brethren, who vote with them, who are,

1   James Kirkwood (fl.1698), Scottish teacher at a school in Linlithgow from which he was dismissed after 15 years for refusing to attend the Presbyterian kirk. A long litigation followed, an account of which was subsequently published by Kirkwood. Finally he received substantial damages from his former employers.

2   Thomas Tenison (1636–1715), Archbishop of Canterbury from 1694, he was known for his moderation towards dissenters. Although Mary Astell rightly corrected Defoe here – it was Sharp and not Tenison who was the incumbent at St. Giles – Tenison apparently played an active part in getting the suspension on Sharp removed.

3   John Sharp (1645–1714) was said to have been provoked 'by the tampering of Roman Catholics with his parishioners', and preached two sermons in 1686 that were said to reflect on the King. As a result his suspension was ordered.

under GOD and the Queen, her Support; and their Temper is moderate in a true and Christian Sense. But I deny that they are *Short-ways Men of Moderation*, and therefore he's under a great mistake in supposing them to be so.

Tenthly, *Short-ways* is also under another mistake, when he tells us that Dissenters *chose War for our sakes, against King* James II. The Man would say, if he has any Meaning, for these People seldom express themselves in the Common Dialect; but he should say, that they chose our *Offices and Employments in Corporations*, to which by Law we only are entitled, and every body knows upon what terms they were admitted to them. He should say, they at last began to smell a Rat, and when they perceiv'd they were not like to be the Building, nor to rear up Presbytery upon the Ruines of the Episcopal Church, then they thought it time to shrink from under their Drudgery, and would be no longer the Scaffolding of Popery. So much for his Mistakes, for I will not at present screw them up to Fourteenthly.

Now give me leave to laugh a little, and 'tis at his telling us, That *The* Scots *have an undoubted Right to the Presbyterian Establishment*, because forsooth! *'tis the Original Protestant Settlement of that Nation.* Dont ye think that the Papists furnished him with this Argument and pay him for venting it? For allowing Original Settlement to be a Right, 'tis like they may have a better Claim than the most antient *Presbyterial Consistory.* Unless Dominion is founded in Grace, and that no Rights or Settlements are of any value, except those which some People more peculiarly call *Protestant!* *Episcopacy is an English Encroachment upon them,* says our mighty Reasoner, our Protestant Dissenter; so is the Reformation, say the Papists. And neither Poor Episcopacy nor Reformation it self, have any thing to offer in their own Defence, save certain Arguments taken out of the Bible, and from the Practise of the Primitive Church. Whereby they pretend to prove, that their Charter allows them to take footing wherever they can obtain it peaceably and Christianly, that is, by dint of Argument, and by patient and heroick Sufferings, or else by Authority of the Lawful Magistrate, and this without being guilty of any Encroachment, or any the least Injury to the Peoples Rights.

But if Episcopacy is not to be restored in *Scotland,* against the Constitution of the Nation, by the same Rule it is not to be destroyed in *England,* since it is our Constitution. And then what becomes of that *Moderate Episcopacy,* those *Comprehensions* and *Uniting Projects,* which your *Moderation a Vertue*,[1] your *Calamys*[2] and other Dissenters are so full of? Certainly *English Men* have as good a Right to their Constitution as the *Scots* have to theirs, and, as we think, better Arguments to defend it, to be sure we have a longer Prescription. Nor know I what can be offer'd to the contrary, except that irresistible Argument, *Club-Law*, which pull'd down Episcopacy in 42, and unless the People, even the Scum of them, have a Native Right to set up what they please (how contrary soever to the Laws of the Land or to the Gospel) whenever they are but strong enough to execute their Projects.

Short ways is grievously pinch'd when Mr. *S appeals to the History of our Kingdom, whether ever they gave the Church the least Favour or Quarter, when they had her under their Power*; and therefore no wonder that he winches and slings to some purpose in a senceless Exclamation; tho Mr *S's* words are modest and cool, there being nothing, except the Truth of them, that can excite his Passion; for it is his own and not Mr *S's* Conclusion, that *Because they never shewed us Quarter*, therefore *We will revenge our selves*. Nor is there, it seems, any great hurt in Retaliation, when from a *Presbyterian* hand; *Shortways* himself can find a Reason for't in a neighbouring Kingdom, p.17. But he may please to remember, that he and his Brethren have been told over and over, and I think our Practices in 1660 did shew we were in earnest, that the *Church of England* knows too well *what Spirit she is of* to *render Evil for Evil*. There can be no reason therefore why they are afraid of our Vengeance, but only because they are conscious that they justly deserve it.

Short ways helps us to an extraordinary piece of News, *viz.* that *the whole House of Peers, including the Lords Spiritual themselves*, have told us that *the Dissenters are no Schismaticks*.[3] Suppose they had, which is more than he will be able to prove these two days, what then? it was never yet allow'd by any Christian Church, no nor by the *Presbyterian Consistory*, except when they got by't, that Lay men have a Right to determine such Points as these. As for Schism, to all those Authors he mentions, I'll oppose the single *Charge of*

---

1 Rev. James Owen, *Moderation a Virtue; or the Occasional Conformist justified*, 1703.
2 Edmund Calamy (1671–1732), biographical historian of non-conformity best known for his abridgement of Richard Baxter's life of 1702.
3 Anon., *Dissenters no Schismaticks*. A second letter to ... Robert Burscough, about his Discourse of Schism., 1702.

Schism continued,[1] which he and his Authors may answer if they can. But it is no new thing to hear Men cry out for new Proof, and to take no notice of the old, tho it be more than enough. This is the Ingenuity of the Church of *Rome*, and that dearest Spawn of hers our English Dissenters. But before they make new *Challenges*, and threaten us with what they *will do*, it may become them to Answer, if not the Arguments, which perhaps may be too tough, at least, the plain Matters of Fact that are produced by Mr *Wesley*,[2] the *New Association*,[3] the *Woolf*[4], Etc. to say nothing of my Lord *Clarendon's* History, and the Accounts of their Antient Practises.

But these peaceable Men who would persuade the World that they are *only upon the Defensive*, that they only oppose our *own Attempts upon their just Freedom*, do it seems take this *just Freedom* to consist, in writing and spreading about among the People, *Abridgments, New Tests*, the *True-born English-man, Shortest Ways, Legions* and a long *Etcaetera* of the like stuff;[5] full of bitter Invectives, notorious Falshoods, and scurrilous Lampoons, on the Establish'd Church, the Government, and even the whole Nation, except a few Choice Men of their own Fraternity; and would have us believe that they have a Charter not to stand corrected, either by the Publick or Private Hands. 'Tis their *Just Freedom*, good Men! and what pity they should be depriv'd of it! to combine against the Constitution, to get into Offices by violating the Intention of the Laws, and so at last into Parliament, that they may be able to Repeal them; whilst no body ought to take notice of these Practices, or to give them any interruption! For one may safely appeal to every sober and considerate Person in the Kingdom, to every one who is not led away by Noise and Prejudice, whether any other Attempts have been made than a necessary provision against their Rude and Open, as well as their Clandestine Attempts upon others? I would therefore desire them before they pretend to bring any Accusations against their Neighbours,

1 Edward Stillingfleet, *The Charge of Schism renewed* etc., 1680.
2 Samuel Wesley (1662–1735), divine, father of the methodist leader, who although attending Morton's dissenting academy became strongly anti-dissent, and in 1703 in *A Letter to a Country Divine etc.*, attacked the dissenting academies.
3 A reference to two pamphlets by Charles Leslie: *The New Association of those called Moderate Church-Man (sic) with the Modern Whigs and Fanatics etc.*, 1702, and *The New Association*, Part II, 1703, both violently attacking dissenters.
4 See footnote under Charles Leslie p.207.
5 References to work by Edmund Calamy and Daniel Defoe. See footnotes pp.218, 221.

to be pleas'd to Answer a few plain Queries. Not that they are the Tyth of what might be asked, but they are such as arise from the Pamphlet before me.

1.   Whether the Ecclesiastical Commission issued out in 1689, the first year of the *Nations Deliverance*, was not intended *to Invite and Compliment the Dissenter*? and if not pray what was its meaning?

2.   Whether one may not very innocently *beware of false Prophets*, who come in *Sheeps Cloathing*, since Truth itself has taught us that *inwardly they are Ravening Wolves*?

3.   Whether *he who enters not in by the Door, but climbeth up some other way*, is any thing else but *a Thief and a Robber*?

4.   Whether any Man can lawfully Preach, who is not lawfully sent? and consequently, let the *Doctrine* and *Faith* be what it may, there can be no true Ordinances, where there is no true Ministry, nor any true Ministry, but where the Succession and Authority is derived from Christ and his Apostles.

5.   Whether a Causeless Separation from the Church be not Schism, and therefore whether *Occasional Conformists* at least, if not other Dissenters, are not Schismaticks?

6.   Whether Dissenters who us'd to exclaim so loudly against Lord Bishops, and the whole Antichristian Hierarchy as they call'd it, are reconciled to the Order and Dignity of *my Lords the Bishops*, or only to the Person of my *Lord of Salisbury*,[1] Etc?

7.   Whether it is consistent with that Piety and Strictness, to which Dissenters have all along pretended, to Burlesque the Holy Scripture, and an Expression particularly applied to our Saviour (*the Zeal of thy House has even eaten me up*) rather than lose an insipid Jest upon Mr. *Sachevereľ*?

8.   Whether it be Decent or Honest for those to accuse others of *foulness of Language* and *bitter Invectives*, Etc. who are most notoriously guilty of the same themselves? and whether it were not fitter for them to take our Lord's Advice, and to begin with the *Beam in their own Eyes*, e'er they attempt to give out the *Mote in their Brothers*?

9.   Whether a Man does not want Common Sense as well as Logick, and is not fitter to Cry Pamphlets about the Streets than to write them, who is not able to distinguish the *Phanaticism of the Dissenters*,

1   Gilbert Burnet (1643–1715), Bishop of Salisbury.

or even the Popery of the Papists, from that which is Christian and Good in either?

10.   Whether Dissenters were only on the Defensive and not the Aggressors, shall I say, in 41? I need not go so far back, even within this two years? Now to *State this*, I hope I may as freely *have recourse* to a *New Test of the Church of* England's *Loyalty* as *Short ways* has to the *Occasional-Bill*. And we find in that Temperate and Uniting Treatise, writ a few months after her Majesty's Accession to the Throne, and before there was a word of a Bill, or any thing had been done or said against Dissenters; that "tho' *Names* of Contempt have been often changed on either side; as Cavalier and Roundhead, Royalist and Rebels, Malignants and Phanaticks, Torys and Whigs, yet the Division has always been barely *the Church and the Dissenter*, and there it continues to this Day."

11.   Whether those Church men who brought about the late Revolution did Well or Ill in't? If they did Well, why is it thrown in their Dish, why are they eternally reproach'd with it? If Ill, what's to be said but that they Repent, and for the future Detest and Abjure the Men and Principles that led them into it. But however it be, neither Papists nor Dissenters have any reason to reproach them, with that which was so conformable to the Principles and Practices, both of the one and of the other. And this leads me to the next Query;

12.   Whether that same Revolution was founded upon Church, or upon Dissenting Principles? If the former why are Church men upbraided with forsaking their Principles, and breaking their Oaths, and so contemptuously used upon this Account, by the *New Test-maker*,[1] *Short-ways and their Fellows? For upon that Supposition, their Accusations are all meer Malice, Forgery* and *Slander!* But if the Managers of those Times did not act by their own, but by the Dissenters Principles; then pray is this the best Usage you can afford your Brethren for coming over to your Principles and Practices? Does not the *Injustice*, the *Treachery*, the *Insults* lie at your own Door? Certainly if this is your method, and that you are firmly resolved against Joining or Uniting in any case, unless upon your own terms; and that it is not enough to comply with you in some things, unless we come over in all; your Exhortations to Peace, Union and Modera-

---

1   A reference to Defoe as author of two pamphlets: *New Test of the Church of England's Loyalty*, 1702 and *New Test of the Church of England's Honesty*, 1704.

tion, are only meer Cant, and have no meaning but to persuade or wheedle, to fright or force us out of our *own* Principles, that when you have gain'd your Point, you may laugh at us as Knaves or Fools for quitting them.

13. Whether those who by breaking down the Fences, admit such into the Church as are firmly resolved never to unite with her, till they have fashioned her after their own Model, do not indeed and most effectually, whether or no they design to do so, betray and weaken, and by consequence destroy her?

14. Whether, except we mean to wear the Bib and the Rattle you design us, it can ever be fit to forget 41, unless you will first condescend to forget the fatal Principles and Practices of those unhappy days? And now I think *Short-ways* has his *Numbers* returned him in full tale, and let him make his best o' them.

As for his *French Parallel*, p.4. it is a mighty Compliment, and of the just size of the Men of his Party, towards the Queen and Church of *England*, whom he must think quite as well of as he does of the *French Monarch* and the Church of *Rome*, or else he could never dream of such an odious Comparison. If he pleases I'll direct him to a more *parallel* Case, even the Practice of his great Forefathers in the *never to be forgotten 41*. Never to be forgotten, because they will not suffer us to forget it, since they repeat its Methods every day. Hideous Outcries of Popery and Persecution, when there was no fear of either from any but themselves, who intrigu'd with Papists at the same time that they falsly accused the King of it; and had it in their Hearts to persecute their Brethren, for we saw they did it with a vengeance when they got the Power. Scurrilous Libels and Lampoons spread throughout the Nation, neither better nor worse than our *Short-ways*, our *Legions*,[1] and a whole Swarm of Wasps from the same hive, which I will not lose time to mention. They had their *Pryns*, *Burtons* and *Bastwicks*, as we have out *Tutchins*, *Stevens's* and *Defoes*,[2] to corrupt the People and fire the Mob. With an unprecedented Insolence they arraign'd the Proceedings and invaded the Privileges of Parliament, Bully'd the House by posting up the

---

1 In 1701 a Kentish petition was presented to Parliament in favour of supporting William in a war against France. When the petitioners were imprisoned by the Tory majority in the House of Commons, Defoe responded with the *Legion Memorial* – so-called because of the signature: 'Our name is Legion, and we are many', which he presented to the House. The petitioners were released.

2 *See foot of next page.*

Straffordians, which their Successors have imitated in their *Black Lists*, to expose all who were not as mad as themselves, to the Fury of the Rabble; they had their Petitioners and Tumults, as we have had our Petitioners and Legions; they garbled the *House of Lords*, as others would now the *House of Commons*, till they got one after their hearts desire. There being no Difference, that I can find, between those Times and these, but that their Fathers had the Nation's Purse in their Hand, which, GOD be thanked, their Sons are not like to finger, so long as such an *Honest and Loyal House of Commons*, as the Nation is at present blest with, fills St *Stephen's* Chapel; and this is the true Reason of all their Rage against this House, a House that us'd to be so much their Darling. But when their Forefathers had got the Purse and Power into their hands, which is all that is wanted by their Successors, what followed? I tremble to think! a bloody Civil War, the Destruction of all Laws and Rights, and of the whole Constitution Ecclesiastical and Civil; Anarchy and Confusion, Tyranny and Oppression alternately; the most detestable Murder of the best of Kings, and, as far as their Power would reach, the Extirpation of the whole Royal Family. And if this is not Truth, or if it is not a very just and sufficient Reason, tho not to retaliate, yet to secure our selves and the Constitution by all lawful and probable Methods, against the like Violence for the time to come, I desire *Short-ways* will be pleased to inform me. For that this was not the *readiest Method*, the *Shortest Way* with the Church and the Government, I hope even Defoe himself has not the Face to deny. And I must always be of opinion that this is the only effectual way to that *Peace and Union* they so heartily desire, this is what in truth they aim at, and mean by't, even bringing all Opposers to truckle under them. "But that these Gentlemen should pretend to (nay really tread in) those very Steps, and yet at the same time be angry to be told they design the rest, is imposing Things upon the World, too gross to go down."

And now, after all that has been said, I leave my Reader to infer, and I think the Premises will warrant the Conclusion, that to lay

2   William Prynne, the Rev. Henry Burton and Dr. John Bastwick who were savagely punished in 1637 for their attack on bishops. John Tutchin (1661?–1707), Whig pamphleteer who defended Defoe over *The Shortest Way with the Dissenters*. William Stephens (1647?–1718), a divine with strong Whig principles who recommended discontinuing the observance of the anniversary of the execution of Charles I.

open the Secret Designs of the Dissenters, which are conceal'd under the Colour of Conscience, and a world of other plausible Pretences; to pull off these Disguises, and to make all the good Laws we can, to defend us from their Treachery, as well as from their more open Attempts; as it is a necessary Duty which we owe to our Sovereign, our Church, and our Country, and even to our own Preservation, so it is in reality the greatest Service can be done Dissenters. For besides, that it preserves the Publick Peace, in which they also have a share, it restrains them, if not from a *Malicious Inclination* towards that detestable Sin of Persecution, at least from being actually Guilty of it. A Sin which the good Men so much exclaim against, and which therefore no doubt the Devil is most apt to tempt them to. And consequently by some seasonable Laws, we may prevent that Destruction which this Crime will Infallibly bring on them, in this World perhaps, but to be sure in the next.

Excerpts from *Moderation*
Truly Stated:Or, a Review of a Late Pamphlet, Entitul'd Moderation a Vertue.[1] With a Prefatory Discourse to Dr. D'Avenant, Concerning His Late Essays on Peace and War, 1704.[2]

[In the Prefatory Discourse the argument for and against the bill opposing Occasional Conformity is put by William Styles and John Nokes who engage in a dialogue on the subject. Mary Astell's own views are represented by Styles.]

pp.lii–liv But whilst they were thus disputing, a Lady in the Company having obtained Audience, "Whatever other Arts, says she, you Gentlemen may excel in, methinks you have not given your selves much trouble in studying the Art of Decorum and good Manners, since in a Lady's Reign, and even in Books that you dedicate to Her Majesty, you take upon you to tell the World that *in this Kingdom no more Skill, no more Policies are requisite, than what may be comprehended by a Woman.*[3] As if there were *any* Skill, *any* Policy that a Woman's Understanding could not reach! So again, if Women do any thing well, nay should a hundred thousand Women do the greatest and most Glorious Actions, presently it must be with *a Mind* (forsooth) *above their Sex!*[4] Now if Women seem such despicable

---

1   Rev. James Owen, *Moderation a Virtue*; or the Occasional Conformist Justified, 1703.
2   Charles D'Avenant, *Essays upon Peace at Home and War Abroad*, In 2 parts, 1704.
3   Ibid. p.364.
4   Ibid. p.180.

Creatures, pray what's the plain English of all your fine Speeches and Dedications to her Majesty, but *Madam we mean to Flatter you?* But I would gladly be inform'd how many Men there are that Act above their Sex, or even equal to it?

They pretend to prescribe *Measures* to Her Majesty to tell Her what is *Right and Safe*, and what her *Gracious Wisdom and Noble Compassion* ought to do. As if she were not much better able to discern what is fit for Her to do, than these Wise Men are to inform Her?...

Tho' you Gentlemen are the Historians, yet give a Woman leave to say, that neither your *Trajans*, your *Constantines*, your *Theodosius's* etc. nor any of your Male-Princes, deserve loftier Panegyricks than her Majesty, or will make a Nobler Figure in History, if Men's Envy do but do her justice. But her Royal Name is Prophan'd by such polluted Pens, as scatter their Incense indifferently upon every Altar...

If therefore these Men would leave Her Majesty to Her own Superior Judgement, and the Integrity of Her *own English Heart*, would they let Her exert Herself, according to Her own Good Sense, Right Principles, and Generous Inclinations, with that undaunted Courage and Royal Magnanimity, that has never been wanting to those Ladies that have adorn'd the English Throne, I make no question but we shall be a Most Happy People, and the Envy of all our Neighbours. But if they will be Medling, Advising, Triming, and Perplexing the Case, I know not what will become of us. Only I comfort myself in this, that Her Majesty will give them full Demonstration, that there's nothing either Wise, or Good, or Great that is above *Her Sex."*

The Men began to stare upon each other, and having silenc'd the Lady with some difficulty, Mr. *Styles* went on: The Lady has some Reason on her Side, and I have often thought... that the only way to make *England* happy, is by Enacting an *Anti-Salique* Law, entailing the Crown, I mean, upon the Females...

Nor is it improbable but that such a Law as this may charm the Dissenters, who you know Love Novelties, and have great Influence over the Female Sex, ever since St. *Paul* wrote to *Timothy*... 'Tis dubious whether we may have a good King hereafter, for among 26 that have sat upon the Throne since the Conquest, there are not many that our Learned Historians will allow to be Good Ones. Whereas 3 of our 4 Queens have been the Glory of the Nation, and the Delight of their People, so that we have three to one, nor was the fourth ill in her own Temper, but as she was influenc'd by her Popish Clergy.

On Moderation (pp.5–6)

To be *Moderate* in Religion is the same thing as to be Luke-warm, which God so much abhors, that he has threatened to spew such out of his Mouth. To be *Moderately* Honest is to be Honest no longer than 'tis for our turn, or till we can hope to play the Knave securely. To be *Moderately* Sober, is to guard our Temperance so long as Inclination, Company and Example don't tempt us out of it. *Moderate* Courage is the bearing Evil when we are forced to do so; and *Moderate* Valour is the fighting when we can't help it, and have no Back-doors to run away by. A *Moderate* Friend is one that will do you no hurt, which as the World goes is a considerable Favour, but he will do you as little good, he will not step out of his Way, or incommode himself in the least to serve you, nor tell you of your Faults for fear of disobliging you; for he judges of others by himself, and is certainly disobliged if you venture to meddle with his. A *Moderate* Christian indeed is a very fashionable and wellbred Person, he is not troublesome with his Religion, he keeps it to himself and will not suffer it to go out of his Closet, you may without any restraint from his Presence, or fear of any dislike that he should shew, either affront God, revile Religion, or Calumniate your Neighbour, as you are dispos'd. And the Truth is they have a little to say for this sort of *Moderation*, for no wise or good Man would willingly pass for a Hypocrite, and there are a sort of People who have been so forward to reprove other Men's Faults, and so backward in mending their own, that a Man who has so much Modesty as to think his own Innocence and Piety not at all conspicuous, will not be over-ready to pull the Mote out of his Brothers Eye, lest he should meet with that just Reprimand of beginning with the Beam in his own. And as for *Moderation* in a Parent, what is it I pray but the letting a Child go on in his Faults without Correction? a very proper Way of expressing your Kindness! A *Moderate* Judge is one who may hit the Case sometimes and do Justice, and as often miss it. And a *Moderate* Magistrate is one who lets the laws fall under Contempt by a remiss Execution of them.

What then is *Moderation* good for you'll say, and when is it to take place? for at this rate it is good for nothing. Why that *Moderation* which the Scripture enjoins, and the only way of rendering *Moderation* a Vertue, is the *proportioning our Esteem and Value of everything to its Real Worth*. When we are warm and assiduous about such things as deserve our Solicitude and indifferent to that which is not worth our Application and Care, we are then *Moderate*. As on the contrary the being remiss in Matters of the greatest Moment, and very eager and industrious about such as a Christian should despise, whatever it is, is not *Moderation*.

Excerpts from *An Impartial Enquiry into the Causes of Rebellion and Civil War in this Kingdom*: In an Examination of Dr. Kennett's[1] Sermon, Jan.31.1703/4. And Vindication of the Royal Martyr, London, 1704

pp.58–64   There is still a Party, and that a restless and busie one, who act by those very Principles that brought the Royal Martyr to the Block; and there are yet too many, for be they ever so few, they are too many, who, instead of deploring that Crying and National Sin, justifie and rejoice in it. How then can it become a Minister of the *Church of England* to do that which Hugh Peters[2] and his Fellows us'd to be set about, 'the vilifying his Majesty in Print, running thro' all the Misfortunes of his Reign, still implying that his own Sins [or Mistakes, the *Influence* of others over him, or the *Opportunities* he gave them, etc.] were the occasion of them all?' ...

In the Name of Wonder, what do these People mean, who are at present so loud against Popery and Arbitrary Power! ...

... sad Experience has taught us to decypher their Gibberish! we know too well, that in their Dialect *Popery* stands for the *Church of England*; the *Just* and *Legal Rights* of an English Monarch are call'd *Arbitrary Power*; ... *Liberty of the People*, in their Language, signifies an unbounded Licentiousness, whereby they take upon them, when-

---

1 White Kennett (1660–1728), Bishop of Peterborough, historian and antiquarian. See Introduction pp.46–7.

2 Hugh Peter or Peters (1598–1660), Independent divine. Although he denied royalist claims that he had been one of the instigators of Charles I's trial and execution, his sermons during and after the trial justified the sentence of the court.

ever they think fit, to Oppose, or even to Remove their Governours, provided they are strong enough to compass their wicked purpose; . . .

To come then to account for the Causes of our deplorable Civil Wars, we may be allow'd to do it in this manner: Tho' Government is absolutely necessary for the Good of Mankind, yet no Government, no not that of God himself, can suit with their deprav'd and boundless Appetites. Few govern themselves by Reason, and they who transgress its Laws, will always find somewhat or other to be uneasie at, and consequently will ever desire, and as far as they can endeavour, to change their Circumstances. But since there are more Fools in the World than Wise Men, and even among those who pass for Wise, that is, who have Abilities to be truly so, too many abuse and warp their Understandings to petty and evil Designs, and to such Tricks and Artifices as appear the readiest way to attain them. Since Riches and Power are what Men covet, supposing these can procure them all they wish; Hopes to gain more, or at least to secure what one has, will always be a handle by which Humane Nature may be mov'd, and carry'd about as the cunning Manager pleases. And therefore of *Necessity* in all Civil Wars and Commotions, there must be some Knaves at the head of a great many Fools, whom the other wheedle and cajole with many plausible Pretences, according to the Opportunity, and the Humour of those they manage . . ..

I will not pretend to justifie all the Actions of our Princes, but it is much more Difficult; nay, it is impossible to justifie, or honestly excuse the Behaviour of our People towards them. Tyranny and Oppression are no doubt a grievance; they are so to the Prince, as well as to the Subject. Nor shou'd I think a Prince wou'd fall into them, unless seduc'd by some of his Flattering Courtiers, and Ambitious Ministers; and therefore our Law very Reasonably provides, that these, and these only, shou'd suffer for it. But are Sedition and Rebellion no Grievances? they are not less, perhaps more Grievous than Tyranny, even to the People; for they expose us to the Oppression of a multitude of Tyrants. And as *we here in this Nation* may have suffer'd by the former, so have we oftner and much more grievously by the latter . . ..

PART V
EPILOGUE

Mary Astell's Preface to the *Embassy Letters; The Travels of an English Lady in Europe, Asia and Africa*[1], by Lady Mary Wortley Montagu 1724 & 1725

Let the *Male-Authors* with an envious eye
Praise coldly, that they may the more decry:
Women (at least I speak the Sense of some)
This little Spirit of Rivalship o'recome.
I read with transport, and with Joy I greet
A Genius so Sublime and so Complete,
And gladly lay my Laurels at her Feet
                    M(ary) A(stell)

Appendix III from *The Complete Letters of Lady Mary Wortley Montagu*, Robert Halsband (ed.), 1965, in 3 Vols., Vol I. (Reference Harrowby Manuscript Trust, 254).

In 1724 Lady Mary Wortley Montagu lent Mary Astell the edited collection of her Embassy letters. Mary Astell read them and was very enthusiastic in their praise. She begged the author to let them be published but Lady Mary decided against publication during her lifetime. When the letters were returned to Lady Mary, Mary Astell had written a preface in the blank pages at the end of the volume (see Introduction to *The Complete Letters*, p.xvii).

It should be noted that the prefatory poem was not included with Mary Astell's Preface in the earliest editions of the *Letters*.

According to Robert Halsband, the *Letters* with the Preface were published without authorisation in 1763. James Dallaway, the editor of the 1803 edition of the *Works*, claimed that the Preface had subsequently received the authorisation of Lady Mary Wortley Montagu.

To the Reader

I was going, like common Editors, to advertise the Reader, of the Beautys and Excellencys of the Work laid before him; to tell him that the Illustrious Author had opportunitys that other Travellers, whatever their Quality or Curiosity may have been, cannot obtain, and a Genius capable of making the best Improvement of every opportunity. But if the Reader, after perusing *one* Letter only, has not discernment to distinguish that natural Elegance, that delicacy of Sentiment and Observation, that easy gracefulness and lovely Simplicity (which is the Perfection of Writing) and in which these *Letters* exceed all that has appear'd in this kind, or almost in any other, let him lay the Book down and leave it to those who have.

The noble Author had the goodness to lend me her M.S. to satisfy my Curiosity in some enquirys I made concerning her Travels. And when I had it in my hands, how was it possible to part with it! I once had the Vanity to hope I might acquaint the Public that it ow'd this invaluable Treasure to my Importunitys. But alas! The most Ingenious Author has condemn'd it to obscurity during her Life, and Conviction, as well as Deference, obliges me to yield to her Reasons. However, if these Letters appear hereafter, when I am in my Grave, let *this* attend them, in testimony to Posterity, that among her Contemporarys, *one* Woman, at least, was just to her Merit.

There is not anything so excellent but some will carp at it, and the rather because of its excellency. But to such Hypercriticks, I shall only say --------------

I confess I am malicious enough to desire that the World shou'd see to how much better purpose the LADYS Travel than their LORDS, and that whilst it is surfeited with Male Travels, all in the same Tone, and stuft with the same Trifles, a *Lady* has the skill to strike out a New Path, and to embellish a worn-out Subject with variety of fresh and elegant Entertainment. For besides that Vivacity and Spirit which enliven every part and that inimitable Beauty which spreds through the whole, besides that Purity of Style for which it may justly be accounted the Standard of the *English* Tongue, the Reader will find a more true and accurate Account of the Customs and Manners of the several Nations with whom the Lady Convers'd than he can in any other Author. But as her Ladyship's penetration discovers the inmost follys of the heart, so the candour of her Temper passes over them with an air of pity rather than reproach, treating with the politeness of a Court, and the gentleness of a Lady what the severity of her Judgement cannot but Condemn.

In short, let her own Sex at least, do her Justice; Lay aside diabolical Envy, and its Brother Malice with all their accursed Company, Sly Whisperings, cruel backbiting, spiteful detraction, and the rest of that hideous crew, which I hope are very falsely said to attend the *Tea Table*, being more apt to think they frequent those Publick Places where Virtuous Women never come. Let the Men malign one another, if they think fit, and strive to pull down Merit when they cannot equal it. Let us be better natur'd, than to give way to any unkind or disrespectful thought of so bright an Ornament to our Sex, merely because she has better sense. For I doubt not but our hearts will tell us, that this is the Real and unpardonable Offence, whatever may be pretended. Let us be better Christians than to look upon her with an evil eye, only because the Giver of all good Gifts has entrusted and adorn'd her with the most excellent Talents. Rather let us freely own the Superiority of this Sublime Genius as I do in the Sincerity of my Soul, pleas'd that a *Woman* Triumphs, and proud to follow in her Train. Let us offer her the *Palm* which is justly her due, and if we pretend to any Laurels, lay them willingly at her Feet.

December 18th, 1724   M.A.

> Charm'd into love of what obscures my *Fame*,
> If I had wit, I'd celebrate Her Name,
> And all the Beauties of her Mind proclaim;
> Till Malice, deafen'd with the mighty sound,
> Its ill-concerted Calumnies confound,
> Let fall the mask, and with pale Envy meet,
> To ask, and find, their Pardon at her Feet.

You see, Madam, how I lay everything at your Feet. As the Tautology shows the poverty of my Genius, it likewise shows the extent of your Empire over my Imagination.

May 31. 1725.